FOREWORD

When I was much younger and attending Bible School we were taken verse by verse through the book of John, six to seven lectures each week, for a whole year. It was a rich time. However, at the end of the year, the lecturer apologised to us that we were only able to complete up to chapter 16 as time had run out. Subsequently, over the years, I have studied, contemplated on, been taught from, had insights and even revelations from the book of John that have been incredibly foundational and inspiring during the forty years of ministry that has formed mine and Denise's lives.

However, one thing that I had never understood, which now seems to be so obvious, is this. Because John was the one disciple that understood more than the others the great reality of God's love as revealed in Jesus, in order to really understand the depths of this beloved disciple's writings, a greater revelation of God's love is necessary in the *reader*! The reader needs to 'see' with the same eyes as the writer!

In these days, we in the Body of Christ are experiencing an outpouring of the love of God the Father in a way that is unprecedented in history. We are 'seeing' the Father and experiencing His love for the world in personal and profound ways. As the Father's love was manifested more significantly to the Apostle John through Jesus (Romans 8:39 puts it, "…the love of God which is in Christ Jesus…") it is beginning to be manifested broadly across the Body of Christ by the Holy Spirit again today.

Stephen Hill has had a wide involvement in many branches of Christianity, which gives him a unique perspective. From a childhood of intense daily church attendance, Bible study and teaching of the Word to the freer styles of spiritual worship and Holy Spirit power encounters, Stephen has come into profound experiences of God's love for him in personal and significant ways. His deep spiritual insights into the Word of God, since he was very young, have matured through experiencing God the Father's love as the apostle John did. Out of this has come a clarity of understanding that has often fed me, inspired me and encouraged me.

Because of his past life and experiences, Stephen sees the contrast between Christianity based in the tree of the knowledge of good and evil and Christianity based in the tree of life more clearly than most. He speaks and writes with a prophetic edge that can, at times, be so sharp that we might reel from its intensity. He challenges many accepted ideas and popular teaching perspectives that we have accepted for long years, exposes them for the mistakes they are in the light of greater revelation from the Word of God, and then presents the truth in simple and obvious one-liners that is honestly joyfully wonderful. Stephen is a Bible-focused teacher totally relying on the Word of God to explain the Word of God in the light of the Holy Spirit's revealing.

JOHN

A Prophetic Revelation

Stephen Hill

©2017

John - A Prophetic Revelation - by Stephen Hill
Published by: Stephen Hill - Ancient Future 2017

Printed in the USA/NZ

Cover design by Tom Carroll

ISBN: 978-0-473-38832-4

This book is also available from Amazon: www.amazon.com in Paperback and Kindle formats.

More resources can be found at: **www.ancientfuture.co.nz**

ANCIENT
FUTURE

"Many thanks to Becky Hill, Alice Adams and Tom Carroll for your work. I couldn't do this without you."

CONTENTS

I recommend this book to all who desire to understand what the gospel really is and wish to advance in their walk as Christians into personal Christlikeness and effective ministries of anointed power. Spiritual power ministry alone without a personality drenched in the love of God will not represent Christianity. Jesus is our model of life and ministry. His identity was in His sonship with God His Father and His ministry was a manifestation of His Father's love working in this fallen world, in supernatural power, of course. Stephen's book, *John - A Prophetic Revelation*, is a great tool to help us all on our journeys in Christ. Thank you Stephen!

— M. James Jordan
Taupo, New Zealand, 2017

PREFACE

This book has been more than a year in the making. It began one evening in early 2015. I was suffering from a stiff neck from bending over my computer too much and my wife, Becky, thought it would be a great idea to spend an evening computer-free. After struggling with restlessness and boredom for an hour, I randomly opened my Bible at John 17. Something happened: a stream of revelation cascaded into my heart. Four hours later, I had written twenty-three pages about Jesus' prayer to His Father.

Not long after that, I began to write about other chapters in John. Gradually, it dawned on me that I should tackle the whole book. What initially seemed like a huge undertaking has become possible and is now a reality.

John's Gospel is the keystone of the revelation of God the Father. It was penned by a man who leant on the breast of the One who lived in the bosom of the Father. By leaning on the breast of Jesus, John heard His physical heartbeat. You could say that John was soaking: He was resting in the place where he could receive the substance of the Father's love. John knew that a relationship with God was about receiving the down-flow of love that comes from the Father.

It is also likely that John's Gospel was one of the last books of the New Testament to be written. Some scholars believe that John wrote it as an old man, long after he was exiled on Patmos. If that is true, it is highly significant that the early Christians were left with such deep revelation about the Father ringing in their ears. Their launchpad into abundant life was the revelation of the Father that is found in John's Gospel. The Bible is not meant to be a book to live by, but a place to meet God, and then live our lives in the Spirit.

The Gospel of John is all about a spiritual transition from the old to the new. More accurately, it is about showing that the 'new' is actually more ancient than the 'old.' What is new is actually primordial because it is from the beginning. It is the reconnection with Source-life, Source-love and Source-reality. The contemporary and the traditional have both fallen short and are found impoverished, unable to sustain the deep echoing longing of the human heart. The human heart is eternal and can only be satisfied with that which appears from eternity and leads back to eternity.

A vast amount of scholarly debate about the Bible exists. John's Gospel is no exception. Theologians speculate about its authorship, casting doubt that it is John. I am not entering into that debate; this commentary assumes that John is the author of the book based on the affirmation of the early Church. They are the most reliable witnesses. Irenaeus, who was acquainted with John's disciple Polycarp, wrote in *Adversus Haereses* (*Against Heresies*) circa 180 AD:

"Now the Gospels, in which Christ is enthroned, are like these. For that according to John expounds His princely and mighty and glorious birth from the Father, saying, 'In the beginning was the Word, and the Word was with God, and the Word was God,' and, 'All things were made by Him, and without Him nothing was nothing made.' Therefore this Gospel is deserving of all confidence…"

These meditations are revelatory to me, Stephen Hill, from where I am at as they are written. I sit down with the Bible and read through the passage and write freehand as it is 'quickened' to me. I am not claiming any more than that, but I am confident that the life of the Spirit can be seen through my human flaws and weaknesses. I write from my personal perspective, shaped by the life that I have lived to this point.

It must be said that this is not an academic commentary. I did not, for the most part, consult any commentaries or writings. I have used some sources, but only to support the revelation that God gave me. Although it was available to me I did not consult in detail the original Greek translation. I have read considerably in the past and do have a certain amount of knowledge. I use this knowledge only as the Spirit quickens it to my mind. I do not study; I approach this in a very relaxed manner, with an open and 'light' mind, writing freehand as words flow through my mind. My unique perspective is through the paradigm of the Father's love and of sonship. I also write from my own life experience, my upbringing, my influences, my successes and my failures. All of this constitutes a seed-bed from which this book has grown.

I am not being held within the chapter divisions. They are not part of the original text as the biblical writers wrote. I do not claim to know what John intended as he structured his writing, but I am dividing it as it speaks to me.

This book is in four main parts:

Part 1 - A NEW GENESIS, from Chapter One to Chapter Six, deals with the beginning, the coming of the Son from the bosom of the Father, and His first signs. This section ends with many disciples leaving Him after Jesus declares that they must eat His flesh and drink His blood.

Part 2 - A NEW CULTURE, from Chapter Seven to Chapter Twelve, looks at the turning of Jesus' ministry into something more subversive than popular. There we find a continuation of signs to open blind eyes and raise the dead, combined with an indictment of religious leadership.

Part 3 - A NEW FAMILY, from Chapter Thirteen to Chapter Seventeen, explores the eve of Jesus' arrest, trial and crucifixion, and the opening up the supreme revelation about the Father, the Son and the Spirit.

Part 4 - A NEW CREATION, from Chapter Eighteen to Chapter Twenty-One, charts the closing out of Jesus' life on earth, His disappearance from the eyes of the orphan system, but the opening of the door into resurrection life and the ever-expanding life of sonship beyond death.

As you read this book, we will dive into the stories and engage with their theology. John's Gospel is unapologetically deep and theological but it is not intellectual. It speaks to the heart and to the spirit. I trust that this book will offer a different perspective on John's Gospel. I trust that its spiritual depths will be plumbed and its richness internalised so that it will become a resource for the Body of Christ.

— STEPHEN HILL
Taupo, New Zealand, 2017

PART ONE

A NEW GENESIS

A NEW GENESIS

~

*In the beginning was the Word and the Word was with God
and the Word was God. He was in the beginning with God.
All things were made through Him, and without Him was
not anything made that was made. In Him was life and the
life was the light of men. The light shines in darkness and
the darkness has not overcome it.* — JOHN 1:1-5

When I read the opening words of John's Gospel I cannot
help but recall the opening words of the book of Genesis.
Both books start with the words, "*In the beginning*". Both books are
foundational. The book of Genesis is the "book of beginnings," taking
us to the inception of human history. The opening words of John's
Gospel, however, are actually proto-Genesis. They tell of a beginning,
a *genesis* that is *before* the creation of the universe. John takes us back
to the source of everything that is, back to the Fountainhead of *all*
existence, and there we discover the inception of life eternal. John's
Gospel is the "book of beginnings" for the New Creation, for the
creation that needs to be entered upon by faith, through resurrection

life, by coming to the Father in the person of the Son.

We need to understand that 'new creation' is indeed *new* from the perspective of human history but it is simultaneously more *ancient* and more *primordial* than the natural creation. The source of our life in God is deeper and previous to the source of our life on earth, and indeed to *all* human life on earth. Our life in God begins in the Father's heart eternally. John's Gospel reveals the genuine Source of all that exists. When we find ourselves connected to that Source, we discover the life of the new creation.

John writes to those who are familiar with Jesus of Nazareth. They had seen Him, touched Him and heard Him. When they began to realise who He truly was, they contemplated His glory which was the glory of the Only Begotten with the Father. In his opening statement, John shows that the Word, the Revelation, is equal to the Essence. The Word was with God and the Word was God.

In the beginning, before time began, Essence eternally issued forth Expression. The Word was eternally begotten of God.

Kallistos Ware of the Eastern Orthodox Church has written the following in his book, *The Orthodox Way*:

> *"The first person of the Trinity, God the Father, is the "fountain" of the Godhead, the source, cause or principle of origin for the other two persons."* [1]

---

1. K Ware, *The Orthodox Way*, St. Vladimir's Seminary Press, Crestwood, New York, 1995.

On earth, this remained unchanged. The Word, Jesus, uttered a full expression of what the Father is like. The Essence and the Expression cannot be divided.

Everything that Jesus spoke and did, in message and *modus operandi*, was the exact expression of the One from whom He eternally proceeds. The Word was the expression of the Source, as the flower is the expression of the root. In the beginning was the Expression, and the Expression was with the Source, and the Expression was equal to the Source. The Son is the expression of the Father.

The Son did not come after the Father, yet He issued from the Father. Begotten, not created. The Father is more essentially 'Source' than the Son, and the Son is positioned downstream from the Source but the living essence is the same. The water of a river has the same essence, but there is a source and there is flow. A river has headwaters, a course, and floodwaters.

"BOOK OF BEGINNINGS"
FOR THE NEW CREATION

The Gospel of John is a new Genesis. It is a 'book of beginnings', outlining the story of a *new* creation that begins in the presence of the Father, a new creation which can renew the heavens and the earth with its potency.

New Creation is brought forth with a similar process to the original creation of Genesis. New Creation is not primarily physical and natural; but it is a spiritual creation that influences and renews the natural order. The simple comparative table below shows the similarities in the birthing of each type of creation. By looking at this we can see some of the parallel themes in the Book of Genesis and the Gospel of John.

GENESIS	GOSPEL OF JOHN
Natural creation	Spiritual new creation
In the beginning, God created through His Word	In the beginning was the Word
Tohuwabohu[2] = darkness and chaos	Darkness and Chaos - absence of the creative-prophetic word from God
Spirit of God hovers/ vibrates over the waters	Spirit of God overshadows Mary[3]
Light-energy "Let there be light"	"The true light which enlightens"
Word spoken	Word manifested
Days of creation	Ongoing new creation
Creation subjected to fall	New creation never fallen
Inception of war against feminine	Redemption of feminine
Loss of dominion becomes domination	Restoration of dominion - Structures of domination lose their power
Life touched by death	Resurrection life beyond death

2. The Hebrew term *tohu wabohu* conveys 'confusion,' 'emptiness,' 'futility,' 'waste.'
3. The angelic annunciation to Mary is not mentioned in John's narrative. Nevertheless it is important to mention this.

In contrast to Genesis, which says, "In the beginning, God…," the Gospel of John opens with the words:

> *In the beginning was the Word and the Word was with God and the Word was God.* — JOHN 1:1

This is an interesting way to begin the "Genesis of the New Creation," because John's starting point is the place of God and the Word in this eternal and original existence prior to Genesis. John is deliberate in starting with the nature of the Trinitarian community that pre-exists all creation.

God is the Source of everything that exists. The Word was in the beginning with God, and so eternally emanates from God. The Word is God's eternal expression. God's expression cannot be anything separate from God's nature. God and the Word have the same substance and are indivisible from one another.

Similarly, the Father's expression is in the Son. The Son, co-eternal and co-equal in substance with the Father, nevertheless is (in the words of the Nicene Creed) "eternally begotten" of the Father. The stance of the Son is eternally downstream from the Father. The Father is eternal Source, the Son is eternal Expression. The Father is the eternal Fountainhead, and the Son is eternal Waters. This reality is mediated further in creation itself and in the human heart by the Holy Spirit, who is the Spirit of the Father and the Spirit of the Son.

John, in his epistle, tells us that the substance of God is both *love* and *light*.[4] If you were to take a DNA sample from God and put it under the microscope in the pathology lab, what would it show up? The divine DNA sample would invariably show up *light* and *love*. Light and love are metaphysical realities. They are the basic components of all that is life.

In declaring that the Word *was with* God, and *was* God, John is asserting beyond any doubt that the fully human Jesus of Nazareth is also fully divine. The God of light and love eternally expresses Himself *as the Word*.

No doubt John is writing at a time when the early Church is establishing the reality that the Carpenter of Nazareth was actually the Eternal Pre-Existent One who was with God in the beginning. The early Church had to establish the truth that Jesus of Nazareth is *consubstantial* with the Father. This revelation of Jesus as Son needed to be absolutely verified so that we would have enough confidence to access the Father through Him.

> *All things were made through him, and without him was not anything made that was made.* — JOHN 1:3

John repeats his words here to emphasise beyond all questioning that Jesus, the Son, is the Father's expression who has brought all things into being. The apostle Paul evokes a similar picture in Colossians. In Colossians 1:15-17 he writes of Jesus:

> *He is the image of the invisible god, the firstborn of all*

---

4.   1 John 4:8, 1 John 1:5.

creation. For by him all things were created, in heaven and on earth, visible and invisible, whether thrones or dominions or rulers or authorities - all things were created through him and for him. And he is before all things, and in him all things hold together.

Instead of 'Word' as expression of God, Paul uses 'image' to mean the expression of God. Paul is expressing the same reality as John. *Word* and *image* are synonymous. The Son, Jesus of Nazareth, is the exact expression of all that the Father is as the Source, and is the same substance yet they remain separate persons. The revelation of God in time is not essentially different to the way He is in eternity. In the words of the theologian Jurgen Moltmann: "The triune God can only appear in history as He is in Himself, and in no other way. He is in Himself as He appears in salvation history, for it is He Himself who is manifested, and He is just what He is manifested as being."[5] Paul's assertion that God "cannot deny Himself" (2 Timothy 2:13) includes the Incarnation. How God appears in human history is precisely how He exists in eternity.[6] Any questioning of this denies the validity of God's revelation of Himself in Jesus.

Jesus, as the Word, is the primordial light of all creation. 'Primordial' means "existing at or from the beginning of time." Many theologies are not primordial enough; they do not go to the beginning of everything. As a result, we are left with an incomplete foundation from which to live. The revelation of the true nature

---

5. Jurgen Moltmann, *The Trinity and the Kingdom*, Fortress Press, Minneapolis, 1993, p153.
6. "We assume that the economic Trinity is the immanent Trinity. The immanent Trinity (God in Himself) is revealed by the economic Trinity (God in history), from which we learn that God is Father, Son and Spirit." C. Pinnock, *Flame of Love: A Theology of the Holy Spirit.*, InterVarsity Press, Downers Grove, Illinois, 1996.

of God that Jesus brought is the *original* truth that God is Father.

> *In him was life, and the life was the light of men. The light shines in the darkness, and the darkness has not overcome it.* — JOHN 1:4,5

The life that is in the Son brings revelation to the human heart. Genuine revelation is always creative. Revelation has the energy to create what the revelation speaks of. What a liberating breakthrough to know that light is always more powerful than darkness! It is impossible for darkness to resist the light. The darkness does not snuff out the light but the increasing light dispels the darkness. The light of revelation and openness cannot but prevail. The creative life of God will redeem the destruction of darkness.

CLOSING OUT THE OLD - USHERING IN THE NEW

> *There was a man sent from God, whose name was John. He came as a witness, to bear witness about the light, that all might believe through him. He was not the light, but came to bear witness about the light. The true light which enlightens everyone was coming into the world.* — JOHN 1:6-9

John, the Gospel writer, now focuses on the historical events which occurred. He contextualises John the Baptist within the cataclysmic event of God appearing on earth.

After four hundred years of darkness and silence, within which no authoritative prophetic voice was heard, another prophet is sent by God. This ragged and wild man, John, appears at the most strategic point in cosmic history. John is the hinge between two epochs, closing out the old but pointing the way to the new. He appears both as a symbol of continuity and of rupture: Continuity, because he is in the prophetic tradition, one like Elijah, the last prophet of the Old Testament era; Rupture, because there has been a change in God's speaking to Israel. Before God enters anew into a situation, there is almost invariably a rupture. Before one epoch begins, there needs to be an intentional departure from the old, if not physically, at least in spirit.

The Holy Spirit is very intentional in putting John the Baptist in his rightful historical context. John is misunderstood to be Elijah the Prophet or even the expected Messiah. But John is neither of these. He has a specific purpose in his prophetic vocation. His sole purpose is to close out the old era and make way for the coming of the Son into the realm of human experience.

> *He was not the light, but came to bear witness about the light. The true light, which enlightens everyone, was coming into the world.* — JOHN 1:8,9

These five words "[*John*] *was not the light*" are seemingly innocuous but they are, I believe, one of the *blazing headlines* of the New Testament. It is remarkable how the Holy Spirit is able to use sparse words that are so easily glossed over and readily dismissed, but, by a flash of revelation, show something that changes our whole way of seeing things. Why are these words, "He was not the light" so important?

John the Baptist was the ultimate and the high point of the prophets. He was the greatest of the prophets. He was greater than Moses, Elijah, Elisha, David, Isaiah, Jeremiah, Ezekiel, Daniel… and all the rest. Jesus Himself commented of John, "I tell you, among those born of women there is no one greater than John." (Matthew 11.11; Luke 7:28). This sets the background for what is a stunning analysis by the Holy Spirit through the stylus of John the Gospel writer.

John the Baptist - *was - not - the - light.*

These words "…He was not the light" are the Holy Spirit's commentary on the *entire* Old Testament. They place the Old Testament revelation where it belongs; in shadow.

If John the Baptist is indeed the greatest of the prophets, and the zenith of Old Testament prophecy, all of the words of Moses, Isaiah, Jeremiah, Ezekiel, and every other person beforehand are shifted into the proper perspective. Their revelation of God was *not* the true light. It was in shadow, diminished, and obscure because the True Light was still to come to the world. *John the Baptist is the last signpost on the road to the destination.* No sensible person will stop at a road sign to admire the words which inform them of the distance to the city to which they are travelling. No, they will drive *past* the signpost until they arrive at the place of their destination.

Many people struggle to reconcile the Old Testament portrayal of God with how Jesus and the New Testament writers portrayed Him. This statement that John the Baptist was "not the light" settles the debate. The writers of the Old Testament were *not* the true light.

The true light came out of the bosom of the Father.

We are often faced with the question; is not God equally Judge or sovereign King as He is Father? Many Christians take their theological framework equally from the Old Testament as from the New. By doing that, they unknowingly reject the New. By equating God as Judge and God as Father, they unwittingly admit that the New Testament has no greater revelation than the Old. If you really get down to it, making the Old Testament of equal standing with the New Testament makes Jesus and His words irrelevant. Therese Martin, later known as St. Therese of Lisieux, sliced through the Gordian knot of theological confusion with this remarkable observation:

> *"If God had simply wanted obedient, fearful servants, it would have been enough for God to have sent only the writers of the Old Testament."* [7]

The very existence of the New Testament is enough to show, beyond all doubt or argument, that God desires to be revealed as only Jesus can reveal Him—as a loving Father.

When the love of the Father is manifested and experienced in our hearts, the substance of that love is life-altering. Love sees all things in the light of love and with an unveiled face. When the love of God comes in, distorted paradigms fall away and the blurred reality comes into focus. The light enters the darkness and the darkness cannot withstand it.

---

7.   Quote taken from Joseph F. Schmidt FSC, *Everything is Grace: The Life and Way of Therese of Lisieux*, The Word Among Us Press, Ijamsville, Maryland, 2007.

John the Baptist was not the light, but he appears to bear witness to the True Light who was coming imminently. John is like the police motorcyclist who rides ahead of the presidential motorcade stopping all traffic because the motorcade is bearing down upon them imminently. The presence of the police motorcyclist signals the impending arrival of what the gathered crowds are waiting for. The presence of John signals the impending arrival of the True Light which enlightens every man. When the True Light comes, there is no longer a dimmed perception of reality, there is no longer shadow. The True Light reveals things as they really are.

THE COMING OF THE TRUE LIGHT

What is the function of the True Light? *To enlighten, to illuminate.* The light itself is *not* to be focused on. Looking into the sun will cause damage to the eyes. We are meant to see what the light enlightens. You don't look *at the light*, you look *away from the light* to everything that it sheds its light upon. What does the True Light reveal? The True Light, Jesus, reveals the nature of reality. He reveals who God truly is, who we really are, and what the world really is. He reveals the original, the problem, and the solution.

There is a popular phrase in evangelical Christianity which says, "So-and-so has *seen the light.*" The truth, however, is that we don't really "see the light." Rather, it is the light which helps us to see everything. The light of Christ's glory is so bright that it is instantly blinding, as Saul of Tarsus discovered on the road to Damascus. What the light does is that it changes how we see everything else. The light influences our perception of reality. It determines how we see God, how we see ourselves and others, how we see life and truth.

Reality can only seen by the True Light. The reality of who God is can only be revealed by the Son who is in the bosom of the Father. From the bosom of the Father, God's true nature is made known and demonstrated. Any revelation that does not originate and flow from the bosom of the Father is either false revelation or inferior revelation. The Old Covenant revelation of God is not at all false but *it is* shadow-revelation. The Old Testament revelation of God is a flickering candle by which we can only see truth dimly. The Old Covenant is, like John the Baptist, only a witness to the true light which is to come.

In order to get a proper perspective on the Scriptures we need to see them by the light of revelation. We must allow the "true light, which enlightens every man" to shine upon the Bible. The true light, through which the Scriptures are understood, is the perspective *from* the heart of the Father.

Old ways of seeing, which are not from the paradigm of the Father's love and of sonship, will give a skewed perspective on the Scriptures. It is our experience, in this revelation of the Father, that the Bible is being seen in a new and truer light. The writings of the apostle Paul, which have and continue to be so problematic to many, are now seen from a different viewpoint. When we understand what kind of person Paul was, how deeply broken and burned out on religion he was yet how deeply comforted he became, we begin to understand more accurately what he wrote. The statements that Paul made, which have caused many disagreements, are now to be seen in the context of a community living in an environment of the outpoured love of the Father.

Seeing with the eyes of the heart as a beloved son gives a much more accurate perspective on the written text of the Bible. In fact, I would go as far as to claim that the Bible can only be fully understood from the perspective of sonship. The only true interpreter of the Scriptures is the resurrected Son through the Holy Spirit. That may seem like an ambitious claim but it is borne out by Luke 24:27:

> *And beginning with Moses and all the Prophets, he interpreted to them in all the Scriptures the things concerning himself.*

Jesus Christ in resurrection has a complete and wholly integrated revelatory interpretation of the Scriptures. This is the only interpretation that we need. Coming into union with Christ in His sonship will ultimately give us access to the proper interpretation of *all* the Scriptures.

GOD APPEARS IN HUMAN HISTORY

> *He was in the world, and the world was made through him, yet the world did not know him. He came to his own, and his own people did not receive him. But to all who did receive him, who believed in his name, he gave the right to become children of God, who were born, not of blood nor of the will of the flesh nor of the will of man, but of God.*
> — JOHN 1:10-13

Even though the Creator of the world is present in the world, the world does not recognise Him. More specifically, His 'own people' (Israel) do not know Him or receive Him. Knowing and receiving God is an issue of our hearts. So prevalent is this world's system with orphanness that their hearts are closed and not able to recognise the Son appearing from the Father's bosom. The appearance of God into human history and circumstance is never recognised by a heart which is closed, for God appears in humble disguise. God does not appear in the way that the religious heart expects Him to. One of the great paradoxes of Christianity is that the in-breaking of God into human history came in the form of a helpless baby. God has not changed His *modus operandi*. He still appears in the form of foolishness and weakness, when we least expect it, in the ordinary and the subversive. We need the eyes of the heart to be opened to recognise the appearance of God.

> *And the Word became flesh and dwelt among us, and we have seen his glory, glory as of the only Son from the Father, full of grace and truth.* — JOHN 1:14

The most significant single event in all time up to this point is when the Word becomes flesh. It trumps every prior revelation of God in the Old Testament.

I am convinced that the full impact and ramifications of this particular reality—the clothing of the Divine in human flesh—have yet to fully dawn on the Church. Christian theology uses the word 'incarnation' to describe this reality. Incarnation literally means "the taking on flesh, the material manifestation of an entity, god or force whose original nature is immaterial."[8] The word 'immaterial' here means to be without matter, without tangible or physical substance.

---

8. Wikipedia

Now, let us pause to consider this. God, the eternal and pre-existent source of everything, who expresses Himself eternally in the Word, decided from His heart to become human. The Word *became* flesh. Go and look at yourself in the mirror. Feel your skin, pass your hand through your hair, press your bones. Let your fingers run over your muscles and the contours of your physical form. Many people have a certain amount of shame or even disdain for the human body but the human body, and the human soul is the place where God has purposed to live.

The Trinity has immense pleasure in becoming incarnate. Colossians 1:19-20 puts it like this:

> *"For in him all the fulness of God was pleased to dwell, and through him to reconcile to himself all things, whether on earth or in heaven…,"*

The coming of Jesus, the Eternal Expression, the Word, is for the purpose of *reconciling all things on earth and in heaven*. The reconciliation and rejoining of earth and heaven is top of God's priority list. The corollary of that is that the division, the keeping apart of earth and heaven is top of Satan's priority list. Heaven and earth are separated through the lies and allegations of the Accuser, through the hegemony of the knowledge of good and evil.

To look upon ourselves, and then to feel ashamed at our nakedness and attempt to cover our perceived nakedness with 'fig leaves,' is to divide earth from heaven. Self-rejection, self-repulsion and self-discrimination are that which divide earth from heaven.

The nakedness of the baby in the manger in Bethlehem is the divine response to the fig leaves. The lack of self-consciousness in a newborn baby is a striking reminder of what it is to be without shame. A little baby does not have any consciousness of being told that it is naked. A newborn baby has no choice but to accept how lovely it is. It is only in the 'orphan/adult' awareness of the knowledge of good and evil that we reject our worthiness to be the dwelling place of God.

"And dwelt among us." (v.14) The force of this expression is that the Word 'tabernacled' or 'tented' among us. However, there is more to it than that. Human flesh is *itself* the tent. Here's how it reads literally in the Greek:[9]

> *"And the Saying flesh became and booths (tabernacles)*
> *in us..."*

There you have it! He pitches His tent in us. The Fulness-of-Godhead inhabits you and I. Yes, He had his own physical body, He possessed the full range of human emotions and more. He is fully human, fully God, but my point is that God is *incarnate in us.*

Theology has overwhelmingly sought, and rightly so, to hold the tension between the human and the divine in Jesus, but it has skimmed over the fact that the Divine actually came to live *within* the human. That divine yearning to unite with humanness has not diminished or receded. It continues today. The outpouring of the Spirit in the New Covenant is the entry of God into His desired

---

9. www.scripture4all.org

home. God has always had a "dream home," and that dream home is us! The promise in Ezekiel 36:27 declares, "...and I will put my Spirit *within* you."

> "...and we have seen his glory, the glory as of the only son
> from the Father, full of grace and truth." — JOHN 1:14

The version I am using (the *English Standard Version*) uses the word 'seen,' but that doesn't adequately reflect what John really means. As a lover of literature and of words, I prefer the older word 'beheld.' What John is really saying is that they *gazed prolongedly upon* the glory of Jesus as the Only Begotten from the Father. John has a burgeoning revelation of Jesus *as the Son of the Father*. By the time he comes to write his Gospel, he is as immersed as he could possibly be in true Christianity. When John is with Jesus, when he is in the company of 'the Word,' he gazes upon Him and contemplates who He is.

To look upon someone's glory is to be much more than a casual observer. It is to deeply savour and contemplate the full expression of who they are. John observes Jesus' personality and behaviour very closely. He does not analyse Jesus in the way that psychologists do but he observes, ponders and reflects on Jesus at close quarters and also from a distance. John is a connoisseur of Jesus. More accurately, however, he is a connoisseur of the *sonship* of Jesus. He does not contemplate Jesus as much as he contemplates Jesus *in relation to the Father*.

In gazing upon the Father-Son relationship, John sees that it is full of *grace and truth*. In other words, the relationship between the Father and the Son is predicated on *gift* and *reality*. *Everything* is gift, nothing is earned. Nothing is held back or needs to be bought. And everything is reality. It could be said that Trinitarian relationships are the epitome of being 'naked and unashamed.' The persons of the Trinity do not judge or assess one another on the basis of right and wrong. They see in absolute reality.

The gift and reality of the Father-Son-Spirit relationship spills over to us. John the Beloved gazes upon the grace-gift and the reality, and he becomes caught up in it, so much so that he habitually rests his head on the chest of Jesus. He knows full well that receiving comfort-love from Jesus is to receive comfort-love from Jesus' Father. John leans on the chest of Jesus, and *leans into* the bosom of the Father.

> *(John bore witness about him, and cried out, "This is he of whom I said, 'He who comes after me ranks before me, because he was before me.)* — JOHN 1:15

In case there is any doubt, John the writer reiterates again that Jesus precedes and outranks John the Baptist. He repeats that we have now entered a new era but the new era is actually rooted in eternity. There can be no hankering after the talismans of an old paradigm. Just in case anyone is still fixated on the diminishing figure of John the Baptist, the man himself is quoted as declaring that Jesus is greater:

> *And from his fulness we have all received, grace upon grace. For the law was given through Moses; grace and truth came through Jesus Christ. No one has ever seen God; the only Son, who is in the bosom of the Father, he has made him known.* — JOHN 1:16-18

The fulness that is in the Son spills over into us. In his lifetime, John gulped mouthfuls of it, let it splash over him and became inebriated in it. John became drunk with the fulness of sonship. He became intoxicated with the grace-gift that flows from the Father. John the Beloved was plunged into a life in which grace was heaped upon grace. This only comes to us in a state of rest, of having given up trying to earn approval.

John, the Gospel writer, sets out a clear contrast between Moses and Jesus Christ. This is the contrast between servant and Son. The Law comes through Moses the servant, but grace and truth come through Jesus Christ the Son. Seeing in the light of the Father's love gives John, the Gospel writer, a more accurate perspective about Moses. Moses was indeed the Lawgiver but the deeper and more ancient realities of grace and truth come through Jesus Christ.

The writer of the Book of Hebrews makes a similar contrast between Moses as a faithful servant *in* God's house and Jesus Christ as a faithful Son *over* God's house (Hebrews 3:5). The faithfulness of a servant can only be measured within the parameters of law-keeping, that is, within a system of command and obedience. Sonship, however, is not measured in terms of command and obedience; it is measured in terms of the ability to receive grace-gift and the capacity to live in truth-reality. Maturity in sonship is becoming more able to receive and live out of love.

> *"No one has ever seen God; the only Son (some versions say 'God' instead of 'Son') who is in the bosom of the Father, he has made him known."* — JOHN 1:18

There is a connection between this verse and the preceding verse. The connection is as follows:

MOSES = SERVANT = LAW

The result of "not seeing God"

JESUS CHRIST = SON = GRACE AND TRUTH

The result of being in the bosom of the Father

Exodus 33.11 and other references tell us that God spoke "face to face as one speaks with a friend." That is true in one sense but it does not contradict what John is saying here. In comparison with the revelation of who God *really is* as Father, John the Gospel writer views Moses as *not* having seen God. When Jesus comes from the bosom of the Father and declares who God truly is, it is an unprecedented revelation.

Freedom from the Law is inextricably linked to the revelation that flows directly out of the bosom of the Father. The truth about God can only be revealed by the Son who abides within the Father's nurturing heart. To receive a revelation from the Son is to truly 'see' God. No one has ever perceived who God really is because the reality of who He is can only be communicated by revelation, and the purveyor of that revelation is the Son who lives continually in the Father's heart.

BREAKING WITH THE STATUS QUO

And this is the testimony of John, when the Jews sent priests and Levites from Jerusalem to ask him, "Who are you?" He confessed, and did not deny, but confessed, "I am not the Christ." And they asked him, "What then? Are you Elijah?" He said, "I am not." Are you the Prophet?" And he answered, "No." So they said to him, "Who are you?" We need to give an answer to those who sent us. What do you say about yourself? He said, "I am the voice of one crying in the wilderness, 'Make straight the way of the Lord,' as the prophet Isaiah said."

(Now they had been sent from the Pharisees.) They asked him, "Then why are you baptising, if you are neither the Christ, nor Elijah, nor the Prophet?" John answered them, "I baptise with water, but among you stands one you do not know, even he who comes after me, the strap of whose sandal I am not worthy to untie." These things took place in Bethany across the Jordan, where John was baptising. — JOHN 1:19-28

John the Baptist has come to the attention of the religious system. The headquarters in Jerusalem has been informed and they need to know what this preacher is about. From a human perspective, John has just appeared out of nowhere. They have absolutely no concept of John's true mandate—to prepare the way of the Lord.

The religious system always wants to fit us into its own particular box. It has a need to contextualise everything and fit everything into its scheme. That is why they say to John the Baptist, "Who are you?" The prophetic person can never be neatly packaged and defined. The true prophetic is extremely frustrating to those who want to label everything and give a title to everything; to those who demand to know and control everything. Paul the apostle makes a telling observation when he says that the spiritual person "is discerned of no man," (1 Corinthians 2:15). In other words, the truly spiritual person exists outside of all categories.

John the Baptist will not allow himself to be categorised just to satisfy the cravings of the religious system. He will not be placed in any box. He is above and beyond definition. He cries out in the wilderness that the Lord is coming. John baptises in the wilderness because those who want to listen to him must travel out to a place which is stripped of all the expectations and exigencies of everyday life. To really receive prophetic promise there needs to be a departure from the norm and a journey to a place of rupture. John baptises repentant people in the wilderness because repentance is required to switch direction; moving away from pursuing God in a religious way and becoming a person whose heart is open enough for the Lord to enter in. The prophetic movement of God cannot be experienced unless we are prepared to make a clean break with the status quo.

MOVING BEYOND EVANGELICAL AND PENTECOSTAL REVELATION INTO SONSHIP

The next day he saw Jesus coming toward him, and said, "Behold, the Lamb of God, who takes away the sin of the world! This is he of whom I said, 'After me comes a man who ranks before me, because he was before me.' I myself did not know him, but for this purpose I came baptising with water, that he might be revealed to Israel." And John bore witness: "I saw the Spirit descend from heaven like a dove, and it remained on him. I myself did not know him, but he who sent me to baptise with water said to me, 'He on whom you see the Spirit descend and remain, this is he who baptises with the Holy Spirit.' And I have seen and have borne witness that this is the Son of God."

The next day again John was standing with two of his disciples, and he looked at Jesus as he walked by and said, "Behold, the Lamb of God!" The two disciples heard him say this, and they followed Jesus. Jesus turned and saw them following and said to them, "What are you seeking?" And they said to him, "Rabbi" (which means Teacher), "where are you staying?" He said to them, "Come and you will see." So they came and saw where he was staying, and they stayed with him that day, for it was about the tenth hour.
— JOHN 1:29-39

John the Baptist stands between two eras. He is simultaneously the final prophet of the prophetic era as well as the forerunner of the new era. This new era has a new mode of revelation; God is now to be revealed in His Son which means that He is to be revealed as Father.

The book of Hebrews is founded on this truth:

"Long ago, at many times and in many ways, God spoke to our fathers by the prophets, but in these last days he has spoken to us by his Son..." — HEBREWS 1:1

The mode of God's communication shifted from what was delivered by prophets to what was declared and manifested *by the Son*. Jesus said of John the Baptist that he (John) was the greatest of the prophets (Matthew 11:9-11), *yet John didn't perform any signs.* John the Baptist himself is the sign that the era of God's revelation through individual prophets has finished. John the Gospel writer shows the reality that the Old Testament train has finally pulled out of the station and John the Baptist is the last carriage to pull away from the platform.

John the Baptist received the revelation from the One who sent him. As an authentic prophet, his sense of being sent would have been of utmost importance to him. The primary function of a prophet is to be God's spokesperson. God had commissioned John to make a way in the desert for the incoming Messiah. John would recognise the authenticity of the Messiah by the fact that the Holy Spirit would descend and remain upon Him.

John the Baptist says, in verse 34, *"I have seen and have borne witness that this is the Son of God."* The title 'Son of God' is not, in itself, an indicator that John had a revelation of Jesus' sonship to the Father. The term 'Son of God' was an honorary title for the 'Sent One,' the Messiah. Just because he uses the word 'son,' it does not necessarily follow that there is a revelation of the Father. The Revealer of the Father is about to appear.

As John sees Jesus approaching him (v.29), he blurts out the revelation that has impacted him. He declares *"Behold, the Lamb of God, who takes away the sin of the world!"* This revelation is a cornerstone of evangelical Christianity which has established itself around the central revelation that Jesus is the Saviour who has atoned for sin by His death on the cross. This revelation extends as far as naming and recognising that Jesus is the one through whom we have salvation through faith in His shed blood.

John's revelation, however, does not stop at the purely evangelical and salvific stage of recognising Jesus. He makes a further pronouncement that Jesus is the one who will baptise with the Holy Spirit. This is what I would call a Pentecostal revelation. If Evangelical Christianity has established itself round the central doctrine of justification by faith, then Pentecostal-Charismatic Christianity has established itself around the doctrine and experience of the baptism of the Spirit. There is, however, much more to Christianity than this. There is a revelation of sonship; a revelation which subsumes the previous revelations.

WHERE DOES JESUS LIVE?

The next day again John was standing with two of his disciples, and he looked at Jesus as he walked by and said, "Behold, the Lamb of God!" — JOHN 1:35

As Jesus passes by, the prophetic impulse grips John and he declares what he sees. In that moment, in the understanding of John's two disciples, Jesus *increases* and John *decreases*. John points away from himself and diminishes in doing so, in order that the profile of Jesus would increase (John 3:30). John the Baptist points to the next sign; he tells the two disciples to go to the next sign, Jesus. We may have thought that Jesus is the destination, but what then happens with these two disciples opens up the new era that Jesus has come to announce.

The two disciples, who had followed the Baptist, now begin to follow Jesus. Jesus becomes aware of this, and turning to them, asks them what they are seeking. Their reply, in verse 38, is this:

"Rabbi, where are you abiding?"

I use the beautiful word 'abide' because it carries the meaning of living and remaining in a place of rest and home.

This is another one of those easily overlooked words that carry an abundance of revelation. Somehow the two disciples are glimpsing a reality about Jesus. In asking to go to His home, they have a dawning realisation that Jesus, the Lamb of God and the Baptiser in the Holy Spirit, *is not His own source.* They have an epiphany that Jesus comes from somewhere, that He has an abiding place, a context and an environment that He operates out of. Jesus has *a home,* one that does not consist of bricks and mortar. That home is the bosom of the Father.

The two disciples progress beyond an 'evangelical revelation' that Jesus is the Lamb of God who takes away the sin of the world. Then they progress beyond a 'pentecostal/charismatic revelation' that Jesus is He who baptises with the Holy Spirit. They move into a 'union revelation' of abiding with Jesus in *His* home. The revelation of the

Father's love and of sonship brings them to the place that Jesus lives in the bosom of the Father.

This has been my experience. I grew up as an evangelical Christian. At a young age I knew, beyond doubt, that my sins were forgiven. I submitted my life to Jesus as my Lord. Then I came into a revelation and experience of the baptism of the Spirit. Jesus filled me with the Holy Spirit and I began to enter into the gifts of the Spirit. I had powerful supernatural experiences. Yet I never thought to ask Jesus where *He* lived. I never thought to go to the place where He came from, and drew His life and power from. I never even considered that He had a context and an environment out of which He lived and ministered.

It wasn't until I collapsed in total burnout and moral failure, in late 2007, that I began to follow the way of these two disciples. In August 2008, I finally asked Jesus the question, "Lord, where do *You* abide?" and He replied, "Come and see." Then He took me home to His abiding place in the bosom of the Father.

THE CALLING OF THE TWELVE

One of the two who heard John speak and followed Jesus was Andrew, Simon Peter's brother. He first found his own brother Simon and said to him, "We have found the Messiah" (which means Christ). He brought him to Jesus. Jesus looked at him and said, "You are Simon the son of John. You shall be called Cephas" (which means Peter). — JOHN 1:40-42

The two disciples who went to Jesus' home immediately become witnesses. They naturally witness within the sphere of their intimate relationships. Andrew goes and finds his own brother Simon, telling him immediately that the hoped-for Messiah has been found. Andrew's time with Jesus has convinced him beyond all doubt that the Hope of Israel is now among them. Andrew testifies to Simon on the basis of revelation and Simon catches the excitement of Andrew's spirit. When Simon meets Jesus he is given another name. Jesus bypasses Simon's family inheritance and speaks Simon's true identity into him. Jesus immediately recognises Simon Peter as a living stone, something that can be used in the building of a spiritual house.

Jesus, knowing within Himself that He is the cornerstone of the building of a new temple that is built with spiritual stones, calls forth Simon Peter as a living stone in the new building. From this point on, Peter and his ministry are defined by this new identity as a spiritual building block. Years later, Peter writes in his letter:

> *"As you come to Him, a living stone rejected by men but in the sight of God chosen and precious, you yourself like living stones are being built up as a spiritual house."*
> — I PETER 2:4,5

The spiritual house that is now being built is the Father's house on earth. Jesus, rejected by men (John 1: 10,11) is already the Cornerstone of the house and, by naming Simon as Cephas (Peter), He aligns one of the first stones to Himself the Cornerstone. The spiritual house will now be built on that basis. The spiritual house that the Trinity will inhabit will be built out of those whose hearts are aligned to the Son, who are the outcasts of the world, set aside by the builders of orphan structures as useless and redundant.

Jesus is very intentional in who He chooses to be part of the foundation of what the Father is building. These men are to be the foundation of a completely new epoch built upon the foundation of sonship. These are the men that the Father gave Him out of the world, to whom He would manifest the Father's name (John 17:6). The foundation of the spiritual house is to be built upon the revelation of who the Father is. Anything that is not built upon the revelation of who the Father is will not be a spiritual house. This is why orphanness always defaults to building man-made structures and organisations.

It is remarkable that, after Jesus returned to heaven, God was willing to entrust the whole plan for redemption to these twelve disciples. There were others, of course; approximately 150 on the day of Pentecost, then Paul. The plan for the redemption of the universe has been entrusted to weak humans. The point is, God implicitly trusts His sons and daughters for the redemption of the universe. There is something profoundly impacting about a weak human being filled with the love of God. Universal and cosmic redemption requires nothing more than that. The cross is the ultimate portrayal of this reality.

CAN ANYTHING GOOD COME OUT OF NAZARETH?

The next day Jesus decided to go to Galilee. He found Philip and said to him, "Follow me." Now Philip was from Bethsaida, the city of Andrew and Peter. Philip found

Nathanael and said to him, "We have found him of whom Moses in the Law and also the prophets wrote, Jesus of Nazareth, the son of Joseph.

Nathanael said to him, "Can anything good come out of Nazareth?" Philip said to him, "Come and see." Jesus saw Nathanael coming toward him and said of him, "Behold, an Israelite indeed, in whom there is no deceit!" Nathanael said to him, "How do you know me?" Jesus answered him, "Before Philip called you, when you were under the fig tree, I saw you." Nathanael answered him, "Rabbi, you are the Son of God! You are the King of Israel!" Jesus answered him, "Because I said to you, 'I saw you under the fig tree,' do you believe? You will see greater things than these." And he said to him, "Truly, truly, I say to you, you will see heaven opened, and the angels of God ascending and descending on the Son of Man." — JOHN 1:.43-51

Jesus is very intentional. He decides to go to Galilee to look for Philip. Philip, an evangelist by calling and gifting, is to be a key player in the building of this spiritual building. The book of Acts tells us of Philip's adventures in being led by the Spirit to gather people into the community of love. Philip is to become an expert gatherer of living stones, whether by preaching and miracle-working (Acts 8:5-8) or by strategic witnessing to one person, the Ethiopian eunuch (Acts 8:26-38). Philip's future ministry will be characterised by supernatural happenings (Acts 8:39).

Philip's enthusiasm spills over to Nathanael. Nathanael has a more reserved personality. His immediate response is to doubt that the

Expected One can come from Nazareth. Nazareth was obviously a town which was despised, a sleepy, country town of not much more than 500 people. It was insignificant and looked down upon.

This is almost invariably the way God works. It is a very natural response, when hearing of something that God is doing, to say, "Can anything good come out of…?" We need to be careful not to equate what God sees potential in, with what human nature sees potential in. I am realising more and more the enormous potential in what has been written off by the natural mind. The assessment of the Tree of the Knowledge of Good and Evil is flawed. Much of what is admired as having potential is on the basis of human good/bad judgements. I love the fact that God has chosen the weak to shame the strong. "God has chosen what is low and despised in the world, even things that are not, to bring to nothing things that are." (1 Corinthians 1:27,28) The time will come when we will be shocked to discover how God has built an eternal reality on the foundation of what is weak, low and despised. This brings tremendous hope to those who find themselves in spiritual crisis.

Nathanael doubts that the Messiah can even come from Nazareth but his doubts are quelled when Jesus speaks to him and calls forth his true identity. Jesus saw Nathanael before Philip even spoke to him. Nathanael is not Philip's choice; Nathanael is chosen by Jesus. The Father is orchestrating the gathering of the followers of Jesus. All Jesus needs to do is connect with a few people of particular gifting and then let them do what they naturally do. The Body of Christ today is overly micro-managed, basically because the gifting of God in people is neither seen nor trusted by leadership. Jesus works in a very 'non-managerial' way. Jesus playfully dances His way through the work that the Father has set for Him to do.

HEAVEN AND EARTH RECONNECTED

"And he said to him, Truly, truly I say to you, you will see heaven opened, and the angels ascending and descending on the Son of Man." — JOHN 1:51

Nathanael is promised the sight of an opened heaven. To see heaven opened is to see beyond the categories of human assessment. When we see heaven opened, we see that everything is settled and complete. From the foundation of the world, the one and only eternal reality issues forth. The Gospel is to bring us back to what is eternally ancient yet ever new. The Gospel is a story of redemption which originates in heaven and restores the connection of heaven and earth.

Nathanael would immediately recognise this picture of the angels ascending and descending. He would have known the story of Jacob's dream in the Torah:

"And [Jacob] dreamed, and behold, there was a ladder set up on the earth, and the top of it reached to heaven. And behold, the angels of God were ascending and descending on it." — GENESIS 28:12

The angels who ascend and descend convey the reality of the ongoing heaven-earth connection. When Jacob had this dream he was promised an inheritance on earth, an inheritance in the land. This promise has been misunderstood as being something political and national. Rather, it is the promise that the earth itself is to be inhabited by those who originate in heaven. Heaven's purpose is to bless and redeem the groaning creation. Rather than gaining a political inheritance the sons and daughters of God are to be conduits of heaven's activity. Jesus, as Son of Man, is the pioneer and exemplar of the redeeming of creation. Redeemed humanity is to become the ladder upon which the angels ascend and descend. Sonship in human form is the conduit of heavenly presence and action upon the earth.

As the Gospel of John unfolds before us we will see the connection between heaven and earth restored. We will become participators in the emergence of the ancient future. We will see revelation dawning upon the darkness and the green shoots of resurrection life spring up. The 'book of beginnings' for the new creation ushers us into the beauty of what it means to be with Christ in the bosom of the Father.

NEW WINE, NEW TEMPLE

~

THE WEDDING AT CANA

On the third day there was a wedding at Cana in Galilee, and the mother of Jesus was there. Jesus also was invited to the wedding with his disciples. When the wine ran out, the mother of Jesus said to him, "They have no wine." And Jesus said to her, "Woman, what does this have to do with me? My hour has not yet come." His mother said to the servants, "Do whatever he tells you."

Now there were six stone water jars there for the Jewish rites of purification, each holding twenty or thirty gallons. Jesus said to the servants, "Fill the jars with water." And they filled them up to the brim. And he said to them, "Now draw some out and take it to the master of the feast." So they took it. When the master of the feast tasted the water now become wine, and did not know where it came from

(though the servants who had drawn the water knew), the
master of the feast called the bridegroom and said to him,
"Everyone serves the good wine first, and when people have
drunk freely, then the poor wine. But you have kept the
best wine until now." This, the first of his signs, Jesus did at
Cana in Galilee, and manifested his glory. And his disciples
believed in him. — JOHN 2:1-11

John the storyteller, launches Jesus into His ministry in the context
of this wedding at Cana. John's Gospel is full of signs, and this
is the first sign. It is well recognised by biblical commentators that
John deliberately highlights the miracles performed by Jesus as
'signs.' Many commentators limit themselves to the supernatural
miracles when they talk about the signs, but I believe the signs
throughout John are not necessarily limited to the miracles. From
God's perspective, miracles are normal. Miracles are there to convince
us when we struggle to believe, but when we begin to believe we
will see signs throughout the whole book. In fact, Jesus is *the* sign
pointing to the Father so we can view everything that He does as
a sign which has deeper meaning attached.

All the signs are significant. The big question is: what do the signs
actually say and where do they direct our attention to? Where do
the signs point? A sign is not an end in itself; it points towards a
destination. One of the problems that we human beings have, is a
tendency to mistake the sign for the destination. We tend to over-
emphasise the sign and establish our camp around the sign. This is
like stopping the car at a road sign which says '100 km to London'
and writing postcards telling our friends that we have already
arrived in London. We would then take photographs of the road

sign and post them on Facebook with the album title "Our holiday in London." In our Christian life, we have tended to elevate the sign and miss out on the destination.

A few years ago, I was in a church meeting in one of the most beautiful locations in the world. Looking out the window, the ocean rolled in onto a sandy beach. When the service started, net curtains were drawn across the view. This was understandable because the pastor didn't want people to be distracted from his sermon. An ironic thing happened when the service finished, however. After the ministry time, the worship leader invited everyone to sit and relax in the presence of God. Soaking music was put on and he asked the technical guy to put a video on the overhead screen. Do you know what the video was? It was a grainy video of ocean waves crashing on a beach! We watched this inferior image while the awesome splendour of the real thing unfolded behind the drawn curtains. In the same way, we tend to camp round 'virtual reality' and miss out on 'substance-reality.'

Every sign that Jesus performs is intended to point to the Destination, directing us to the reality of the Father. Until this day, when the revelation of the Father is beginning to be made known, the Body of Christ has mostly been encamped around the Sign. We have become bogged down on the way to the Father. However, as Scripture is being opened up in the light of the Father's love, we are seeing the signs for what they really are and allowing them to lead and propel us towards the destination. As we journey through this book of John, we will discover what the signs say about the Father.

THE THIRD DAY AND THE FIRST SIGN

"On the third day." (v.1) There is a significance in 'the third day.' To me, this speaks of resurrection into a new era; it signifies a new beginning beyond death. When John wrote this book he would have known full well that Jesus rose from the dead on the third day.

The third day is also a day of renewal. It is the fulfilment of the prophecy of Hosea:

> *"Come, let us return to the Lord.*
> *For he has torn us, that he may heal us;*
> *He has struck us down, and he will bind us up.*
> *After two days he will revive us;*
> *On the third day he will raise us up,*
> *That we may live before him."*
> — HOSEA 6:1-3

When he speaks of 'the third day,' John is heralding a new beginning. He is introducing the dawning of newness, of restoration, of revelation that brings healing and the binding of wounds. The "beginning of signs" happens on the third day. The signs begin when the death of the old is complete.

When we are awakened to the 'third day,' we are also awakened to the 'signs.' When we see from the perspective of 'the third day,' we will recognise that our life and all our circumstances are actually signs that point to another reality.

"And the mother of Jesus was there." (v.1) Mary is important.

Protestantism has thrown out the proverbial baby with the bathwater when it comes to Mary. Mary may not be an object of veneration as such but she is worth far more attention than she has been given by the Protestant tradition. *Mary herself is a sign,* a sign of what the Father wishes to incarnate Himself in. Mary is the only human being who ever carried the incarnate Trinity physically within her.

The presence of the mother of Jesus at this wedding emphasises the importance of the Incarnation. Her role in the sign demonstrates that it takes a partnership between heaven and earth to work the miracle. She shows that the Father is to be manifested in human flesh. Mary is savvy enough to tell the servants to do whatever Jesus instructs them.

Jesus is invited to the wedding with His disciples. The significance of the wedding is the coming together of two persons in union, the joining of male and female, of the masculine and the feminine. In this revelation of the Father's love, we know that the true image of God is equally masculine and feminine.[10] The dominion given to humanity in Eden was given to the image of God, the man *and* the woman. Since the Fall, there has been an irreconcilable division between the sexes. Since that time there has also been a constant struggle to rejoin male and female, and vice versa.

God has also sought to keep the relational bond with His people. God's covenant with Israel is likened to a marriage. The Law kept the nation of Israel bound in covenant relationship to God. The

---

10. Denise Jordan sets this out in her book, *The Forgotten Feminine,* published by Fatherheart Ministries, Taupo, 2013.

point that John is making here is that the celebration and vitality of the union is interrupted. The wedding of God and humanity has ground to a halt because the wine has run out.

> *When the wine ran out, the mother of Jesus said to him,*
> *"They have no wine." —* JOHN 2:3

Nothing spoils a party like the wine running out. That is probably enough to provoke a riot. The wedding guests may be half drunk already, and the celebration is in full swing.

The vivifying energy of the Old Covenant has run out; there is no more life in it. The Old Covenant, based around a view of a God that demanded obedience, no longer has the energy to make the heart glad. The wine running out speaks of burnout, of weariness and emptiness. What is needed to keep the party going cannot be relied on any more. We are left high and dry and our lack of inner energy and life is very obvious.

The old *must* run out before the sign of the new era can begin. The old wine *has to* run dry before Jesus provides the new wine. This has been my experience personally. My connection with God was energised by legalism. In 2007, the wine that kept me going ran out. It ran out to such an extent that in my distress I turned to illegitimate means for comfort and stimulus. From this passage, John is showing that the comfort and stimulus of the old era of servant-hearted Christianity, of 'Old-Covenant' Christianity, has run out. The wedding celebration has stopped until the Son initiates a new thing and demonstrates a sign.

MARY - A CATALYST FOR DIVINE ACTION

And Jesus said to her, "Woman, what does this have to do with me? My hour has not yet come." — JOHN 2:4 [11]

Those who wish to downplay the role of Mary assert that Jesus' calling her "Woman" is a putdown. I do not believe for a moment that Jesus is dishonouring His mother. I want to suggest that His addressing of her as "Woman" can also be seen as highlighting the end of the war against the feminine. To get the gist of what I am suggesting, you need to read *The Forgotten Feminine* by Denise Jordan.[12] In that book, Denise Jordan brings out the truth that Satan has a specific strategy against the feminine image of God. There is a deep systemic misogyny from the very beginning to undermine and attack all that is feminine.

Mary's role at the Cana wedding feast highlights that it is the woman who announces the end of the old era and the start of the new era. Mary is part of that company of women who announce the good news (Psalm 68:11).

Mary, the 'woman,' stands at the threshold of the new era. Her son's response to her is that His hour has not yet come. It is not His time. Yet, 'His hour' is literally just minutes away! The new era is pounding on the door. Despite the words of Jesus, Mary knows that the working of the miracle is imminent. Where others would be put off by Jesus' statement that His time has not yet come, Mary

---

11. Some versions have Jesus saying, "Woman, what does this have to do with *you?*" which suggests Jesus disrespects His mother. I am sticking with the ESV translation as "Woman, what does this have to do with *Me?*' (italics mine).

12. Available from Fatherheart Ministries, www.fatherheart.net

has the faith to pull the future into the present. She instructs the servants to be ready and do whatever Jesus tells them to do. Mary can smell the whiff of a miracle.

Mary's faith pulls the future into the present. Hebrews 6:5 tells us of those who had "tasted…the powers of the age to come." The restoration of the true feminine carries with it the faith to taste the powers of a coming age.

THE MIRACLE BEGINS TO UNFOLD

Now there were six stone water jars there for the Jewish rite of purification… — JOHN 2:6

In Biblical understanding, the number 'six' signifies incomplete human effort.[13] The quantity of six represents what man has generated in his own strength.

The six stone water jars are, like the old wine, another symbol of the religious system. As we go through his Gospel, we will find that John records specific details to represent the system of religion. The water jars are intended to bring external purification but they cannot purify the human heart. Religion emphasises outer purification in order to be acceptable to God. If you get the externals right, then you can be united with God. Jesus really hammered the point to the Pharisees that they looked right on the outside but were rotten on the inside. True purity is a purity of the heart.

---

13. The Hebrews used the number 'seven' as code for 'completeness' or 'fulness' (in God), and the number 'six' as code for the incomplete effort generated by humanity. In the Hebrew mind, 'seven' is God's number, 'six' is man's number.

The sign begins to unfold. Jesus proceeds to act out the conditions for the miracle to occur. I need to ask; did Jesus respond to His mother's faith here? Did she cause Him to move? Maybe she did. My knowledge of God is that He initiates, but He *also* moves in response to our faith. The glory of the Incarnation is that God can respond to the initiative of our faith. This doesn't contradict the statement that the sons of God are led by the Spirit (Romans 8:14). God is always the initiator but in the outworking of faith, He is looking for a people who trust Him enough to take a step into the unknown. Mary demonstrated trust in the heart of God and she instructed the servants to be ready for what Jesus would direct.

Jesus rolls out the miracle. He instructs the servants to fill the jars with water. He uses what is already available and what is to hand.

A NEW FEAST-MASTER REPLACES
THE OLD FEAST-MASTER

And he said to them, "Now draw some out and take it to the master of the feast." So they took it. When the master of the feast tasted the water now become wine, and did not know where it had come from (though the servants who had drawn the water knew)... — JOHN 2:8,9

John highlights the 'master of the feast' here. He is the chief administrator and organiser of the wedding. In this passage, he is shown in a poor light. He seems to be unaware of the problem of an inadequate supply of wine. The wine has run out on his watch. If a hotel manager allowed the bar to run dry in the middle of a wedding party he would be in a lot of trouble. The 'master of the feast' appears to us as incompetent.

On another level, the master of the feast is out of touch with the working of the miracle itself. The servants who pour the water into the jars are in on the miracle. They know that water went in but wine is coming out. They also know that they are following the instructions of another 'master of the feast,' Jesus. The new 'master of the feast' has caught the old 'master of the feast' on the hop!

This 'master of the feast' represents religious officialdom. He is the administrator of the old system that has run out of energy and life. He is out of touch and his communication with the bridegroom has broken down. He actually castigates the bridegroom for keeping the good wine under wraps.

It is fascinating that Jesus doesn't explain the sign. In his rebuke of the bridegroom, the 'master of the feast' verbalises what the sign is supposed to convey:

> *"Everyone serves the good wine first, and when the people have drunk freely, then the poor wine. But you have kept the best wine until now."* — JOHN 2:10

The old era of religion, of obedience under the Old Covenant (we could include servant-hearted/orphan-spirited Christianity in this) begins with 'good wine.' At the beginning we enjoy it and drink freely of it. We get tipsy on it. We are enlivened and stimulated by calls to radical obedience, by great visions, by activities and programmes for improvement. Personally speaking, I freely drank and became inebriated on the 'good wine' of servant-hearted Christianity.

Somewhere along the line, however, the 'good wine' runs out and the 'poor wine' is introduced. At first we are so drunk on the good wine that we do not notice that the 'master of the feast' has introduced poor wine to keep the party going. Ultimately, however, the poor wine begins to take its toll. Merriment turns to nausea, a feeling of wellbeing turns to dizziness. Then we discover that there is *no more* wine, not even the inferior stuff. The party is over.

The reality for me was that I *had tasted* the 'good wine' of genuine moves of God. The Spirit had undoubtedly moved in power. But, unknown to me, the 'good wine' ran out and was replaced with 'poor wine.' What is represented by the 'poor wine'?

Because the power of the Spirit is no longer evident in many churches, something else has been introduced to keep the party going. No amount of highly sophisticated programmes, of musical talent, along with slick presentation and ultra-cool preachers can compensate for the loss of tangible anointing and presence within meetings. Churches that once experienced the tangible presence of God with demonstration of the supernatural have run out of this 'good wine.' To keep the show going, to keep attendance high, to pay for buildings and salaries, a 'culture of excellence' has been introduced. The 'culture of excellence' is poor wine and it is running out.

"But you have kept the best wine until now." These nine words encapsulate what the sign is. The revelation of the love of the Father and of our relationship to Him as sons and daughters is the *best* wine. It is the wine that comes from the heavenly vineyard. The inadequacy of man's effort is transformed by the touch of Jesus into the vivifying reality of God.

This episode of Jesus turning the water into wine is precisely what has played out in my life. My attempted union with God was presided over by the 'master of the feast,' that is, by legalism. My Christianity was following the same course. The good wine was replaced by poor wine, then the wine ran out. The rug was pulled out from my desire for union with God. The music and the dancing were abruptly halted.

However, out of my attempts to become pure in my own strength, something was touched by Jesus, the Son. My water was turned into His wine. He introduced me to His Father, the Source of the never-ending supply of new wine. Sonship to the Father provided the energy, stimulus, and the richness that I always longed for.

The wedding celebration can now resume, energised and enlivened by the new wine, the Sprit who pours out the love of God within the human heart. It is the Spirit of sonship that energises our Christianity.

> *This, the first of his signs, Jesus did at Cana in Galilee,*
> *and manifested his glory. And his disciples believed in him.*
> — JOHN 2:11

It is not surprising, given what we now understand, that the *first* of Jesus' signs occurs at a wedding. Biblical history began with a wedding between a man and woman, and it will end with a wedding between Christ and the Church. This final and ultimate union can only be energised by the revelation of sonship. When we come into the reality of our sonship on an individual level, the Bride will begin to be seen on a corporate level. First sons and daughters, then the Bride!

MANIFESTING GLORY

"…and manifested his glory." The display or manifestation of glory, is very important to John. Glory is the full expression of a person's true nature. To use the expression 'manifest glory' is to *strongly emphasise* what happened. It is an expression of intensification. Throughout his writings, John makes a great deal of the manifestation of glory.

- *"…and we have contemplated his glory, a glory as of the only begotten of the Father."* — JOHN 1:14

- *"The only Son, who is in the bosom of the Father, has declared [manifested] Him."* — JOHN 1:18

- *"Father,…glorify your Son, that the Son may glorify you."* — JOHN 17:1

- *"That which was from the beginning, which we have heard, which we have seen with our eyes, which we looked upon and have touched with our hands, concerning the word of life - the life was made manifest, and we have seen it, and testify to it and proclaim to you the eternal life, which was with the Father and was made manifest to us…"* — 1 JOHN 1:1,2

The glory of Jesus is manifested to John. The glory of the Father is manifested to John through gazing at the Son. I am convinced that John (and later Paul) excelled in contemplating the glory of the Father and the Son, and the glory transformed them. When

John writes that Jesus "manifested His glory," he fully means that the glory of the Father is manifested through Jesus. We need to gaze into the words of the Gospel to see the glory that is shining through the language.

> *"After this he went down to Capernaum, with his mother and his brothers and his disciples, and they stayed there for a few days."* — JOHN 2:12

John has highlighted Mary as the human catalyst for the miracle at Cana, co-working with the Father to make room for the Son to work the miracle, and he continues to note Mary's presence with Jesus, travelling with Him.

When John was writing his gospel narrative, he would have already lived with Mary for a number of years, caring for her as his mother. Remember that, on the cross, Jesus gave Mary and John to each other as mother and son. As we shall see, Mary's influence in the spirituality of John is evident. The feminine quality of John's gospel is recognisable.

THE RELIGIOUS CULTURE OF TRADING MUST GIVE WAY TO THE FATHER'S CULTURE OF GIVING

> *The Passover of the Jews was at hand, and Jesus went up to Jerusalem. In the temple he found those who were selling oxen and sheep and pigeons, and the money-changers sitting there. And making a whip of cords, he drove them all out of the temple, with the sheep and oxen. And he poured out the coins of the money-changers and overturned their tables.*

And he told those who sold the pigeons, "Take these things away; do not make my Father's house a house of trade." His disciples remembered that it was written, "Zeal for your house will consume me." — JOHN 2:13-17

We can be somewhat disturbed by the violence of Jesus' actions here. He is not meek and mild when He drives out the moneychangers and overturns their tables. It must have been remarkable to witness this scene, but what happens in the temple carries a far more profound meaning than the actual event.

Jesus, the Son, is acting prophetically here. His actions are the actions of a prophet, violently overturning what is false and misleading about God. To borrow Paul's phrase, in 2 Corinthians 10:5, Jesus is "destroying everything that is raised against the knowledge of God."

I have written about the prophetic nature of sonship elsewhere.[14] The prophetic carries a destructive element within it but this violence is the violence of love. It is the Son's zeal for the Father's house. The Father is being grossly misrepresented here by the trade within the temple court. The Father's house has become a house of trade, a house of merchandise.

In this context, the concept of trade is not limited to selling things for money to make a profit. To understand what is happening here, we need to know that the basic principle of trading is that you receive something in exchange for a payment. The concept of trade

14. *What Does it Mean to be Prophetic?* by Stephen Hill

is the very antithesis of what characterises the Father's house; Jesus overthrows the tables so violently because the practice of trading so misrepresents who the Father really is. The Father's house works on principles that are diametrically opposite to the culture of trading. Payment in exchange for a benefit or favour is part of the religious set-up, whereas the Father's house works on the basis of *giving and receiving*. In the Father's house there is a constant flow of grace-gift emanating from the heart of the Father.

Religion, in its essence, is really an issue of trading. According to Ezekiel 28:16, one of the charges put to Lucifer was this:

> *"In the abundance of your trade, you were filled with violence in your midst, and you sinned."*

The "abundance of trade" was the corrupted wisdom (Ezekiel 28:17) of Satan. Satan believed that, by trading, he could become like God. Godlikeness was something to be earned, to be bought. This is the very beginning, and the core principle, of religion. You give in order to receive. The Father's house is the exact opposite: You receive His gift and then give out of that receiving.

When Jesus drives out the moneychangers with His whip and overturns their tables, He is destroying the very heart of the religious deception.

THE NEW TEMPLE REPLACES THE OLD TEMPLE

> *So the Jews said to him. 'What sign do you show us by doing these things?' Jesus answered them, 'Destroy this temple, and*

in three days I will raise it up.' The Jews then said, 'It has taken forty-six years to build this temple, and you will raise it up in three days?' But he was speaking about the temple of his body. When therefore he was raised from the dead, his disciples remembered that he had said this, and they believed the Scripture and the word that Jesus had spoken.
— JOHN 2:18-22

This sign is the sign of the new temple replacing the old temple. It is another sign of the transition from the old era to the new era, from law to grace, from servanthood to sonship, from old wine to new wine. Now we have the transition from the old wineskin to the new wineskin. The old structure which 'housed' God under the system of religious trading is dealt a blow by the Son's prophetic actions.

Jesus radically redefines the temple, the dwelling place of God. He dismisses the edifice that sustains rituals based on a wrong view of God and reveals that the *real* temple is the body of the Son. God's real dwelling place is the temple of the humanity of sons and daughters. He does not dwell in temples made with hands (Acts 17:24). Instead of *going to church,* we begin to realise that we *are* the Church. Yes, we gather together, but we are still temples when we are not gathered. This is the scandal and glory of incarnation. God is pleased to dwell in a human person. The temple of the Father is in the human person of the Son, and now, by the indwelling of the same Spirit, in sons and daughters.

For those who have eyes to see, every sign in John's Gospel shows the stark contrast between an old, servant-hearted connection with

God based on law observance, and a new sonship relationship with
the Father based on receiving His gift of life.

THE NEW BIRTH

~

NICODEMUS SEEKS ANSWERS

*Now there was a man of the Pharisees named Nicodemus, a
ruler of the Jews. This man came to Jesus by night and said
to him, "Rabbi, we know that you are a teacher come from
God, for no one can do these signs that you do unless God is
with him." Jesus answered him, "Truly, truly, I say to you,
unless one is born again he cannot see the kingdom of God."
Nicodemus said to him, "How can a man be born when he
is old? Can he enter a second time into his mother's womb
and be born?" Jesus answered, "Truly, truly, I say to you,
unless one is born of water and the Spirit, he cannot enter
the kingdom of God. That which is born of the flesh is flesh,
and that which is born of the Spirit is spirit. Do not marvel
that I said to you, 'You must be born again.' The wind blows
where it wishes, and you hear its sound, but you do not know
where it comes from or where it goes. So it is with everyone
who is born of the Spirit." — JOHN 3:1-8*

John introduces Nicodemus to the story. As a member of the Sanhedrin, Nicodemus is part of the religious system but he is to be found later bringing spices and ointments to embalm the body of Jesus (John 19:39). Nicodemus is on a spiritual journey to find deeper meaning and satisfaction for his soul.

> *Now there was a man of the Pharisees, named Nicodemus, a ruler of the Jews. This man came to Jesus by night and said to him, "Rabbi, we know that you are a teacher come from God, for no one can do these signs that you do unless God is with him."* — JOHN 3:1,2

Before we get to Nicodemus, notice the *modus operandi* of *Jesus*. In relation to the crowds who followed Him (John 2:23-25), He is compassionate but He is also *passive* in the sense that He waits for the approach of those who are hungry enough to want to progress further in revelation. He does not attempt to force something upon them that they are not ready for. Nicodemus, however, is evidently hungry enough to press in beyond the externals, to discover what is going on at a deeper level. His approach to Jesus, albeit stealthy, shows the desire that is in his heart to know more.

Nicodemus is a "ruler of the Jews," a good example of a 'master of the feast.' He is an administrator and official of the religious system which thrives on the misapprehension of who God really is. Without a revelation of the Father, he is bound to rules and external formulae. However, Nicodemus's heart is opening. The beautiful reality of grace is such that a tiny opening of the heart will let in enough love to give the heart sufficient confidence to open up more. Nicodemus is open enough to see the signs and go to where the signs point.

He moves beyond the crowd that Jesus didn't entrust Himself to.

Nicodemus comes to Jesus by night. He comes subversively, presumably because he is afraid to be seen. Jesus still agrees to spend time with him. Love needs to expand within us to drive out fear. Fear is driven out to the extent that love comes in. It is obvious that the love of God drove out fear in Nicodemus because he is later seen speaking for Jesus within the Sanhedrin, leading them to conclude that he had joined Jesus' followers (John 7:50-51).

Nicodemus' visit is evidence that he is beginning to interpret the signs. Rather than just being impressed by the wonders that Jesus is doing, Nicodemus recognises that Jesus is a teacher *come from God*. He sees that God truly is with Jesus. Nicodemus is hungry, but he does not receive any further revelation until he sits down to dialogue with the Revelator who has come to reveal the Father. Jesus, the Son, takes Nicodemus beyond the sign and begins to show him how to follow the sign, to connect with the true God, the one revealed as *Father*.

REBORN FROM NEW PARENTAGE

Jesus answered him, "Truly, truly, I say to you, unless one is born again he cannot see the kingdom of God." Nicodemus said to him, "How can a man be born when he is old? Can he enter a second time onto his mother's womb and be born?"
— JOHN 3:3,4

If the phrase 'born again' didn't mean *exactly* what it says, it would be tempting to use a different term altogether. The best way to grasp its full meaning is to use our imagination to picture what childbirth actually is. What is birth? The Oxford Dictionary defines birth as:

- the emergence of a baby or other young from the body of its mother; the start of life as a physically separate being;

- the beginning or coming into existence of something;

- A person's origin, descent, or ancestry.

This is precisely what happens in the new birth, in the *spiritual* realm.

Nicodemus is not as stupid as we have sometimes made him out to be when he asks Jesus:

> *"How can a man be born when he is old? Can he enter a second time into his mother's womb and be born?"*

Nicodemus is beginning to understand the radical nature of Jesus' statement and its ramifications.

This issue of being "born again" points to *the Father*. It is about a literal, yet not physical, *regeneration,* a reconnection with a *parentage* that is beyond natural parentage. Being born again is not so much about being 'saved' (in the sense of saying 'the sinner's prayer' as it is about coming into the reality of sonship. In 1 John 3:9 (NASB), John says, *"No one who is **born of God** practices sin, because His seed abides in him; and he cannot sin, because he is **born of God**."* This is a stunning statement. The original Greek word used for 'seed' here is *sperma,* from which we get the word 'sperm.' In other words, the very life-force of God is within us, generating and giving birth to us. This is enough to realise that the whole issue of being born again is much deeper than a label or an evangelical cliche. To be 'born again' is to be generated from the *sperma* of God the Father.

Nicodemus' questions highlight that the new birth is exactly like the natural birth. There is a conception, a pregnancy, a labour, and a birth. If we realised this, we would be more tuned to the spiritual process in people who come to Christ. We would be more like midwives. After the birth, we would ensure that the newborn are connected to the comforting and nurturing mother heart of God.

THE SPIRITUAL NATURE OF THE NEW BIRTH.

> *"Truly, truly, I say to you, unless one is born of water and the Spirit, he cannot enter the kingdom of God. That which is born of the flesh is flesh, and that which is born of the Spirit is spirit." —* JOHN 3:5,6

Jesus clearly delineates between natural conception and birth, and *spiritual* conception and birth. Spiritual conception and birth has *nothing* to do with human parenthood; it has *everything* to do with *God's* parenthood.

> *"Do not marvel that I said to you, 'You must be born again.' The wind blows where it wishes, and your hear its sound, but you do not know where it comes from or where it goes." So it is with everyone who is born of the Spirit." —* JOHN 3:7,8

This image of the wind has often been used to illustrate the apparently unpredictable movements of the Spirit. I do not believe that is what these verses mean. I want to suggest that they simply mean that we cannot identify by natural observation, such as a birth certificate or even a DNA test, the origin or destiny of the person who is born of the Spirit. Just as it is impossible to identify where the wind starts and finishes, it is impossible by natural deduction to identify where the son or daughter of God starts and finishes. Their origin is in the Father and their destination is in the Father. The person who is 'born of the Spirit' has heavenly genetics.

> *"Nicodemus said to him, 'How can these things be?' Jesus answered him, 'Are you the teacher of Israel and yet you do not understand these things? Truly, truly, I say to you, we speak of what we know, and bear witness to what we have seen, but you do not receive our testimony. If I have told you earthly things and you do not believe, how can you believe if I tell you heavenly things?"* — JOHN 3:9-12

Jesus shifts the focus away from an earthbound, natural mindset to a heavenly, spiritual mindset. Nicodemus, still within his natural intellect, is confused. Revelation must dawn in order to perceive the spiritual reality.

Jesus highlights the lack of enlightenment in Nicodemus. Notwithstanding Nicodemus' status as a 'teacher of Israel,' he really knows nothing of what Jesus is saying. Outside of revelation, he just doesn't understand.

The words, "Truly, truly, I say to you...," alert us to the fact that Jesus is about to make an important statement. It seems to suggest that Nicodemus had previously been sceptical about Jesus. Nicodemus' heart had been closed to Jesus. A hardened heart cannot receive revelation; only an open heart is receptive to revelation when it comes. Now here comes the important statement:

> *"No one has ascended into heaven except he who descended from heaven, the Son of Man. And as Moses lifted up the serpent in the wilderness, so must the Son of Man be lifted up, that whoever believes on him may have eternal life."*
> — JOHN 3:13-15

No one has ascended into heaven except He who *descended from heaven*. This is explosive. This statement sums up the whole cosmic issue of religion and Christianity. True Christianity is actually something which *descends from heaven*. Christianity cannot be achieved; it must be received. To attempt to 'ascend to heaven' without first recognising that heaven has descended to us is to go on the same trajectory as Lucifer. Lucifer, in Isaiah 14:13, purposed in his heart to "ascend to heaven." Everything that is from God has descended from heaven, having originated in Him. I am not denying that we can be lifted up and taken into His presence, but it is only as we know that our origin is in the Father. The orphan way of 'ascending to heaven' is a religious movement generated in self-effort.

Jesus reminds Nicodemus of Moses lifting the serpent up in the wilderness. The lifting up of the serpent was a sign. By looking at it, the Israelites received the substance of healing. The people were given something to look at to help them access the metaphysical reality beyond. The lifting up of the Son of Man upon the cross is to have the same effect. By faith, we can appropriate what He died for, the life which is eternal.

"...*that whoever believes in him may have **eternal** life.*" Believing in Jesus gives access to eternal life. To believe means that we invest and entrust our spiritual wellbeing to Him.

What is the eternal life that we receive? It is to come into a relationship within the Trinitarian community of love. In John 17:3, Jesus defines 'eternal life' as a heart-knowing of "*Father,...the only true God, and Jesus Christ whom you have sen*t."

SAVED FROM CONDEMNATION

"For God so loved the world, that he gave his only Son, that whoever believes in him should not perish but have eternal life. For God did not send his Son into the world to condemn the world, but in order that the world might be saved through him. Whoever believes in him is not condemned, but whoever does not believe is condemned already, because he has not believed in the name of the only Son of God."
— JOHN 3:16-18

Let me put this verse in a different light than what we are used to. Because this is such a well known verse we tend to skim over it and miss out on its revelatory potential. A verse like this has become too familiar and familiarity often breeds contempt.

A big issue of salvation is freedom from condemnation. It may be that freedom from condemnation is more important than freedom from sin and here is why: When the man and his wife ate from the Tree of the Knowledge of Good and Evil in Eden, they became aware of something that they were never intended to become aware of. They were made aware of their nakedness. God didn't have a problem with their nakedness, before or after the Fall. However, *they* had a problem with their *own* nakedness. They became condemned in their own eyes. God did not look at them any differently (except with sadness and compassion for what was happening to them) but they looked at themselves and each other differently.

It is a well-known fact that *sin* entered into the world when they took of the forbidden tree. But let us think of it in this way: *condemnation* entered the world when they ate the fruit of the forbidden tree.

Condemnation is a precursor for sin. What robs us of eternal life is sin, yes, but, more fundamentally, it is *condemnation*. It is condemnation which fuels sin and when the root cause of sin is removed, there is no longer a sin issue. The root cause of all sin is the knowledge of good and evil.

Perishing is inextricably linked to condemnation. When we eat from the wrong tree we automatically begin to 'perish,' to fall into decay because we are cut off from the Tree of Life. When we move away from our dependence on the Tree of Knowledge we move into the Tree of Life where there is no condemnation. The bloodstream of eternal life can flow once again.

The primary reason for God sending His Son into the world is to reverse condemnation.

COMING TO THE LIGHT

"And this is the judgement: the light has come into the world, and people loved the darkness rather than the light because their deeds were evil. For everyone who does wicked things hates the light and does not come to the light, lest his deeds should be exposed. But whoever does what is true comes to the light, so that it may be clearly seen that his deeds have been carried out in God." — JOHN 3:19-21

The Greek word for judgement here is '*krisis*.' This judgement is not personally punitive, coming from a God who wishes to vent His displeasure. The appearance of the Light into the world brings a crisis; a watershed between those who respond to the Light and those who don't. All revelation brings a crisis because you either open your heart to it or keep your heart closed. This is the judgement. When God brings the light of revelation to us we can open our hearts to that revelation, thus becoming more Christlike. If we do not open our hearts to the 'crisis' that new revelation brings, we remain untransformed.

The person who "does what is true," who is authentic and committed to being increasingly authentic, is not afraid to open their heart to the Light. When the light of revelation enters and transforms the heart, the resulting actions will have been "carried out in God." Love produces fruit and that fruit is described by Paul in Galatians 5:22, 23:

"Love, joy, peace, patience, kindness, goodness, faithfulness, gentleness, self-control"

The light of love also exposes that which is 'wicked.' We need to understand that descriptions like 'wicked' or 'evil' are not restricted to what is morally reprehensible. From God's perspective doing 'good' out of self-righteousness is also 'wicked' and 'evil.' The motivation to do 'good' rooted in the knowledge of good and evil is also 'wicked.' Religious moralists are afraid to come to the light, because the light of love and of revelation will expose the motivation of their hearts. When the crisis of God's light comes it exposes the motivations of the human heart.

THE FRIEND OF THE BRIDEGROOM

After this Jesus and his disciples went into the Judean countryside, and he remained there with them and was baptising. John was also baptising at Aenon near Salim, because water was plentiful there, and people were coming and being baptised (for John had not yet been put in prison).

Now a discussion arose between some of John's disciples and a Jew over purification. And they came to John and said to him, "Rabbi, he who was with you across the Jordan, to whom you bore witness — look, he is baptising and all are going to him." John answered, "A person cannot receive even one thing unless it is given to him from heaven. You yourselves bear me witness, that I said, "I am not the Christ, but I have been sent before him. The one who has the bride is the bridegroom. The friend of the bridegroom, who stands and hears him, rejoices greatly at the bridegroom's voice. Therefore this joy of mine is now complete. He must increase, but I must decrease." — JOHN 3:22-30

When John the Baptist's disciples question him about the growing numbers of people going to Jesus, his response is very clear. Unless a person or a ministry anointing comes from heaven, it is worthless.

Gift is always initiated from a higher place. If a spiritual 'gift' is offered from somewhere that is not heaven, we cannot really receive the gift. John the Baptist discounts himself as the gift but affirms that he has been sent ahead of the Gift to help humanity become ready to receive the Gift. In one sense, John the Baptist helped to prise open the clenched fist of a humanity that was so orphaned that it had no ability to receive.

John the Baptist is the fulfilment of Malachi's prophecy:

> *"Behold, I will send you Elijah the prophet before the great and awesome day of the Lord comes. And he will turn the hearts of fathers to their children and the hearts of children to their fathers, lest I come and strike the land with a decree of utter destruction."* — MALACHI 4:5,6

The Baptist is turning the hearts of fathers back to their children and the hearts of the children back to their fathers. He is preparing an open hand to receive what is given from heaven.

John is the friend of the Bridegroom. As with the wedding in Cana, the motif of marriage is repeated here. The friend of the bridegroom has played a vital role in the preparation of the nuptials and now he hears the shout of the bridegroom as the bridegroom arrives at the banquet. John the Prophet has participated in preparing the Bride by laying the axe to the root of the Tree of the Knowledge of Good and Evil. He has also helped to prepare the Bride by restoring the child-father connection (Malachi 4:6). The restoration of individual hearts is a vital component and the principal catalyst in the preparation of the corporate Bride.

Softened and opened hearts on an individual level will compose a soft and open Bride who will be ready to receive the Bridegroom on the wedding night. Authentic prophetic ministry, by softening and opening the hearts of individuals, has a central role in the preparation of the Bride. When prophetic ministry ceases or is stifled, the readiness of the Bride takes a backward step.

The Church only comes out of sonship. There must be individual identity as sons and daughters in the Father's family who then become the corporate Bride. The Father has promised Jesus a Bride, formed out of His sons and daughters. The Bride is the daughter of the Father presented to the Son on His wedding day. There is only one bride. The Bride is a corporate identity, not an individual one. The paradigm through which every Christian needs to see themselves individually is that of beloved son or daughter.

When the Bride receives the Bridegroom and the wedding takes place, the ministry of the prophet is complete. But not before! Prophetic speech is needed as long as the Church remains unmarried to Christ. When the increase of the Bridegroom becomes established enough to be irreversible the ministry of the prophet can decrease.

HE WHO COMES FROM ABOVE

"He who comes from above is above all. He who is of the

*earth belongs to the earth and speaks in an earthly way. He
who comes from heaven is above all. He bears witness to
what he has seen and heard, yet no one receives his testimony.
Whoever receives his testimony sets his seal to this, that God
is true. For he whom God has sent utters the words of God,
for he gives the Spirit without measure." — JOHN 3:31-34*

The true direction of spiritual authority flows from heaven to
earth. The closer the connection to heaven, the greater the spiritual
authority. If a person is self-generated and is sent from earth without
heavenly connection, their speech will have no life-generating
power. The authority of one sent from heaven cannot be revoked.
Even when prophetic speaking is not received because it does not
fit our conservative mindsets and is either shouted down, ignored
or contextualised. The speech of heaven prevails over the categories
of our status quo.

*"For he whom God has sent utters the words of God, for he
gives the Spirit without measure. The Father loves the Son
and has given all things into his hand" — JOHN 3:34,35*

Jesus the Son, sent by God, speaks every word that the Father
utters. The words of Jesus can be trusted to be absolutely true and
absolutely from God. Why? Because God has given to Jesus His Spirit
without measure. The Father has not hesitated to pour within the
human Jesus the fulness of the Godhead-spirit and the completeness
of His personality. Paul verifies this when he writes:

*"For in him all the fulness of the Godhead was pleased to
dwell." — COLOSSIANS 1:19*

The fact that Jesus utters the words of God, flowing from the fulness within, demonstrates that the Son is loved by the Father. As we increase in likeness to Jesus, and as we become more merged with His sonship, we begin to realise that all things have been given to us. This is the journey of faith; to continuously explore the expansiveness of the gift that has been given by the Father to the Son. We are that gift but we also participate in receiving the gift. The gift is *all things*.

THE SON IS GIVEN EVERYTHING

"The Father loves the Son and has given all things into His hand." — JOHN 3:35

This statement sums up the essential core of the Trinity. The flow of love and gift is directed from its eternal Source, the Father, to its eternal Beneficiary, the Son. The love never ceases to emanate from the being of the Father, and the Son is always perfectly aligned to receive that love and to do something creative with it. The Son is not a passive recipient of the love. He pours it out to others by the Spirit. Jesus never moves out of His alignment with the Father who *is* love. The fruit of that patrial-filial relationship is the giving of all things into the hand of the Son. It cannot be any other way for love; for love wants to give all things into the hand of the one who is its object.

How does the One who is Son receive that love? Is the reception of all things entirely passive or does it need to be earned in any way? Does sonship have to qualify to receive something, according to its maturity in sonship? In some way, according to Philippians 2,

Jesus did 'qualify' to receive all things. He qualified by descending as deep as death on the cross.

The point that I wish to make here, however, is this: Even the qualification to mature from childhood into responsible and virile sonship is gained by still remaining in the down-flow of the Father's love. All a child really needs to do to mature into full sonship is to stay in the flow of receiving and responding to parental love. The perfect parental love of God our Father will do the work that is intended to bring us to a place of receiving all things, receiving the inheritance of our Father.

Sometimes we resort to striving to receive from the Father, but all we really need to do is to continue to be aligned with the love of the Father. No matter what age, receiving a gift is the same. True maturity as God intended it can only come in the environment of the Father's love. The sons of Luke 15 bear this out. For the younger son, it took a return to his father's house to come back to his inheritance. He had squandered it, but it still awaited him. The older son also needed to return to his father's house by leaving the field of self-righteousness.

It was only sonship that enabled Jesus to go to the cross and become sin. Whatever way you look at it, the life, death and resurrection of Jesus only makes sense through sonship. It was the knowledge and continuing awareness of the Father's love that sustained Him, through the downward movement, to the place of exaltation and receiving the name above all names. Whatever that name is, it was not given to Him beforehand. The Father's love carried Jesus to the depths, through the depths, and up from the depths to receive all things from His hand.

ETERNAL LIFE OR WRATH?

"Whoever believes in the Son has eternal life; whoever does not obey the Son shall not see life, but the wrath of God remains on him." — JOHN 3:36

Believing in the Son automatically connects us to the Source of eternal life, the Father. Eternal life is described later in John 17:3 as "[knowing] you, the only true God, and Jesus Christ whom you have sent." To believe in the Son is to believe in the Father; obedience to the Son is to submit to His directive in bringing us to the Father.

When the Fall marred creation, orphanness became the default condition of the human race. Access to the Tree of Life was revoked and Tree of the Knowledge of Good and Evil automatically became the food source. Since the Fall, all creation has been disconnected from the Tree of Life and from the parental love of God the Father.

I do not believe that the wrath of God is direct and punitive, coming out of divine petulance. The wrath of God is the default position of being disconnected from His life and love. To refuse belief in the Son is to fail to apprehend eternal life; it is to be blinded to where eternal life comes from. The eyes of the heart are not open to perceive the Tree of Life and so the wrath of God remains. The wrath of God manifests as corruption, as the removal of eternal life. In other words, the wrath of God is to remain living in the Tree of the Knowledge of Good and Evil with all its ramifications.

Paul, the apostle, writes in Romans that the "wrath of God is revealed from heaven." (Romans 1:18) It is not revealed against human beings but it is revealed against their "ungodliness" and their "unrighteousness." Therefore God's wrath is against what causes human beings to be independent from His love. In verses 24, 26 and 28, Paul repeats the phrase "God gave them up to…" The wrath of God, therefore, is God allowing human beings to do whatever they want, to be self-generated and self-energised, to be disconnected from the Father as source. The 'wrath of God' is the state of orphanness. God sent His Son into the world to rescue us from that, and to restore us back to the loving embrace of divine parenthood.

THE WELL IS WITHIN

~

In the shimmering heat, along the dusty road, He walks. With Him, His band of kindred spirits who have abandoned everything to follow Him. They are on the move from Judea towards the inland sea; their route will take them through the land of the despised apostates, Samaria. But the roads of contemptible Samaria are no dustier than the roads of Judea or Galilee; they blister the feet, parch the lips and exact their relentless toll on the travellers just the same. As the sun soars to its height, in the middle of the day, the group approaches the Samaritan village of Sychar.

A NEW FRONTIER

"Now when Jesus learned that the Pharisees had heard that Jesus was making and baptising more disciples than John…, he left Judea and departed again for Galilee. And he had to pass through Samaria. So he came to a town of Samaria called Sychar, near the field that Jacob had given to his son Joseph. Jacob's well was there; so Jesus, wearied as he was

from his journey, was sitting beside the well. It was about the sixth hour." — JOHN 4:1-6

The opening statement of this story of Jesus meeting the woman at the well verifies that John the Baptist is, as predicted, decreasing, and that Jesus is increasing:

"Now when Jesus learned that the Pharisees had heard that Jesus was making and baptising more disciples than John..."

John, the burning and shining lamp, is diminishing, and Jesus, the true light of dawn, is brightening. Inevitably, the previous move of God must make way for the new.

The Pharisees have a problem with the fading of John the prophet and the brightening of Jesus the Son. The religious persona attaches itself to a residue of the past while the Spirit of God has *already* transitioned to a new place. This new place is to be introduced by Jesus in His encounter with the woman at the well.

Jesus sits at the well alone. Fully human, He is exhausted from travelling, trudging along dusty tracks under scorching sun. The disciples have left Him to go to the village to buy provisions. After a while, Jesus is joined by a woman who has come to draw water from the well. This woman, like Jesus' mother at Cana, is set to become a catalyst for a major revelation about the Father. She is a rank outsider, a *woman* and a *Samaritan*. The Jews, *including* the disciples of Jesus, hated and despised the Samaritans, judging them as pagans and apostates.

Almost without exception, I have found that the blessing of God lies on the other side of a prejudice. What do I mean by this?

In my understanding of Scripture and Church History, and in my own personal experience, in order to enter into something new in God, I had to overcome my inbuilt pre-judgements. It wasn't that I had to *earn* God's blessing, but that I had to *humble* myself to be able to participate in what the Father wanted to do.

Oftentimes, the channel through which God's blessing came, was a person, a situation, or a cultural expression that was distasteful to me. Invariably it went against the grain of what I thought God approved of and was invested in. God definitely confounds the wise and uses the simple. He always takes us beyond what *we think* He is like in order to reveal Himself. Two biblical examples of this spring to mind:

- In 2 Kings 5:11-12, Naaman was offended and became enraged because he had a prejudice against the River Jordan. In his mind, the Abana and Pharpar rivers were superior to the muddy Jordan. Until he humbled himself on the advice of his servant and overcame his angry prejudice, he was not healed of his leprosy.

- In Acts 10:9-16, the Lord had to deal with an inbuilt prejudice in Peter before a new spiritual landscape could be opened up. Peter's vision of the great sheet filled with unclean animals, birds, and reptiles (which he was commanded to eat) hit at the very heart of his own tightly held assumptions of what God did and didn't approve of. Peter had to overcome guilt, offence and repulsion (which is how he would have viewed the Gentiles) to open up a new frontier of the Spirit's operation.

I use this to show the significance of this dialogue with the Samaritan woman. Jesus transcends cultural and religious prejudices to engage with her and to open up a frontier of revelation. This frontier of revelation, on the other side of prejudice, is a revelation about the Father.

THE GIFT OF GOD

The conversation begins when Jesus asks her for a drink of water. She immediately brings up the division between Jews and Samaritans:

> *"How is it that you, a Jew, ask for a drink from me, a woman of Samaria?"*

Then Jesus answers her:

> *"If you knew the gift of God, and who it is that is saying to you, 'Give me a drink', you would have asked him, and he would have given you living water."* — JOHN 4:10

This, like the wedding at Cana, is another 'sign' about the movement from religion to *life*. Jesus begins to talk to her about *living* water. If only she knew "the gift of God," and that the man talking to her is the distributor of the gift. The Father that Jesus is revealing is radically different from the God that she knows, and the distinguishing difference is that He is a God of *gift*. *Her* God, the *religious* God, does not give any gifts. The "gift of God" is a radical departure from what the woman's experience of God would have been. To this woman, the very idea of 'gift' is something totally foreign. She is downtrodden with serving the six men with whom she had lived throughout her life. She has no idea how to receive any gift.

The work of the Son is to distribute the gift from the Giver, the Father. Jesus' request for a drink to quench His thirst is a lead-in to offering the gift of living water to the woman. As we will see, water is a major theme in John's Gospel, because it is a symbol of life.

> The woman said to him, "Sir, you have nothing to draw with, and the well is deep. Where do you get that living water? Are you greater than our father Jacob? He gave us the well and drank from it himself, as did his sons and his livestock." — JOHN 4:11,12

At this point, the woman is still locked into her own paradigm. Revelation has not yet broken across her way of seeing reality.

"You have nothing to draw with, and the well is deep." This sentence sums up the way that religion constantly keeps us at arm's length from anything that truly satisfies the deep cry of the heart. The well is deep, the water cannot be got at, and there is nothing to get it with. The answer to your heart's cry, according to religion, is well-nigh impossible to access. The majority of people have no ability to access the solution to the problem of their thirst. The religious system thrives because it keeps people suspended in the horns of a dilemma.

The human race desperately needs comfort, but comfort is constantly elusive. Religion presents God like a mirage in the desert. As soon as you think you are approaching the oasis of union with God, it fades and shifts again. Eventually you collapse, utterly exhausted, and die of heatstroke and thirst. The religious system will always ask you to pay something for a bucket to let down into the well that it controls all access to.

THE WELL IS WITHIN US

The gift of living water, which springs up eternally *from the inside*, is the Father's response to an inaccessible well and a vessel that is impossible to purchase. The gift of the Father's love in the human heart is continual and it slakes the thirst *from within*. Living water, bubbling constantly from within, dispenses with the need to keep coming to the well. The New Covenant internalises the line of supply so that all the answers to human desperation come with the indwelling Spirit.

The central issue here is about a father and what he has given to his children. For this woman, it was "our father, Jacob." The problem is that, in our dislocation from the true Father, we attach our expectation to other fathers. But provision from fathers who are in themselves the source is running out. Any supply that is not from the *eternal* Source will inevitably run dry.

Jesus came to reveal the Father from whom all fatherhood derives its name.[15] All true fathering takes its nature and character from

---

15. One way of reading Ephesians 3:15 can be, "For this reason I bow my knees before the Father, from whom all *fatherhood* in heaven and on earth derives its name." (my italics).

the Father, the original Source. When the woman declares that the well was given by Jacob, Jesus' response to that statement is to say, in effect, "Let me show *you* the well that the Father, your *real* father, gives. It is freely accessible and it never runs out."

> *Jesus said to her, "Everyone who drinks of this water will be thirsty again, but whoever drinks of the water that I will give him will never be thirsty again. The water that I will give him will become in him a spring of water welling up to eternal life."* — JOHN 4:13,14

Everyone who drinks this water will be thirsty again. They will be thirsty because they are drinking from a well that comes from a father who is not eternal. The source of eternal water, the water that gives life which flows from the innermost being, is the source of all. That Source is the Father of Jesus. Drinking from the well of "our father Jacob" has a definite limit, but drinking from the well issuing from *our* heavenly Father is limitless. In fact, all the other fathers are invited to draw from that well too.

"The water that I will give him." This is the water that Jesus *Himself* drinks from. Jesus drinks from the bottomless well of the Father's love. He gives to us out of what He receives.

"…will become in him a spring of water welling up to eternal life." Jesus the Son, activates in us the spring of eternal life by giving of the water that is *within Him*. He takes the spring of clear water which eternally bubbles in His own heart and puts it into us. It is the water of life, the *one* life, and the only life which sustains everything. It is the God-life. From His Spirit, Jesus puts that God-life into our

spirits and that life has its own innate energy. Receiving living water from Jesus connects us to the Source of the living water, His Father.

We must go inwards to find the living water. There is a movement in this passage from an external source of water to an internal source of water. This is what is happening in Church history at this time. For many centuries, Christians have looked to *external sources* to quench spiritual thirst. The revelation of the Father brings with it a revelation of the Spirit who *indwells*. Old Covenant revelation does not go any further than a Spirit who acts externally but the New Covenant Spirit lives and acts from inside the believer. When we look within, we will find that the spring of life is bubbling up from the deepest place. The Holy Spirit within us is pouring out the love of God. Deep in the depths of my heart and your heart, is the Source. It is not originating in us; rather it is the love of God poured out into our spirits by the Spirit who cries "Abba, Father!" (Romans 8:11) "The Spirit himself bears witness that we are children of God." (Romans 8:16)

> *The woman said to him, 'Sir, give me this water so that*
> *I will not be thirsty or have to come here to draw water."*
> — JOHN 4:15

This woman's heart is beginning to open up. Jesus has been speaking prophetically. His words, from the heart and to the heart, have incised the woman's heart and now she admits her need; she is spiritually thirsty and needs to come to the well for water. She mentions the physical well here, but she is talking of her thirst at a spiritual level. She is beginning to realise that the whole topic of conversation runs much deeper than the differences between Jews and Samaritans and much deeper than a well or a water container.

She is beginning to receive revelation. From initially seeing Jesus as a Jew, and expecting Him to ignore her, she then perceives Him as a prophet. Her heart is opening. She is looking to place Him in a context so that she can get a handle on what He is saying to her. She begins to engage Him in a religious debate:

A SEVENTH HUSBAND

Jesus said to her, "Go, call your husband, and come here." The woman answered him, "I have no husband." Jesus said to her, "You are right in saying, 'I have no husband'; for you have had five husbands, and the one you now have is not your husband. What you have said is true." — JOHN 4:16-18

Jesus, speaking again prophetically, gets to the heart of what is hindering her from receiving the Father's love. For these rivers of living water which spring up to eternal life are nothing else but the Father's love. They are the life source and the fountainhead of refreshment. Jesus asks her to go and call her husband. This elicits a response from her that she has no husband. She is speaking here from a place of shame, from the Tree of the Knowledge of Good and Evil. She is deeply condemned and ashamed about her life circumstances of having five husbands and is now living with a man outside of marriage. Speaking as she does from the Tree of the Knowledge of Good and Evil, I wonder does she sense the presence of the Tree of Life?

Jesus, by supernatural knowledge, is able to tell her that He knows what her life is. It is almost certain that this woman, like Mary Magdalene, has been labelled as a prostitute. Yet this woman is a sign and, in her encounter with the Son, she becomes a catalyst for the seismic shift of revelation that Jesus is about to present.

Any reader of John's Gospel, who understands what the signs are really about, will prick up their ears at the mention of 'five husbands.' This detail is not concocted by John to fit his schematic, but it is, nevertheless, intentionally highlighted by the Holy Spirit. The 'five husbands' have the same meaning as the 'five roofed colonnades' in Bethesda in Chapter 5. I see a further connection to the five books of Moses, the Torah. The significance of these numbers would not be lost to the mind of John's readers.

My basic premise here is that the 'five husbands' represent being married to the Law. This woman has repeatedly attempted to fulfil her marital duty and she has repeatedly failed in that. The text does not say whether the five husbands had died or whether they had left her. Perhaps she left them, though, given the culture of her day, that is less likely. Nonetheless, we are left with the impression that she has had five unfulfilling marriages. She no longer has the capacity to stay within the legal obligations of marriage and so she is now living with Number Six who is not her legal husband. Exhausted by the Law, she has resorted to living by her human instincts. Five times she has attempted a successful life by trying to keep the Law; now she is resigned to living in the shame of her failure to keep the Law.

Unknown to her, she has met her 'seventh Husband.' Five husbands, cohabiting with a sixth, and now she meets Jesus. It goes without saying that Jesus is not to be her natural husband. The point is that Jesus redeems everything that she has been searching for but has not found. Jesus restores dignity and identity to her. Without uttering it, He reaffirms her beauty and worth.

WORSHIPPERS THE FATHER IS SEEKING

The woman said to him, "Sir, I perceive that you are a prophet. Our fathers worshipped on this mountain, but you say that in Jerusalem is the place where people ought to worship." Jesus said to her, "Woman, believe me, the hour is coming when neither on this mountain nor in Jerusalem will you worship the Father. You worship what you do not know; we worship what we know, for salvation is from the Jews. But the hour is coming, and is now here, when the true worshippers will worship the Father in spirit and truth, for the Father is seeking such people to worship him. God is spirit, and those who worship him must worship in spirit and truth." — JOHN 4:19-24

Up to this point in Church history, there has been little emphasis on the Father and, as a result, most people only emphasise the concept of *worship* when they read this verse. However, Jesus clearly puts the emphasis on *the Father;* it is the *Father* who is seeking those who will worship Him.

There has never been a shortage of people who worship 'God' but Jesus is connecting worship with knowing *the Father.* Jesus came to earth to reveal and manifest 'God' as 'the Father.' The worship of 'God' (unrevealed as Father) is too generic, too vague, and it gives rise to a systematic formula, leading us to focus on either 'Jerusalem' or 'this mountain.' The revelation of the Father is intimate and specific, and it is *in spirit and in truth*. This means that it is not an outward formula but it is an inward reality.

Worshipping God as 'Father' means that you not only worship Him as almighty and all-powerful, which all religions do, but you worship Him as *Father*; no religion does this. This is what He is seeking. God is looking for those who know Him as 'Father' and worship Him from that place of intimate relationship.

Jesus makes a powerful prophetic declaration to the woman. He declares to her:

> *"Woman, believe me, the hour is coming when neither on this mountain nor in Jerusalem will you worship the Father. You worship what you do not know; we worship what we know, for salvation is of the Jews But the hour is coming and is now here, when the true worshippers will worship the Father in spirit and in truth, for the Father is seeking such people to worship Him."* — JOHN 4:21-23

In this statement, Jesus declares the cessation of the old era and the ushering in of the new era. The old era places the emphasis on what form of worship is appropriate. The new era is not concerned with outward system or form. The new era of worshipping the Father brings us into the realm of spirit and truth.

"The hour is coming and is now here." When we receive the Father's love, it is no longer a question of waiting for a coming revival. The Father's love brings the hoped-for future into present reality.

Jesus overturns the basis on which worship is to take place. In doing so, He confronts the religious mindset. Religion cannot coexist with the revelation and experience of God as Father. What Jesus is saying is that when God is known as Father, worship can no longer be located in Jerusalem or 'this mountain' because its locus is now spiritual. Therefore, no geographical place is any holier than another. Worship is an issue of the inward heart. This is the fundamental difference between Old Testament and New Testament worship.

Have we seen worship in spirit and in truth yet? How will we recognise it when it emerges? All I can say is, the further we grow into sonship, the richer our own personal expressions will be, and those individual expressions will not be muzzled by the current revved-up liturgy in the excellence-driven culture. I suspect that some of the sons, consumed by zeal for the Father's house, will take a proverbial whip of cords and overthrow some things; for the Father's house has become a house of performance, a house of marketing techniques, and a house of merchandise.

These are the worshippers that the Father is seeking; worshippers who are at home in His presence. The prodigal is home from the road, the elder son is in from the field. They are together rejoicing in the Father's house. We have been so distant from His heart. All the trappings of covenant and law are subservient to the family relationship that we have found in Him.

If people only knew what was behind the apparent 'veil,' in the innermost place. The Holy of Holies is actually home! It is a place of rest and joy and communion. It is a place of union, not performance.

Worship within the inner place is relaxed and peaceful, without effort. It is a harmonious synergy of thought, emotion and activity. We are in the ark of the covenant, and the ark of the covenant is within us. This is the hope of glory. We are sunning ourselves in familial union with Father who is 'Abba.' This is what the religious mind cannot take in; the God whom we worship is 'Daddy!' It's really very simple. It offends the mind but it is what the heart longs for. The Holiest of All is *actually* Abba's bosom.

> *The woman said to him, "I know that Messiah is coming (he who is called Christ). When he comes, he will tell us all things." Jesus said to her, "I who speak to you am he."*
> — JOHN 4:25,26

Again we see that what is longed for and hoped for in the elusive future becomes a present reality. Jesus declares unequivocally that He, a weary man sitting at a well, is the One they have been waiting for. The in-breaking of God can be touched, talked to and looked upon. The experiencing of the Father's love in our hearts brings what we long for into reality. We can look into our hearts and hear Jesus saying to us, "Revival is here now. I who speak to you am He. I am living within You."

There is no need to wait for the time when all things will be revealed. When we encounter Jesus sitting beside the well of our hearts, we can hear Him tell us everything we ever did. By faith, take that time now; take the time to gaze into the well inside you and encounter the Person who will release the living water within you.

MY FOOD IS TO DO THE FATHER'S WILL

Just then his disciples came back. They marvelled that he was talking with a woman, but no one said, "What do you seek?" or, "Why are you talking with her?" So the woman left her water jar and went away into town and said to the people, "Come, see a man who told me all that I ever did. Can this be the Christ?" They went out of the town and were coming to him.

Meanwhile the disciples were urging him, saying, "Rabbi, eat." But he said to them, "I have food to eat that you do not know about." So the disciples said to one another, "Has anyone brought him something to eat?" Jesus said to them, "My food is to do the will of him who sent me and to accomplish his work." — JOHN 4:27-34

The disciples return with their provisions and are astounded that Jesus is talking *with a woman*. They are still seeing with the eyes of natural perception, with a cultural and religious paradigm. The truth is that this unknown woman has actually come into more revelation than the disciples.

I find it fascinating how many hidden trails there are in the strategy of God. Here is a woman to whom was revealed remarkable things about true worship and the Father, and yet we never hear about her again! How does John know how the conversation at the well went? Maybe Jesus related it back to him. Maybe Jesus told His mother, Mary, who then told it to John. Is it possible that this Samaritan woman reappeared in the community of faith that followed Jesus and was in the upper room at Pentecost? We can never know for sure. Jesus, however, *did* infect her with a virus of the love of the Father, and she gossiped the good news to the people of her town. When we are liberated from shame, our 'dark side' actually becomes a way of connection for others to receive the love of God. This woman has notoriety in her community, but in the Father's love *everything* is redeemable, and *everything* is redemptive.

The disciples press Jesus to eat some of the food they had purchased (v.31). They had gone to buy it because they were all hungry after walking in the heat of the day. Jesus, however, doesn't feel the need for food any more. He says to them, "*I have food to eat that you do not know about…My food is to do the will of him who sent me and to accomplish his work.*" The 'food' that satisfies Him is doing the Father's will. His co-participation with the Father literally satiates His hunger pangs. This shows that the Father's love is a metaphysical substance. To do the Father's will is to be a channel for the surge of the Father's love towards another, in this case, the Samaritan woman.

I have experienced this metaphysical reality of the Father's love. When I was a charismatic Christian I had quite a few supernatural experiences. They were exciting and stimulating but they were all *external*. They were outside me. I was affected by shaking or weeping, or laughing, or being bounced up and down. But when I first heard James Jordan preach on sonship I had another supernatural experience which was completely different. There was no external manifestation in my body but I felt a substance growing inside me, filling me up as if I had eaten a three-course meal. I couldn't eat any food for the rest of the day; my physical hunger was literally satisfied by the substance of the Father's love.

The love of God is a substantial, weighty reality to the spirit, not a concept to the mind. Jesus *really* doesn't feel hungry any more because the substance of the Father's love is rising up in His innermost being. Jesus *Himself* is living from the rivers of living water that flowed out of His belly (KJV). The substance of the Father's love can be literally felt in the belly. I use the King James terminology deliberately, because our form of Christianity is too often 'head-centric' and not 'belly-centric.' Rather than seeing revealed truth as concept, it is to be seen as reality which is centred in the innermost part, in our human spirit, which then flows outwards to the mind, will, and emotions. The love of God will even affect the physical body.

PERCEIVING THE ABUNDANCE OF THE HARVEST

> *"Do you not say, 'There are four months, then comes the harvest? Look, I tell you, lift up your eyes, and see that the fields are white for harvest. Already the one who reaps is receiving wages and gathering fruit for eternal life, so that sower and reaper may rejoice together."* — JOHN 4:35,36

When we realise that the true Gospel is actually about coming home to the Father, and living in a sonship relationship to Him, our eyes are opened to see that the fields are indeed 'white for harvest.' I am not a natural evangelist and, in the past, it would require a tremendous effort and personal sacrifice for me to 'witness.' However, manifesting the love of the Father to others, whoever they may be, *is* preaching the Gospel. I preach the same good news to 'Christians' and 'non Christians'. This perspective takes the striving out of it.

The other thing that has brought me freedom is the realisation that I am not on my own. It is not my individual responsibility to do everything. Bringing the good news of the kingdom is not primarily an individual responsibility. The work of ministry is a community task given to the Body of Christ. The more that the Body of Christ matures, it will become apparent that it is *us*, the family of God, who are doing the work of the Father. If I can live without condemnation, being my authentic self, that will be an integral part of the witness, but I do not have to be *anything other* than myself. As sonship liberates us to be nothing more and nothing less than our true selves, we find that we automatically become reapers of the harvest. Only the Father's love can open up our perception to see this reality.

> *"For here the saying holds true, 'One sows and another reaps.*
> *I sent you to reap that for which you did not labour. Others*
> *have laboured, and you have entered into their labour.'"*
> — JOHN 4:37,38

It sounds absurd but we only need to reap the harvest that is *already* ripe. Do you mean, Jesus, that we *don't actually* have to do the hard work of breaking up fallow ground and sowing seed? This is precisely what Jesus is saying. This flies in the face of most perceptions of evangelism and mission. 'Missions' and 'reaching the lost' often sound like a lot of hard work. To reach the world's population with the Gospel always seemed to be a titanic undertaking, a Mount Everest to climb. But Jesus doesn't seem to believe that. He declares that there is no problem with the harvest; all that is required is for the disciples to walk through the fields, pick the heavily laden crops, and pluck the ripe ears of grain from the stalk.

It is my conviction that religion has blinded us to this. Our thinking has blinded us to the fact that the world around us is extremely hungry for love. You see, it is not an issue of trying to make people intellectually assent to an evangelical creed. The reaping of the harvest is a matter of connecting people with the manifested reality of the Father's love for them.

Another big deception that religion has foisted upon us is that we are *not qualified* to be harvesters. The truth is, however, that harvesting the ripe fruit is not only for evangelists, pastors and teachers. In fact, it is not even primarily for them. *Everyone* can harvest, and it is God's purpose that everyone will be freed from condemnation into participating in the harvest. Harvesting can be done at many different levels. You simply fill up whatever size of container you have in your hand. You don't have to preach, or call people up to the front of a service to be a harvester. Manifesting the Father is to be done at work, at home, at the school gate, on vacation, or wherever life may take you.

It is only as we move away from seeing Christianity from an individualistic perspective that we can come into the freedom of entering into the labours of others. A wider and deeper perspective helps us to grasp that we enter into the labours of all who have declared the Good News up to this point in the history of the human race. This even includes the 'saints' of the Old Testament era. The New Testament writers never denied the Old Testament Law or sought to undermine it. They saw it in its cosmic and historical context, and entered into what the patriarchs and prophets had sown. In his letter to the Galatians, Paul radically re-interpreted the Law in the light of the Father's love.

I am discovering that *everything,* including my extreme religious upbringing, my experiences of 'un-love,' my own religious zealotry, my shameful moral failures, is all seen differently in the light of the Father's love. In the light of the outpoured love of the Father, all that I have been through is radically re-interpreted in a redemptive way. What is more, everything in our past which is negative, can *actually* be a tool in the reaping of the harvest. When we can be open and unashamed of our weaknesses and speak from a place of honesty, it can be a very effective relational bridge to others.

A few years ago I heard the Lord speak so clearly in my spirit that it was almost audible. He declared, "The harvest is endless and boundless." When I heard it then, reaping the harvest seemed like a mammoth task. Now I see that it is actually an incredible blessing. We will reap the fruits of the Father's love for ever!

STAYING WITH THE SAMARITANS

Many Samaritans from that town believed in him because of the woman's testimony, "He told me all that I ever did." So when the Samaritans came to him, they asked him to stay with them, and he stayed there two days. And many more believed because of his word. They said to the woman, "It is no longer because of what you said that we believe, for we have heard ourselves, and we know that this is indeed the Saviour of the world."

After two days he departed for Galilee. (For Jesus himself had testified that a prophet has no honour in his own home town.) So when he came to Galilee, the Galileans welcomed

him, having seen all that he had done in Jerusalem at the
feast. For they too had gone to the feast. — JOHN 4:39-45

Jesus accepts the hospitality of the Samaritans and stays with them
for two days. He further manifests the Father's love by acting out
what He has already told the woman. True worship is not a question
of the right form or location. Jesus shows Himself to be radically
free from the prejudiced categories of 'this mountain' or 'Jerusalem.'
In lodging with the Samaritans (the despised, the 'unwashed,' the
heretics) for two days, Jesus is incarnating the Father, demonstrating
what it is to be *in spirit and in truth*. He exemplifies worship in spirit
and in truth by accepting the hospitality of the Samaritan village.
A prophet who is not honoured in his home town is honoured by
the outsiders.

Too often our perceived prejudices hold us back from entering
the harvest field. The harvest field to be reaped is often behind the
walls and hedges of our own prejudices. This is almost invariably
true. This is what Peter (in Acts 10) had to be challenged with. The
new ripened fields of the Gentiles lay behind the 'wall of enclosure'
which determined what was kosher and what wasn't kosher. The
love of the Father compels us beyond our deep-seated prejudices
into the ripened harvest.

THE SECOND SUPERNATURAL SIGN

So he came again to Cana in Galilee, where he had made
the water wine. And at Capernaum there was an official
whose son was ill. When this man heard that Jesus had come
from Judea to Galilee, he went to him and asked him to

come down and heal his son, for he was at the point of death.
So Jesus said to him, 'Unless you see signs and wonders you
will not believe.' The official said to him, 'Sir, come down
before my child dies.' Jesus said to him, 'Go; your son will
live.' The man believed the word that Jesus spoke to him and
went on his way. As he was going down, his servants met
him and told him that his son was recovering. So he asked
them the hour when he began to get better, and they said
to him, 'Yesterday at the seventh hour the fever left him.'
The father knew that was the hour when Jesus had said to
him, 'Your son will live.' And he himself believed, and all
his household. This was now the second sign that Jesus did
when he had come from Judea to Galilee. — JOHN 4:46-54

Jesus returns to the region of Cana to perform His second supernatural sign. The town of Capernaum is where Jesus establishes His ministry of declaring who the Father is. According to Matthew 4:12-16, this is primarily Gentile territory. Jesus crossed cultural boundaries to manifest the Father's love. He went to Samaria; now He goes to Galilee to demonstrate love outside the historical parameters of the demonstrated favour of God.

This 'official' holds a place of administrative authority; in our culture he is a high-ranking civil servant. It seems that he is a 'nobleman,' possibly connected to Herod the Tetrarch's court. As such, he is part of the structure that had arisen out of orphanness. The governmental structures of the world, both secular and religious, are orphan structures. Even though we are meant to pray for governmental authority, (1 Timothy 2:1.2) we must realise that governmental structures are not to be equated with the Kingdom of God. The sickness of the official's son is a sign of the dis-ease that orphanness brings and that needs healing.

The significance of this sign of supernatural healing lies in the fact that orphanness has brought a rupture to the father-son relationship; the father and his sick son represent the malady that is endemic to the world system. The boy's father, notwithstanding his high status, is impotent to do anything about his son's illness. He is trapped in a system of rote and formula, a system which does not depend on relationship. Adherence to formula without relationship causes life to die and dis-ease to flourish. The higher up we ascend on the ladder of orphan servanthood, the more advanced our dis-ease becomes until death constantly stalks us, because we are distanced from the Father's heart.

Jesus as a Son is radically free from the system. He is free from the orphan ways of submitting to the system. To quote James Jordan, "Jesus was free from orphan methods of paying taxes." Jesus fulfils His responsibility to pay taxes by telling Peter to catch a fish with a coin in its mouth.

I must make clear that I am not undermining this man as a governmental official or the job that he is in. I am not undermining anyone who works as a civil servant or for an institution. We all live, to a certain extent, within the world system. The point is that the government of God is different, because it operates in love and freedom, and on the principle of giving and receiving. God's way of doing things does not bring dis-ease. The kingdom of God restores sons to their fathers and brings families back together again. This sign, performed by Jesus, is a fulfilment of the closing prophecy of Malachi:

"And he will turn the hearts of fathers to their children and the hearts of children to their fathers..." — MALACHI 4:6

As a result, the official believes with "all his household." (v. 53) The good news of the Father's love is intended to bring redemption to families. The household not only includes the nuclear family but also those who are employed within the house. The family and the employees of this man come under the influence of the Father's love which has worked effectively in healing his dying son. The Good News of the Father's love infects every strata of the social order.

John, the writer of this Gospel, now leaves off numbering the signs. After saying that this was the second sign, he no longer attempts to number the signs performed by Jesus because he has alerted us to be on the lookout for signs. Most biblical commentators limit the number of signs in John's Gospel to seven but I think there are more. I believe that *every* action of Jesus is a sign if we have eyes to perceive it.

CHAPTER FIVE

GET UP AND WALK!

~

They lie in clusters around the pool. Every day, for months, for years, hardly moving. Just waiting. Waiting with muted hope that one day life will be different. It is rumoured that these waters have healing properties. From time to time the waters are agitated by something that makes them become healing waters. They are stirred and churned by an angel. The problem is, however, that only those who get there first are healed. Then the water goes flat and still again. There is more disillusionment than hope in this place yet, in their desperation, they cling to the few strands of hope that remain. Anyway, they cannot move, even if they wanted to. They are institutionalised, lying under the Five Colonnades.

THERE'S NO NEED TO WAIT FOR THE ANGEL - THE SON IS HERE!

After this there was a feast of the Jews, and Jesus went up to Jerusalem. Now there is in Jerusalem by the Sheep Gate a pool, in Aramaic called Bethesda, which has five roofed *colonnades. In these lay a multitude of invalids—blind, lame, and paralysed, waiting for the moving of the water, for an angel of the Lord went down at certain seasons into the pool, and stirred the water: whoever stepped in first after the stirring of the water was healed of whatever disease he had. One man was there who had been an invalid for thirty-eight years. When Jesus saw him lying there and knew that he had already been there a long time, he said to him, "Do you want to be healed?" The sick man answered him, "Sir, I have no one to put me into the pool when the water is stirred up, and while I am going another steps down before me." Jesus said to him, "Get up, take up your bed, and walk." And at once the man was healed, and he took up his bed and walked. Now that day was the Sabbath"* — John 5:1-9*

In this narrative, the pool of Bethesda represents the Old Covenant. Anyone reading this from a Jewish perspective would immediately recognise the five roofed colonnades (alternatively translated as 'porches' or 'porticoes') as representing the Torah (the five books of Moses). The Torah was the foundational structure as well as the overarching umbrella of the Old Covenant.

These five porches presumably form a structure which roofs the bathing pool. This is a healing spa, drawing crowds of sick and disabled looking for a miracle. It exists on the basis of its reputation of sporadic miracles of healing which have already happened there. To grasp what the atmosphere would have been like, I tend to think of some of the shrines in Europe such as Fatima, Medjugorje or Lourdes. These are world-famous places of pilgrimage based around historical occurrence of miracles. I am not making any value judgement on the credibility of these devotional centres, rather, I am using them as examples of what the atmosphere of the pool at Bethesda would feel like. Like Lourdes, the popularity of this pool is dependent on the people's hope that what had happened there years previously will one day happen again. Much of our hope for a move of God *anywhere* is little more than a hope for a sporadic stirring by an angel. What God really wants is to bring an atmosphere of love that will never diminish.

We have an understandable tendency to encamp around the places where we received healing in the past. In doing this, we somehow hope for a touch from God to heal our pain.

In sonship, there is no need to wait in desperate hope for the waters to be stirred up. In sonship, the solution is already available within us. Loving-kindness and compassion are instantly accessible to the heart that is open to the Father's love. The waters of healing and mercy flow continually through the innermost being.

The man at the pool of Bethesda has a similar expectation to those who purchase a weekly lottery ticket, hoping against the odds to win the jackpot. From time to time an angel would stir the water and those who were lucky enough to be in the pool when that happened were healed. Some people are 'lucky' enough to win the lottery and no longer need to lie by the Pool beneath the Five Porticoes.

Bethesda means 'house of mercy.' In religion, the concept of mercy is a lottery. In Christianity, mercy is an ironclad guarantee. Jesus releases the man from needing the help of others to be healed. Jesus tells him to "Rise up," and, in the speaking of those two words, the man sees who he is through the Father's eyes. In the eyes of the Father he is perfectly capable of standing on his own two feet. The religious porticoes never bestow capability on the individual. Religion always likes to keep a lottery running. The hope of someday, somewhere, receiving mercy and healing from God keeps the crippled and lame dependent on the Five Porticoes. Many religious programmes are kept active because people cannot rise up and walk on their own two feet.

TRUE SABBATH

So the Jews said to the man who had been healed, "It is the Sabbath, and it is not lawful for you to take up your bed." But he answered them, "The man who healed me, that man said to me, 'Take up your bed, and walk.'" They asked him, "Who is the man who said to you, 'Take up your bed and walk'?" Now the man who had been healed did not know who it was, for Jesus had withdrawn, as there was a crowd in the place. Afterward Jesus found him in the temple and said to him, "See, you are well! Sin no more, that nothing worse may happen to you." The man went away and told the Jews that it was Jesus who had healed him. And this was why the Jews were persecuting Jesus, because he was doing these things on the Sabbath. But Jesus answered them, "My Father is working until now, and I am working."
— JOHN 5:10-17

The religious system is outraged that the healed man is lifting his bed on the Sabbath. Lifting his bed means that he is working. A man who had been bedridden for thirty-eight years is now healed, and yet the religious leaders accuse him of working! This would be laughable if it wasn't so tragic.

The religious system invariably values the symbol more than the substance. It honours a facade more than reality. The whole point of human relationship with God is summed up in the healing of this man. If the religious leaders only knew it, the whole point of God's covenant and the Law was to actually lead people to the substance of Christ, and through Him to the Father. The tendency of religion is always to camp around the sign, to be stuck on the way, without perceiving the destination.

The Pharisees are more interested in maintaining the symbolic significance of the Sabbath day than living in the ongoing reality of Sabbath rest. It is only the love of the Father that can deliver on the promise of true Sabbath rest. Through the Father's love, rest is established permanently in the human heart. When the love of the Father establishes itself, all is at rest and there is a continual Sabbath.

The Sabbath was intended to be a gift of rest and relaxation, but the Pharisees are enforcing it as a rule. They fail to see the irony, that in enforcing the day of rest legalistically, they are sabotaging the true goal of the Sabbath. To make the Sabbath an external rule is to be working in their own strength to fulfil *what they perceive* as God's requirement. The purpose of the Sabbath, however, is more than just enjoying God. The purpose of the Sabbath is to co-participate with God in *His* enjoyment. The absurdity of religion is that it *forces* us to 'enjoy' God. Sonship genuinely enjoys God but also rejoices with God in the exuberant pleasure that He takes in His creation.

Jesus counters the hypocrisy of the Pharisees by speaking of another reality; the reality that God the Father and the Son are continually in a place of rest but they are also working. The Jews are *working* to maintain the Sabbath from a place of striving. Jesus and the Father are resting, and working *from* that place of rest.

This sign illustrates the radical difference between religion and sonship. Religion, the product of orphanness, has no internal rest so it creates and maintains a system which only self-generated effort can sustain. Jesus declares that sonship can never be self-generated.

WHATEVER THE FATHER DOES, THE SON ALSO DOES

This was why the Jews were seeking all the more to kill him, because not only was he breaking the Sabbath, but he was even calling God his own Father, making himself equal with God. "Truly, truly, I say to you, the Son can do nothing of his own accord, but only what he sees the Father doing. For whatever the Father does, that the Son does likewise."
— JOHN 5:18,19

Here Jesus defines what the Sabbath-rest of sonship is. It is the knowledge that the Son can do nothing of His own accord. When we are utterly broken to our own initiative and energy in spiritual things, we have entered a place of rest. The Son doesn't do any work independently of the Father. The Son works in the Father's business and pursues the Father's interests. The primary aim of the Father's business is to sow and to reap the harvest of His love. The Son is fully included in all of the Father's business plans.

The Father's business is for a son who is mature enough to be given responsibility. This is what adoption, in the biblical sense, actually means. The Hebrew meaning of adoption is "to be placed as a son." This means, among other things, to be brought fully into the business of the father. When Scripture uses the word 'adoption,' it is not referring to a Western concept of it. There is no word in Scripture for 'adoption' as we understand it in our Western culture. The biblical meaning of the word is to be 'son-placed.'

In Hebrew culture, a man 'adopts' his own biological child. In other words, he places his boy into a more mature sonship. The bar mitzvah is the first stage in this son-placing. Placing the son is an affirmation by the father that he recognises the son's potential. It is a rite of passage into responsible manhood for the son. From that time on, the son is brought increasingly into his father's world. He is trained up in the business of his father. The father entrusts the son with his name and with his seal in which the son can conduct negotiations and sign contracts on his father's behalf. Son-placing is the father's seal of approval on the son. The father is prepared to stake his reputation on his son. He introduces his son to his own business associates and affirms that to do business with the son is to do business with him, the father.

The true son works with the father. This is what Jesus does. On earth, He is entrusted with the Father's business, doing what the Father instructs Him to do, moving in harmony with the Father. He has full power to wield the Father's resources.

> *"For the Father loves the Son and shows him all that he himself is doing. And greater works than these will he show*

him, so that you may marvel." — JOHN 5:20

Jesus is stating that the initiative belongs entirely to the Father. The direction of the flow of relationship comes from the direction of the Father. The Father is doing things and showing the Son what He is doing. The Son cannot originate, the Son cannot be a source. The Son must be, as it were, downstream from the Source. To really live as God intends for us to live, we must be downstream from the eternal Source whose substance is continually flowing into our hearts.

Is there anything the Son needs to do? Having the heart of a son is what makes a true son. It is about *being* before *doing.* The heart of a son is a heart that wants the Father to be pleased. The heart of a son is a heart directed towards the Father, not self-centred but primarily centred on the interests of the Father. The principal interest of the Father is to have His sons and daughters come home to Him so that in turn He may present them corporately as a perfect bride for His beloved Firstborn. As the Father and the Son work together, greater works will be demonstrated. Jesus is specifically talking here about the raising of the dead.

LIFE, DEATH AND JUDGEMENT

"For as the Father raises the dead and gives them life, so also the Son gives life to whom he will. The Father judges no one, but has given all judgment to the Son, that all may honour the Son, just as they honour the Father. Whoever does not honour the Son does not honour the Father who sent him. Truly, truly, I say to you, whoever hears my word and believes him who sent me has eternal life. He does not

come into judgment, but has passed from death to life."
— JOHN 5:21-24

What I wish to highlight here is the connection between life, death, and judgement. The work of the Father and the Son is essentially to raise the dead and bring them to life. Since orphanness entered into the world, all creation has been under the rule of death. When Adam and Eve ate the fruit of the Tree of Knowledge, they entered into death. Since that moment, not only humans but the entire created order has been under the tyranny of death, disconnected from the Life-Source.

Judgement is what happens when humans are not in the flow of eternal life. Judgement is the terminus at the end of the path of the knowledge of good and evil. The only means of escape from this pathway to nowhere is to honour the Son. By honouring the Son, by believing into Him, we are reconnected to the Father. Reconnection to the Father's love sets us free from the judgement that brings death. By hearing what the Son says and believing in the Father we pass from the death of orphanness into the life of sonship. Sonship-life is eternal because it draws its life from the Father through the Tree of Life.

> *"The Father judges no one, but gives all judgement to the Son. That all may honour the Son, just as they honour the Father."* — JOHN 5:22,23

This is the exact opposite of what many tend to believe. Because of deeply seated distortions in our paradigm of fatherhood, the Father is generally viewed as a judge. Jesus, on the other hand, is seen as being non-judgemental. The Father judges no one. The Father loves all His creation. However, the Father has given all judgement to the Son. The Son is the way back to the Father. The Father has invested all of His authority in the Son. To undermine the Son is to undermine the Father also. To refuse to honour the Son and the Father is to reject sonship.

Jesus is carrying out the Father's business on the earth. He comes, with the full backing of the Father, to carry out the work of redemption. If a businessman's representative is insulted by his client, then that is also a rejection of the business owner himself. Similarly, not honouring the Son means that the relationship with the Father is broken.

By giving judgement to the Son, the Father places His full confidence in the Son. This relates to the Son's mission on earth. The judgement of Jesus is on the basis of His sonship. The judgement is not a legal judgement such as is handed down in a court of law. Rather, it is a measuring against and distinguishing from who the Son is. The biblical idea of sin is less about moralistic behaviour (which is a symptom) and more about "missing the mark." The 'mark' is to be in an intimate relationship of sonship with the Father. To miss the mark is to fail to come into the redemptive relationship of sonship to the Father. To be in Christ in sonship is to reconnect with the life that comes from the Source.

> *"Truly, truly, I say to you, an hour is coming and is now here, when the dead will hear the voice of the Son of God, and those who hear will live."* — JOHN 5:25

Jesus uses the same expression here as He did in the conversation with the woman at Jacob's well in Sychar. *"An hour is coming - and - is - now - here."* Once more, Jesus collapses the gap between the present and the future, between the now and the not-yet. From His perspective, the potency of His voice to bring life to the dead is ever present.

How can the dead hear? This is a physical impossibility. The dead are beyond hearing any other voice. The Son of God is able to penetrate the total unresponsiveness of the dead. When Jesus stands at the grave of Lazarus, He calls Lazarus by name, and Lazarus, already decomposing, comes out to Him.

The utterance of a command by the Son of God carries in its sound waves an 'electrical current' of resurrection life. The voice of the Son of God is able to penetrate what is impossible in the natural. Naturally it is impossible for the dead to hear *anything* because all physical senses have ceased to function. However, the voice of Jesus resounds into the place where the soul lives beyond the grip of physical death. Jesus speaks to the physically dead and He speaks to the spiritually dead.

How can Jesus do this? The answer comes immediately:

> *"For as the Father has life in himself, so he has granted the Son also to have life in himself. And he has given him authority to execute judgement, because he is the Son of Man."* — JOHN 5:26,27

The "life in Himself" that the Father possesses is the unique quality of eternal life that gives life to everything else. The life of the Father is the life that sustains the universe. 'Son of Man' is a reference to Jesus in His humanity. The Father gives His 'source-life' to Jesus of Nazareth so that He (the Son) can generate eternal life here on earth.

Alongside the bestowal of being a life-source, the Father has also given to the Son the mandate to execute judgement. We may struggle with this terminology because it is not very politically correct, but executing judgement is not to be viewed as totally negative. To 'execute judgement' in this context is to *bring the dead to life, not* the other way round. The execution of judgement by the Life-Giver is a judgement *against* the law of death. It is a judgement which brings forth the dead to resurrection life.

This is a similar form of judgement to what is described in Psalm 149:6,7:

> *"Let the high praises of God be in their throats*
> *and two-edged swords in their hands;*
> *to execute vengeance on the nations*
> *and punishments on the peoples,*
> *to bind their kings with chains*
> *and their nobles with fetters of iron,*
> *to execute on them the judgement written…"*

This is a judgement primarily against principalities and powers, and not so much against individual human beings. 'Nations' and 'peoples' are political entities. They are kingdoms of the world that operate on diametrically opposite principles to the Kingdom of God.

This judgement is a positive judgement because it reverses oppression.

> *"Do not marvel at this, for an hour is coming when all who are in the tombs will hear his voice and come out, those who have done good to the resurrection of life, and those who have done evil to the resurrection of judgement."* — JOHN 5:28,29

I do not want to dive headlong into a debate here about the details of the resurrection and of judgement. However, some comments need to be made.

The terms 'good' and 'evil' here are *not* definitions of moral behaviour within the parameters of the Tree of the Knowledge of Good and Evil. They are *not* moral qualities based on a law code. The words 'good' and 'evil,' when spoken by Jesus, need to be understood from *His* perspective. From God's perspective (the Tree of Life), 'evil' includes *both* the 'good' *and* 'evil' of the Tree of Knowledge. The issue of 'good' and 'evil' as spoken by the writers of the New Testament needs to be seen, not in moral or behavioural terms as such, but rather in terms of love and life. In other words, the issue of 'good and evil' needs to be seen from a Tree of Life perspective. Within the Tree of Life, relationship in the flow of love is 'good,' and lack of relationship outside the flow of love is 'evil,' no matter how morally 'good' that may appear.

The fruits of both states of reality will be evident. Relationship with God and others in love, within the Tree of Life, will inevitably lead to life beyond death. Love sets us free from the principle of sin and death. The consequence of utter self-absorption, outside of the Source of love, will invariably lead to judgement and death.

I CAN DO NOTHING ON MY OWN

Jesus then explains why He has this life in Himself, and why He has been given the authority to execute judgement. It is precisely because:

> *"I can do nothing on my own (or 'of myself'). As I hear, I judge, and my judgement is just, because I seek not my own will, but the will of him who sent me."* — JOHN 5:30

These words encapsulate the essence of what sonship is. Sonship cannot do a single thing independently of its Source. That does not mean that a son has a servile deference to command. It means that sonship is always positioned downstream from the Father. The Son knows that all His identity is in and from the Father. All that a son has become is because of who the father is. This is a universal principle. The essence of orphanhood is to seek its own ends, and to rely on its own assessments. An orphan has no source so he must become his own source. But truth cannot be arrived at independently of relationship with the Father, whose substance is love. It is only the love of the Father that can bring a right assessment (judgement) of everything.

This is why Jesus has confidence in His assessment (judgement) of everything. It is not 'righteous judgement' on the basis of expertise in the knowledge of good and evil. His judgement is 'just' precisely because it is on the basis of hearing the Father's voice. The Son's utter dependence on the Father is an absolute guarantee of a proper assessment of everything. The Son, unable to function independently of the Father, is fully aligned with the Father's reality. This is why the Father can entrust the Son with the responsibility of carrying out His will. Incompetence and lack of self-reliance are the major qualifiers for carrying out the Father's will on earth.

CALLING THE WITNESSES

"If I alone bear witness about myself, my testimony is not true. There is another who bears witness about me, and I know that the testimony that he bears about me is true. You sent to John, and he has borne witness to the truth. Not that the testimony that I receive is from man, but I say these things so that you may be saved. He was a burning and shining lamp, and you were willing to rejoice for a while in his light. But the testimony that I have is greater than that of John. For the works that the Father has given me to accomplish, the very works that I am doing, bear witness about me that the Father has sent me. And the Father who sent me has himself borne witness about me. His voice you have never heard, his form you have never seen, and you do not have his word abiding in you, for you do not believe the one whom he has sent. You search the Scriptures because you think that in them you have eternal life; and it is they that bear witness about me, yet you refuse to come to me that you may have life. I do not receive glory from people. But I know that you do not have the love of God within you. I have come in my Father's name, and you do not receive me. If another comes in his own name, you will receive him. How can you believe, when you receive glory from one another and do not seek the glory that comes from the only God? Do not think that I will accuse you to the Father. There is one who accuses you:

Moses, on whom you have set your hope. For if you believed
Moses, you would believe me; for he wrote of me. But if you
do not believe his writings, how will you believe my words?"
— JOHN 5:31-47

The entire section from verse 19 through to verse 47 is a response
to the accusation by the Jews in verse 18. Jesus is being accused of
crimes of blasphemy and of Sabbath-breaking, undermining the very
heart of the teaching of the Torah. He is before a (formal or informal)
tribunal. In the religious culture of Jesus' day, no accusation could
stick unless it was verified by two or three witnesses (Deuteronomy
19:15).

In this section, from verse 30 to verse 47, Jesus calls upon His
witnesses to establish the truth of who *He* is. He names:

a. **John the Baptist;**
b. **The Father** *(who is unseen, but seen through*
   supernatural signs);
c. **The Scriptures;**
d. **Moses.**

These four witnesses are Jesus' defence against the accusations of
blasphemy and Sabbath-breaking. Let me consider these witnesses
in more detail:

a. **John the Baptist as a witness**

By naming the Baptist as a witness, Jesus places the Pharisees
in the horns of a dilemma. This is the same dilemma that He put

them in when He asked the question (see Matthew 21:25; Mark 11:30; Luke 20:4) whether John's baptism was from heaven or from human origin?

By acknowledging the witness of John the Baptist, the Pharisees then have to agree that Jesus *is* from God. If they do not believe John's witness, then they have discredited John.

John was a burning and shining lamp, but he only illuminated until the true light came. John's lamp faded as it was intended to. The brightening dawn of the True Light which enlightens everyone, rendered John's light obsolete.

b. The Father as a witness

John the Baptist pointed beyond himself to Jesus, but Jesus points to the Father. Jesus becomes the way to the One who sent Him, the Father. Jesus bears witness to the Father, and the Father bears witness to Jesus. All that Jesus says is confirmed by the miracles that His Father works through Him. It is the Father who actually performs the miracles, validating His Son with supernatural attestation.

> *"And the Father who sent me has himself borne witness about me. His form you have never seen, and you do not have his word abiding in you, for you do not believe the one whom he has sent."* — JOHN 5:37-38

The Father is a spirit. He remains eternally in spirit form. No one has seen His form. He is incarnated in His Son and, by extension, in His sons and daughters. The purpose of the Father is not to be limited to a one-off Incarnation in Jesus but to be incarnated forever in His sons and daughters. To have the Father's Word abiding within is to be living in sonship because the Father's Word is equal in substance to His love. Believing in the One whom the Father has sent opens the way for the Father's word to abide in us. By receiving the Son, we simultaneously receive the Word. The Father's Son and the Father's Word cannot be divided.

c.   The Scriptures as a witness

"You search the Scriptures because you think that in them you have eternal life;and it is they who bear witness about me, yet you refuse to come to me that you may have life."
— JOHN 5:39,40

The Father's Word does not necessarily equate to the written text of the Scriptures. The Scriptures, however, bear witness to the Substance, the Person of the Son. The late John Wimber described reading the Bible as akin to going into a restaurant and reading the menu. The menu describes what you can eat, *but it is not the meal itself.* Many Christians try to eat the menu instead of getting what the menu describes. I don't know about you, but I would *much* rather eat a juicy steak than a piece of laminated card! The Bible points to the substance but it is *not* the substance itself.

The Pharisees are chomping on the menu. They are looking to the Scriptures for eternal life, but they fail to order off the menu and taste the actual meal. They are not able to enjoy the succulence of the Eternal Life that the Scriptures point to. Eternal life is a vivifying relationship with the Trinity.

"I do not receive glory from people. But I know that you do not have the love of God within you…How can you believe, when you receive glory from one another and do not seek the glory that comes from the only God?" — JOHN 5:41,42,44

The love of God is a substance. It has to be experienced and substantiated within. As that substance grows more and more in the heart, the less we need glory from people. The need to receive glory from others is directly proportional to our need to receive the substance of the Father's love. Our hunger shows the deficit of the substance of love in our hearts. One of the consequences of receiving the Father's love is that it sets us free from being affected both by the disapproval *and the approval* of others.

The glory that comes from the authentic Source can never be earned. It is reserved for sons and daughters. The Father is pleased to manifest His personality in and through His own offspring.

d. Moses as a witness

"Do not think that I will accuse you to the Father. There is one that accuses you; Moses, on whom you have set your hope. If you believed Moses, you would believe me; for he wrote of me. But if you do not believe his writings, how will you believe my words?" — JOHN 5:45-47

The final witness who verifies Jesus and turns the accusation back on the Pharisees is Moses. It is remarkable that Jesus cites Moses as a witness that He, Jesus, is indeed one with the Father. Where does Moses write about Jesus? How does Moses accuse the ones who are so strident in keeping the Mosaic law? The Pharisees are fixated on keeping the Commandments according to the knowledge of good and evil. Therefore, the Law itself condemns them because it is impossible to keep it fully. Anyone who lives by the Law is already condemned by the very Law that they seek to live by.

I baptised a guy some years ago in the Irish Sea. It was freezing cold! When he came up out of the water I said to him, "Now you have the Holy Spirit inside you and He will be your teacher." I resisted the temptation to take my friend through any discipleship course or even give him any resources to start him off as a new believer. I was interested to see how the Holy Spirit would lead him, without the influence of any person. What happened soon after was remarkable. The Holy Spirit began to reveal Biblical realities to him before he even picked up a Bible. However, this friend of mine soon began to read the Bible, beginning at Genesis. He read through as far as the end of the Book of Judges. Think about what he read! The books of Leviticus and Numbers which appear utterly boring to many; the book of Joshua with its sometimes violent narrative. But here's what is remarkable! Do you know what his conclusion was, after reading through the Pentateuch, and then Joshua and Judges? His conclusion was that God is a loving Father!

"If you believed Moses, you would believe me; for he wrote of me." When the Spirit pours out the love of God inside the human heart, even the reading of the Torah will declare somehow that God is love. The Scriptures and the Law are opened for what their true purpose is. When our eyes are opened to see God's eternal purpose flowing out of His love, we then see how the whole Bible hangs together. The perspective of the Father's love enables us to see the unity of the

written Word. When Jesus is revealed, we understand the nature and purpose of the entire tapestry of the Scripture.

CHAPTER SIX

You Are What You Eat!

~

THE SIGN OF MULTIPLYING BREAD

After this Jesus went away to the other side of the Sea of Galilee, which is the Sea of Tiberias. And a large crowd was following him, because they saw the signs that he was doing on the sick. Jesus went up on the mountain, and there he sat down with his disciples. Now the Passover, the feast of the Jews, was at hand. Lifting up his eyes, then, and seeing that a large crowd was coming toward him, Jesus said to Philip, "Where are we to buy bread, so that these people may eat?" He said this to test him, for he himself knew what he would do. Philip answered him, "Two hundred denarii worth of bread would not be enough for each of them to get a little." One of his disciples, Andrew, Simon Peter's brother, said to him, "There is a boy here who has five barley loaves and two fish, but what are they for so many?" Jesus said, "Have the people sit down." Now there was much grass in the place.

So the men sat down, about five thousand in number. Jesus then took the loaves, and when he had given thanks, he distributed them to those who were seated. So also the fish, as much as they wanted. And when they had eaten their fill, he told his disciples, "Gather up the leftover fragments, that nothing may be lost." So they gathered them up and filled twelve baskets with fragments from the five barley loaves left by those who had eaten. — JOHN 6:1-13

The sixth chapter of John opens with a journey to the other side of the Sea of Galilee. Jesus is followed by a large crowd who have been impacted by the miracles performed by Him. We then have the well-known story of the feeding of the five thousand. This sign is motivated by compassion. Jesus enquires of Philip if there is anywhere nearby to buy bread but the disciples do not have enough money to buy bread. Jesus, however, is testing Philip to see what his reaction will be because Jesus is about to perform another major miracle. He is priming Philip for another sign. He is about to multiply bread and fish to feed the hungry crowd. And so the miracle unfolds.

Andrew finds a boy who will provide the ingredients for the miracle. I'm sure that this young lad left home that morning with no idea what his day would hold. Andrew requisitions his packed lunch and gives it to Jesus. The disciples are perplexed. How will such a paltry lunch feed so many people? How will something so meagre and so mediocre bring sustenance to so many? It will do that, and more, in the hands of Jesus.

Availability is transformed into abundance. Impoverishment of resources becomes overflowing bounty. The multiplication does not stretch to being merely adequate; it carries on until there is enough surplus left over to fill twelve baskets. It does not take much imagination to see spiritual meaning in all this. The heart of a child is willing to give what he has to the disciples. In their adult minds they struggle to grasp what Jesus will do but it does not stop them from participating in the miracle.

THE HUNGER FOR A KING IN A TIME WITHOUT THE FATHER[16]

When the people saw the sign that he had done, they said,
"This is indeed the Prophet who is to come into the world!"
Perceiving then that they were about to come and take him
by force to make him king, Jesus withdrew again to the
mountain by himself. — JOHN 6:14,15

This miracle provokes a predictable reaction. The people immediately latch onto the supernatural demonstration and hail Jesus as the expected Prophet, the Coming One. Signs and wonders always excite the crowd. People are so desperate for contact with the transcendent that they are intoxicated by the miraculous.

This is understandable but Jesus is wary of this reaction. Jesus did not entrust Himself to the crowds (John 2:23-25) because He knew that they fundamentally misunderstood who He was and what He was about. The signs and wonders performed by Jesus answer an immediate and physical need of the crowd. Here we have a classic example of people camping around the sign, without

---

16. I have adapted this terminology from the poet, Robert Bly.

recognising the purpose of the signs, which point ultimately to the destination. This is a very common human reaction to anything that God does. Because of our deep orphanness we have a need to be part of something significant, and we easily get caught up in the excitement of the moment. This need is understandable, but it is a reaction which is essentially orphan.

There is an innate need in the orphaned human heart to attach to something. Because we are cut off from the Source, we attach to things that are not 'Source' and are not therefore spiritually real. When the people clamour to make Jesus a king, they are seeking to meet their gnawing 'father-hunger.' When the leadership, protection and blessing of fathers is absent, that yearning is transferred into the desire for someone to rule. The hunger for a king can never satisfy father-hunger.

Forcing Jesus to become a king is a shortcut to deal with the insecurities and fears within the people, because Israel no longer has a king and is ruled by an occupying power, the Romans. This reaction is not limited to Jesus' time. Our father-hunger (orphanness) puts a desperation into us to look to someone else for security. Christians are not exempt from this. It is not unusual for us to come under an anointed ministry and then try to make that person a 'king' by force. Our disconnection to the Father makes us very vulnerable to creating structures to rule over us. Jesus runs away from this and withdraws to the mountain to be alone.

MASTERY OVER NATURE

When evening came, his disciples went down to the sea, got into a boat, and started across the sea to Capernaum. It was now dark, and Jesus had not yet come to them. The sea became rough because a strong wind was blowing. When they had rowed about three or four miles, they saw Jesus walking on the sea and coming near the boat, and they were frightened. But he said to them, "It is I; do not be afraid." Then they were glad to take him into the boat, and immediately the boat was at the land to which they were going. — JOHN 6:16-21

Jesus is alone on the mountain and the disciples, tired of waiting for Him, decide to go across the Sea of Galilee to Capernaum. In the middle of their journey a squall whips up, forcing them to abandon the sail and take to the oars. I have been part of a crew that once rowed a boat for quite a long distance. Like the disciples, we were a crew of twelve, and we rowed for many hours into a head wind. We expended a lot of energy but hardly seemed to make any progress. It is easy to imagine that the disciples were concerned about their safety.

Walking on the water is another sign. Jesus displays mastery over the elements. He is demonstrating dominion over nature. The water is able to hold His weight. Whatever happened to the molecular structure of the water is the opposite of what happened when He walked through a wall. When He walked through the solid wall the molecules moved apart for Him; this time the molecules come together to make the water solid underneath His feet.

This sign is solely for the disciples' benefit. The crowds are not in on it. Jesus does not perform this like a 'magic trick' to impress the disciples; He comes to them upon the water because He is concerned about their safety. They are struggling in the driving rain and screaming wind. They are even more afraid when they see Jesus on the water, however. According to Mark (Mark 6:49) they think He is a ghost.

His reassuring words, "It is I, do not be afraid" bring immediate calmness. They take Him into the boat, and there is yet another miraculous occurrence: the boat immediately arrives at the other side of the lake. Whenever we go through storms, the only thing that will take away our fear and bring us immediately to haven is the revealed presence of Jesus. Reminding ourselves that we are loved will not do this; it is only the experience of the voice of Jesus and the *reality* of the Father's love that transform rough sea into solid ground.

THE FATHER'S APPROVAL *IS* ETERNAL FOOD

When they found him on the other side of the sea, they said to him, "Rabbi, when did you come here?" Jesus answered them, "Truly, truly, I say to you, you are seeking me, not because you saw signs, but because you ate your fill of the loaves. Do not work for the food that perishes, but for the food that endures to eternal life, which the Son of Man will give to you. For on him God the Father has set his seal."
— JOHN 6:25-27

Jesus and His disciples then arrive in Capernaum, where, before long, they are discovered by the multitude of people. Some of the crowd has even taken to boats to follow Jesus across the lake.[17]

---

17. Lake Tiberias or The Sea of Galilee, sometimes called Lake Gennesaret.

The rest of chapter 6, from verse 25 to verse 71, brings out the meaning of the sign of the multiplication of the bread and fish.

In the opening remark of this passage, Jesus tells them what the essence of eternal food is. Eternal food is the Father's seal of approval, attestation and authentication. This food, substantiated in the human heart, does not grow stale or develop mould. It is the answer to the basic need of the human heart, that of significance and of being loved. When we have an ongoing experience of the Father's approval and know the reality that we belong to Him, we do not hunger again.

There are similarities here with John 4. In John 4, Jesus uses the need for water as one of the staples of life to point to the spiritual need for 'living water.' In John 4, the rivers of living water which continually spring up from the heart are none other than the Father's love. In this sign of the multiplication of bread, He takes another basic human need, the need for bread, and uses it to describe the bread which comes from heaven.

Without a sense of approval and significance from the Father Himself, we will always be forced to feed on that which will not last. Without the seal of the Father's approval, we will never be able to satisfy the gnawing hunger at the very kernel of our being.

The Son, however, *is given* the approval of the Father. What is more, it is the *Son of Man* who is given the Father's approval. This approval is not confined (or even available) within the closed circle of divinity but it comes upon the *human* Jesus. The Father's seal is stamped upon the Son who in His humanity is dependent upon the Father, and who needs to draw constantly from His Source. The seal of the Father's approval is especially crafted to fit sonship in the human condition.

THE WORK OF GOD

Then they said to him, "What must we do, to be doing the works of God?" Jesus answered them, "This is the work of God, that you believe in him who he has sent.
— JOHN 6:28,29

Their question is typical of the seeker after God. It is really a religious question with the emphasis on what *they* need *to do*. It is also a desire to possess the ability to perform miracles. The truth is that seeking after God in order to do His works will invariably lead you in the ways of religion unless you come to believe in "the One who He has sent."

Believing in the One who God has sent is much more than the affirmation of a doctrinal truth. To believe in the 'One' sent by God is to place our confidence in *the Son*. It is to enter *into* the Son as if we were going through a door. In John 10:7, Jesus identifies Himself as 'the door.' This is more than mere metaphor. Jesus must be entered into by faith. Our life must be subsumed into His life, our personality swallowed into His personality. Christianity invites us to become united with Jesus in His life.

When we believe into the Son we will discover that it leads somewhere else. In the same manner that the Way leads to the Destination, the Door leads somewhere. Believing in the Sent One and entering into the Son brings us out on the other side, where the Father is waiting to embrace us.

> *So they said to him, "Then what sign do you do, that we may see and believe you? What work do you perform? Our fathers ate the manna in the wilderness; as it is written, "He gave them bread from heaven to eat."* — JOHN 6:30,31

Like the Samaritan woman at the well of Sychar, they attempt to engage Jesus on the level of theology. They are still stuck in the desire for an outward sign, something to satisfy the senses. As He did in John 4, Jesus cuts to the chase:

> *"Truly, truly, I say to you, it was not Moses who gave you the bread from heaven, but my Father gives you the true bread from heaven."* — JOHN 6:32

This is strikingly similar to His comments to the woman at the well in Sychar. For her, the source of life was "our father, Jacob." For these people, it is Moses who gave them the manna.

Whenever we settle for a source that is not the true source we will end up trapped in a religious paradigm. To attribute a spiritual source to Jacob, Moses or anyone else other than the Father, is to identify a false source to the river. Jesus came to show the true Source of life, His Father.

> *"For the bread of God is he who comes down from heaven and gives life to the world." They said to him, "Sir, give us this bread always."* — JOHN 6:33,34

The Samaritan woman (John 4:15) requested that Jesus give her water to drink so that she would never be thirsty or have to come to the well to draw water. Here, the crowd asks for a continual supply of the bread of God. They are now seeking the *spiritual* food that *Jesus* is talking about. Like the Samaritan woman, they are now looking for spiritual, not physical, sustenance.

I AM THE BREAD OF LIFE

Jesus said to them, "I am the bread of life; whoever comes to me shall not hunger, and whoever believes in me shall never thirst. But I said to you that you have seen me and yet do not believe. All that the Father gives me will come to me, and whoever comes to me I will never cast out. For I have come down from heaven, not to do my own will but the will of him who sent me. And this is the will of him who sent me, that I should lose nothing of all that he has given me, but raise it up on the last day. For this is the will of my Father, that everyone who looks on the Son and believes in him should have eternal life, and I will raise him up on the last day." — John 6:35-40

Spiritual sustenance and satisfaction is found in Jesus. He *Himself* is the substance of life that comes from heaven. By consuming Him into our inner being, into the core of who we are, we will have the kernel of life inside us.

Eternal life is knowing the only true God and Jesus Christ whom He has sent (John 17:3). The substance of eternal life is being caught up in the Trinitarian relationship. The nucleus of all reality is the community of Father, Son and Spirit.

It must be this way because ultimately it is not possible to know the Father apart from the Son. It is also not possible to remain in relationship with Jesus without being led to the Father. Up to now, the majority of Christians have claimed to have relationship with Jesus but have not had a revelation of the Father. However, it cannot remain like this because the Son will *always* lead us to the Father.

The Son's mission is not His own; it is to do the Father's will. Sonship always operates out of a consciousness of being sent by the Father. The mandate of sonship on earth is to steward what belongs to the Father.

I HAVE COME DOWN FROM HEAVEN

So the Jews grumbled about him, because he said, "I am the bread that came down from heaven." They said, "Is not this Jesus, the son of Joseph, whose father and mother we know? How does he now say, 'I have come down from heaven'?" Jesus answered them, "Do not grumble among yourselves. No one can come to me unless the Father who sent me draws him. And I will raise him up on the last day. It is written in the Prophets, 'And they will all be taught by God.' Everyone who has heard and learned from the Father comes to me—not that anyone has seen the Father except he who is from God; he has seen the Father. Truly, truly, I say to you, whoever believes has eternal life. I am the bread of life. Your fathers ate the manna in the wilderness, and they died. This is the bread that comes down from heaven, so that one may eat of it and not die. I am the living bread that came down from heaven. If anyone eats of this bread, he will live forever. And the bread that I will give for the life of the world is my flesh." — JOHN 6:41-51

The Jews grumble because Jesus uncovers His heavenly DNA. He, the carpenter from Nazareth, the 'illegitimate' son of Joseph and Mary, actually has another origin. Jesus shows that the true source of everything is *not* Moses, *not* the Covenants, *not* the Law, *not* Joseph and Mary, but the Father in heaven. The Father pre-exists all the patriarchs. Establishing a direct link to the Father in heaven is the ultimate threat to the religious system.

A direct connection to the Father gives access to the bread that is eternal. How does this work? The Father speaks security, affirmation, and favour into the core of the human spirit. When the heart internalises the Son, the Father's seal of approval is established permanently on the inside. Religious motivation cannot withstand the potency of the permanent approval of the Father in the deepest recesses of the human heart.

Jesus is establishing the fulfilment of what the prophets foretold. He quotes Isaiah 54:13:

"All your children shall be taught by the Lord."

In the New Covenant, revelation is accessible and available to *everyone*. This is undeniably the Father's purpose. Much of our experience of 'church' is that some people are more qualified than others to be "taught by the Lord." In our orphan experience, we have harboured an assumption that it is only leaders, pastors, teachers, evangelists, prophets and apostles who can be taught by God, and they, in turn, teach us. But there is a better reality to come; a reality that *all* of the children will come to a place of receiving direct revelation for *themselves*. The ramifications of this for how we function together as 'church' are staggering, but now is not the time to explore this.

Jesus promises something that the manna could not give. The manna fed the wandering band of Israelites as they traversed through the wilderness. It could not prevent them from dying, however, because it did not contain the substance of eternal life. Jesus promises eternal life to the person who eats the bread of heaven. How will this work?

INTERNALISING JESUS

The Jews then disputed among themselves, saying, "How can this man give us his flesh to eat?" So Jesus said to them, "Truly, truly, I say to you, unless you eat the flesh of the Son of Man and drink his blood, you have no life in you. Whoever feeds on my flesh and drinks my blood has eternal life, and I will raise him up on the last day. For my flesh is true food, and my blood is true drink. Whoever feeds on my flesh and drinks my blood abides in me, and I in him."
— JOHN 6:52-56

These verses are not about cannibalism. That may seem glaringly obvious but the Jews that are listening to Jesus are stuck in a literal interpretation. They cannot see with the eyes of their hearts. To ask the question, "How can this man give us his flesh to eat?" is like the question posed by Nicodemus, "How can a man be born when he is old? Can he enter a second time into his mother's womb and be born?" (John 3:4) These so-called 'dumb' questions (of Nicodemus earlier and the Jews here) do miss the point but we should not be so quick to sneer at them for they do confront us with the reality of what is required for eternal life.

In this chapter, what is required to have the substance of eternal life is not a physical eating of flesh and drinking of blood. A *spiritual* eating and drinking is required. To say that the eating and drinking is 'spiritual' does not take away from the reality of it. It does not mean doctrinal assent or mere lip-service to the *concept* of Jesus as the Son of God. To eat and drink Jesus means the *actual internalising* of His life into our hearts.

To eat means "to chew, to masticate." It means to *fully absorb* the reality of the sonship of Jesus into the core of who we are. It is not only accepting Him but accepting the Source of His life into us as well. In internalising Jesus, we internalise His connection to the Father. When He comes into us, all that He is comes into us. His primary relationship is His relationship with His Father. This relationship will find resonance in the other primary relationship to be consummated in the future, His relationship with His Bride.

Furthermore, to "eat and drink Jesus" is to draw from the source from which *Jesus* eats and drinks, His Father. The next statement makes this very clear:

> *"As the living Father sent me, and I live because of the Father,*
> *so whoever feeds on me, he also will live because of me. This*

is the bread that came down from heaven, not like the bread the fathers ate, and died. Whoever feeds on this bread will live forever." Jesus said these things in the synagogue, as he taught at Capernaum. — JOHN 6:57-59

Relationship with Jesus is inextricably linked with the Father. Jesus eats and drinks of the substance of who the Father is. It is the Father's substance which sustains *Him* in *His* life. We are to avail ourselves of the Son in the same way that He avails Himself of the Father. By internalising the sonship of Jesus into our hearts, we become connected to the source of eternal life. The "bread that came down from heaven" *is* a relationship of sonship to the Father.

THE TRAP OF OFFENCE

When many of his disciples heard it, they said, "This is a hard saying; who can listen to it?" But Jesus, knowing in himself that his disciples were grumbling about this, said to them, "Do you take offence at this? Then what if you were to see the Son of Man ascending to where he was before? It is the Spirit who gives life, the flesh is of no avail. The words that I have spoken to you are spirit and life. But there are some of you who do not believe. (For Jesus knew from the beginning who those were who did not believe, and who it was who would betray him.) And he said, "That is why I told you that no one can come to me unless it is granted to him by the Father." — JOHN 6:60-65

What Jesus has just said is hard to stomach. They must eat Him and drink His blood! It is offensive; it is outrageous! No eternal life unless they chew on His flesh and gulp down His blood? And Jesus knows full well that He has caused deep offence; so deep that many disciples give up following Him at this very moment.

These words of Jesus are scandalous to His listeners. They prove to be a stumbling block, an offence. The Greek word used for this is *skandalon* which literally means "to trip someone up." This word *skandalon* is also used to describe a trap to catch an animal; a sapling of a tree is bent back which then springs up and catches the animal when it steps on it. Jesus' assertion that eating and drinking Him is the only way to gain eternal life becomes a *skandalon*, a bent sapling waiting to catch His listeners.

This *skandalon* brings a watershed, a dividing line in the ministry of Jesus. It is at this point that many of His disciples leave Him. What offends (scandalises) the majority of the disciples is this issue of "eating the flesh" and "drinking the blood" of Jesus. Eating and drinking Jesus—internalising the sonship of Jesus—remains scandalous and offensive. It is still a stumbling block to many who desire to know God.

It is a cause of offence and a trap, not because of its difficulty, but because it reeks of grace. It is a hard saying, not because it is difficult to live up to, but precisely because it cuts against ingrained religion. Ingrained religion depends on 'the flesh,' on human energy and motivation, to make it work, but Jesus declares that the flesh is absolutely useless. This is a stumbling block because we are addicted to trying to achieve eternal life by our own human effort and accreditation.

ONLY THE SPIRIT GIVES LIFE

"It is the Spirit who gives life; the flesh is of no avail. The words that I have spoken to you are spirit and life. But there are some of you who do not believe..." — JOHN 6:63,64

'Spirit' and 'flesh' are fundamentally different. 'Spirit' is that which emanates from the true Source, the Father; and 'flesh' is that which *does not* come from the true Source, the Father. Spirit comes from heaven and flows down; flesh comes from beneath and stretches out to gain dominance.

The words spoken by Jesus come from the Originator of Life, His Father. Those words are original words, creative words, and eternal words. Only what originates in the Father can be creative and eternal. The Son is the conveyer of these words. The words that are spoken by Jesus are anointed words because they contain within them the very substance of eternal life and the very personality of the Father.

(For Jesus knew from the beginning who those were who did not believe, and who it was who would betray him.) And he said, "This is why I told you that no one can come to me unless it is granted to him by the Father." — JOHN 6:64,65

Jesus knows that there are some who follow Him who do not believe. It is possible to follow but not to believe because belief is an issue of the heart. It is possible to follow a movement that appears to be successful yet have no heart connection at all with the core reality of that movement. Jesus knows that there are those (Judas in particular) among His followers who do not have a genuine revelation of who He is.

Authentic revelation about Jesus is given by the Father. Jesus is intentional in connecting everything back to the Father. He confidently establishes that the Father is the 'first cause' and primary mover in the universe. The difference between some who are 'granted' and others who are 'not granted' is in their connection to the Father. In saying this, Jesus emphasises the fact that the Father is the source of all spiritual activity. It is the Father's desire and wooing that brings fallen humanity to the Son, so that the Son in turn can reintroduce humanity to the Father.

WE HAVE NOWHERE ELSE TO GO

After this many of his disciples turned back and no longer walked with him. So Jesus said to the Twelve, "Do you want to go away as well?" Simon Peter answered him, "Lord, to whom shall we go? You have the words of eternal life, and we have believed, and have come to know, that you are the Holy One of God." Jesus answered them, "Did I not choose you, the Twelve? And yet one of you is a devil." He spoke of Judas the son of Simon Iscariot, for he, one of the Twelve, was going to betray him. — JOHN 6:66-71

I want to finish on a positive note, so I will deal with the last line of chapter 6 first. Judas is mentioned for the first time. John identifies Judas Iscariot retrospectively, that is, after the events of his betrayal of Jesus. At this time, none of the Twelve have the slightest clue that Judas will betray Jesus. Perhaps Judas himself has no clue that he will ultimately betray Jesus. The use of the word 'devil' to describe

Judas is slightly misleading. The original word *diabolos* means 'an adversary'; it means someone who is a 'false accuser.' Judas' main problem (for himself and others) is that he misrepresents the true character of Jesus. I will offer the suggestion later in this book that Judas, rather than being deliberately malevolent, fundamentally misunderstands the person of Jesus and the nature of His ministry.

Jesus has developed such a culture of non-judgement within the Twelve that none of them have any suspicions about Judas. Remarkably, Jesus Himself had chosen Judas to be one of the Twelve. That doesn't seem to make sense but we have to live with this mystery. Why did Jesus choose His betrayer? There is no definitive answer but it highlights the supreme confidence of God that ultimate victory is His. God is supremely confident that love will always, and without exception, overcome evil.

This closes the first phase in the ministry of Jesus. Jesus has upped the ante by declaring that we must eat His flesh and drink His blood to gain eternal life. In doing so, He has removed another central tenet of the religious code. The construct of religion does not require the *internalisation of anything*. Religion is generated out of a heart that is closed and it is always externalised. In other words, religion is always about outward conformity and behaviour.

Jesus challenges the Twelve: "Do you want to go away as well?"

Simon Peter's response is: *"Lord, to whom shall we go? You have the words of eternal life, and we have believed and have come to know, that you are the Holy One of God."*

Peter's response shows that he and the others have traversed this particular watershed and have not fallen on the stumbling stone. Their belief is the belief of verse 29, a *believing into* the One who is sent from God. They have "come to know." This knowing is the Greek verb *ginosko* meaning "to become deeply acquainted with, to know intimately." "To know" is a Jewish idiom for sexual intercourse between a man and a woman.

They do not have the full revelation of sonship as yet. The "Holy One of God" is a Messianic revelation. They believe that Jesus is sent from Yahweh; that He is the One that Israel is looking for. They are determined to remain loyal to Jesus. Little do they know where loyalty to Jesus will ultimately take them. It will take them to a place of disillusionment, of the abandoning of hope for an earthly kingdom. But it will bring them beyond disillusionment into a bright new day of co-participation with Jesus in His relationship with the Father.

PART TWO

A NEW CULTURE

COME AND DRINK

~

A MOVE UNDERGROUND

After this Jesus went about in Galilee. He would not go about in Judea, because the Jews were seeking to kill him. Now the Jews' Feast of Booths was at hand. So his brothers said to him, "Leave here and go to Judea, that your disciples also may see the works you are doing. For no one works in secret if he seeks to be known openly. If you do these things, show yourself to the world." For not even his brothers believed in him. Jesus said to them, "My time has not yet come, but your time is always here. The world cannot hate you, but it hates me because I testify about it that its works are evil. You go up to the feast. I am not going up to this feast, for my time has not yet fully come." After saying this, he remained in Galilee. — JOHN 7:1-9

Chapter 7 begins a new phase for Jesus in His ministry of manifesting the Father. Following His assertions in chapter 6, He has now become a target for religious retribution and is charged with blasphemy. The ministry of Jesus now takes a turn towards the subversive. His mission seems to go underground. This is a surprising strategy and is misunderstood by the supporters of Jesus.

His family, presumably His siblings in the family of Joseph and Mary, urge Him to continue as He did before. They fail to see spiritual realities. Their advice is on the 'wrong side' of belief, according to verse 5:

"For not even His brothers believed in Him."

His brothers want to promote His ministry, in spite of the fact that they don't believe in Him. That sounds ironic, but it makes sense to me. Jesus' brothers advise Him against keeping a low profile. They believe that His ministry is about to take off and become wildly successful. The opposite is happening, however. The ministry of Jesus is not about having a high profile or success. The ministry of Jesus is working along diametrically opposite lines to the way that the world thinks. Jesus' 'marketing strategy' is to become more subversive; it is to adopt a *lower*, not a higher, profile.

What is happening here? The ministry of Jesus on earth is entering a phase where it seems to be diminishing. The activities of Jesus are increasingly under wraps. He hides Himself and does things in secret. By John 11:54, He no longer walks openly among the Jews.

The Son's downward trajectory from heaven is descending deeper. The seed cast from the Father's hand can be seen falling into the earth. If this didn't happen there would not be any eternal fruit. On the one hand, the crowd had been trying to force Jesus to become king; on the other hand, the Jews have committed themselves to assassinate Him.

Jesus tells the others to go up to the Feast of Booths (Tabernacles) saying that His time has not yet come. He is living in eternal dimensions while His brothers are living only in the here and now. Their time is "always here." The internal radar of Jesus is set to the cross, to His death and burial, and beyond to His resurrection. He is savouring already the "joy set before Him" (Hebrews 12:2). Jesus' reward is beyond His current lifespan on earth. Already He can see the glittering prize of bringing many sons to glory with His Father.

> But after his brothers had gone up to the feast, then he also went up, not publicly but in private. The Jews were looking for him at the feast, and saying, "Where is he?" And there was much muttering about him among the people. While some said, "He is a good man," others said, "No, he is leading the people astray." Yet for fear of the Jews no one spoke openly of him. About the middle of the feast Jesus went up into the temple and began teaching. The Jews therefore marvelled, saying, "How is it that this man has learning, when he has never studied?" — JOHN 7:10-15

Jesus then goes to the feast, unpublicised. This appears to be underhanded because His actions contradict His words to His brothers. Is He being deceptive? Maybe He is, because they did not understand what He was about. On the other hand, it may be that He has not planned to go and the Father puts it on His heart to go. Either way, His actions do not follow any convention nor do they fulfil the expectations of others. His freedom from doing what is seen to be 'good' and 'right' is increasingly apparent. He acts with resoluteness, challenging conventional wisdom based on the knowledge of good and evil. He is already "as wise as a serpent, as innocent as a dove" (Matthew 10:16). Jesus is functioning in true righteousness, the rightness of relationship to His Father. He continually reverts to His Source, the Father.

When the Jews marvel at His teaching (verse 15), wondering why it is so profound when He has never studied formally in the rabbinical tradition, Jesus acknowledges His source. His teaching comes to Him as revelation directly from the Father. Revelation always outstrips the acquired knowledge of the mind. The interesting thing is that true revelation often confuses and offends the intellect but, at the same time, it sits comfortably within the continuum of historic orthodoxy. Revelation always has an authentic feel to it so that the heart can accept it. Even the Jewish scholars can sense the authenticity of Jesus' teaching. It is somehow consistent with the Torah, the Writings and the Prophets. Rather than contradicting them, the teaching of Jesus unveils them, shining light upon them in a way that scholarship can never do after centuries of study.

MY TEACHING IS NOT MINE...

So Jesus answered them, "My teaching is not mine, but his who sent me. If anyone's will is to do God's will, he will know whether the teaching is from God or whether I am speaking on my own authority. The one who speaks on his own authority seeks his own glory, but the one who seeks the glory of him who sent him is true, and in him there is no falsehood." — JOHN 7:16-18

In attributing all His teaching to His Father, Jesus displays His sonship. All teaching that originates in the heart of the Father will not only be life-giving but will authenticate what the Scriptures already teach. Alignment of the heart with the Father automatically brings out revelation that can only be marvelled at. The Father's wisdom, expressed through the heart of a son or daughter, stuns the intellect.

> *"Has not Moses given you the law? Yet none of you keeps the law. Why do you seek to kill me?" The crowd answered, "You have a demon! Who is seeking to kill you?" Jesus answered them, "I did one deed, and you all marvel at it. Moses gave you circumcision (not that it is from Moses, but from the fathers), and you circumcise a man on the Sabbath. If on the Sabbath a man receives circumcision so that the law of Moses may not be broken, are you angry with me because on the Sabbath I made a man's whole body well?"* — JOHN 7:19-23

The fallout continues from the healing of the lame man at the Pool of Bethesda. The religiously motivated mob is still incensed that Jesus has apparently violated the Sabbath by healing this man. The irrationality of the religious mindset is amazing, but it is not from choice. Its cause is spiritual blindness. When we are trapped in the tendrils of the ancient Tree of Knowledge we will never see things as they truly are. Our whole perception of reality is skewed so that we value a ritual which marks one single body part (circumcision) over a miracle that brings healing to the whole body.

The Jews are incensed that Jesus apparently worked on the Sabbath by healing a man, yet they cannot see that they too are 'working' by performing the rite of circumcision. They are choking on a gnat while swallowing a camel.

> *"Do not judge by appearances, but judge with right judgement."* — JOHN 7:24

The judgement (assessment) of religion is a judgement (or assessment) of external appearances. Judgement within the knowledge of good and evil is purely the assessment of evidence and data. It cannot see the heart-motivation of those that it seeks to judge. Right judgement comes from the Tree of Life. Correct assessment can only be distinguished by the eyes of the heart. The eyes of the heart see that healing someone's body on the Sabbath is not breaking the Law but superseding it!

From verses 25-52 the polemic rolls on between the people and the religious officials. Sometimes the people are swayed by the officials, sometimes they stand up to them and question them. Within the vortex of rancour and confusion, Jesus lies back into the resting place, hiding Himself in the Father.[18]

RIVERS OF LIVING WATER

> *On the last day of the feast, the great day, Jesus stood up and cried out, "If anyone thirsts, let him come to me and drink. Whoever believes in me, as the Scripture has said, 'Out of his heart will flow rivers of living water.'" Now this he said about the Spirit, whom those who believed in him were to*

---

18. I have chosen not to comment on parts of this chapter because I do not want to obscure or take the focus away from the section on 'Rivers of Living Water.' I am writing with a prophetic voice.

receive, for as yet the Spirit had not been given, because Jesus
was not yet glorified. — JOHN 7:37-39

This occurs within the context of a particular Jewish feast, in which the High Priest proceeded through the Temple and approached the altar. Accompanied by the other priests, the High Priest then poured pitchers of water over the altar. The water flowed over the altar and ran in rivulets down to its base. As more and more buckets of water were poured, the rivulets became a stream of water that flowed down the steps of the Holy Place into the outer courts. It would have been a compelling scene to behold.

What were the priests doing? They were participating in a historic ritual which attempted to replicate the vision of Ezekiel 47, where the prophet saw a river of water gushing from under the threshold of the temple. Those waters became a mighty river, deep enough to swim in; a river which brought healing and restoration to all in its path.

As He watches this ritual being played out, Jesus is seized by a powerful inner surge of anointing. He leaps forward and cries out, startling the gathered people:

"If anyone thirsts, let him come to me and drink!"

In doing so, Jesus has identified their fundamental need. The deepest problem of all for the people is that they are desperate for something that will slake their thirsty souls. They listen to Jesus' words because their souls are deeply and permanently parched. They have no moisture in their hearts; their hearts are shrivelled up with a dryness that is much more deeply ingrained than the span of a human lifetime. This arid desert is something they have been born with because it has existed from the time of the 'great rupture' of the Garden of Eden.

Are *we* any less thirsty? You and I have a dusty, arid desert inside us. We are inexorably drawn to see the ritual of water being poured over altars and, for a short while, we feel a little moistness in our souls. But Jesus is making another promise here; the same promise that He made to the woman of Sychar. Jesus' promise, which most of us have still to fully grasp, is that we can be eternally satisfied by rivers which flow from *inside* us.

Whoever believes in Jesus, whoever entrusts their life entirely to the Son, will discover a well of water bubbling up within them. This well of water flows from underneath the threshold of the temple and will not stop.

We have difficulty in locating this well within us because we have difficulty believing that we are the temple. The water still flows from underneath the threshold of the temple, as it did in Ezekiel's vision. However, we are always looking for 'times of refreshing' because we do not understand how the temple has transitioned. The temple, once a building and an institution, is now an organic presence within the human heart. It is within every individual heart and, by extension, within the community of those who are aware of this.

What if we admitted and believed that the Spirit of God can actually indwell us? That you and I are the sanctuary? What if we came to the realisation that we, you and I, are the Holy of Holies? I believe that this is a major sticking point in contemporary

Christianity. We just cannot believe that we, in our mundane ordinariness, are the Holy of Holies. That the tent and the temple of the Old Testament are merely a shadow of the present reality of human skin, blood and bone. But that is what the New Covenant is! When we open our hearts to this reality we will find that there is a gushing river within us, deep enough to swim in.

I had a spiritual vision once in which I could see Jesus standing on the steps of the temple. He was emptying jars of water down the steps, as the priests did on the last day of the feast. The volume kept increasing and then Jesus summoned something from behind Him and a mighty torrent gushed out of the darkness of the temple into the daylight. I feared that Jesus would get swept off His feet, but as the water made contact with His heel, He instantly became larger and the mighty torrent gushed and eddied around His ankles and swirled up to His knees. When the river of revelation hits your image of Jesus, it will increase who He is. As soon as the Spirit 'hits the heels' of your current perception of who God is, He will instantaneously expand your perception.

Sonship is ever moving and ever expanding. It is a constant enlargement in relationship with Father. Every time the flow of the river hits an obstacle, the obstacle will be carried with the river. Everything flows in the same river. Material provision for human needs comes in the flow of the Father's love. Wisdom for the decisions of life comes in the flow of the Father's love. Strength to carry life's burdens is found in the flow of that love.

The heart is not logical. The heart is not taught by rationality and education. No matter what happens, the heart remains at the centre. Life can cause the heart to hide and harden but His love warms and grows it. The heart is the doorway into everything that is heavenly. In Christianity, the Spirt is no longer external; He lives within us in the core of our being. From the depths of our spirits the Holy Spirit connects us with the reality of heaven. Heaven is to be reached by looking inward not upward.

"...for as yet the Spirit had not been given, because Jesus was not yet glorified." The Father has to wait until Jesus is glorified before He can release the gift of the Holy Spirit. The New Covenant of an indwelling God comes beyond the cross, in resurrection life. While Jesus is on earth, the fulness of the Spirit only operates through Him. The entire fulness of the Godhead is channeled through this one opening, the Son. When Jesus is glorified at the Father's right hand, the fulness of the Spirit will be channelled through many openings. The rivers of living water will find a way out through the hearts of multiple sons and daughters throughout history.

This all happens at the Feast of the Tents (The Feast of Tabernacles or Booths). At this feast, people came to Jerusalem and camped out in tents (booths) made of boughs and branches. This feast was one of the three major Jewish feasts, the others being Passover and the Feast of Pentecost. I find it very interesting that the other two feasts have been fulfilled in the experience of the Church. The Body of Christ has come into a revelation of the Passover feast, of the blood of the Lamb who has taken away sins. The Body of Christ has also come into the fulfilment of the Feast of Pentecost, many have had a Pentecostal experience. The Body of Christ has yet to experience what the Feast of Tabernacles really means.

The Feast of Tabernacles is not about who we are in God. It is, rather, about who God is *in us*. The Feast of Tabernacles is the realisation that God, in His fulness, has pitched His tent within us. "Little old me" has become the tent and temple of the Trinity. The Feast of Tabernacles is the realisation that Christ in us is 'the hope of glory' (Colossians 1:27). When this stupendous reality is awakened to our understanding, we will find rivers of life and revelation springing up inside us.

FREEDOM FROM CONDEMNATION BRINGS FREEDOM FROM SIN

~

The crowd parts and makes a path for them to exit. One by one they shuffle out, not able to look anyone in the eye. A small cairn of rocks is left where they have been dropped in the dust. A woman is left in their trail, dishevelled from being caught *in flagrante* (in the heat of the moment) with another man. Her cheeks are stained with tears, rivulets of black kohl running down her face. The woman is glancing at another figure who is stooped on the ground, at eye level with her. He has made markings in the dust. All eyes are upon Him as He rises to His feet…

THE SIGN OF NOT CONDEMNING

Chapter 8 begins with another significant event. I use the

word 'significant' (sign/ificant) because, for me, this episode is unquestionably a sign. It is not a sign recognised by biblical commentators because there is no apparent miraculous element to it, nevertheless what happens is potent with meaning.

> *...but Jesus went to the Mount of Olives. Early in the morning he came again to the temple. All the people came to him, and he sat down and taught them. The scribes and the Pharisees brought a woman who had been caught in adultery, and placing her in the midst they said to him, "Teacher, this woman has been caught in the act of adultery. Now in the Law Moses commanded us to stone such women. So what do you say?" This they said to test him, that they might have some charge to bring against him. Jesus bent down and wrote with his finger on the ground. And as they continued to ask him, he stood up and said to them, "Let him who is without sin among you be the first to throw a stone at her." And once more he bent down and wrote on the ground. But when they heard it, they went away one by one, beginning with the older ones, and Jesus was left alone with the woman standing before him. Jesus stood up and said to her, "Woman, where are they? Has no one condemned you?" She said, "No one, Lord." And Jesus said, "Neither do I condemn you; go, and from now on sin no more."* — JOHN 8:1-11

Once more, as previously in John's Gospel, we have a woman who is a catalyst for a major revelatory watershed and an unveiling of the true nature of God. What is more, she is on the wrong side of the moral protocol.

This woman is in an acute situation, caught red-handed in the act of adultery. It is almost superfluous to ask where the man is. Why is *he* not brought before Jesus? It is indicative of the systemic misogyny within society and, even more starkly within the religious system, that the man is not mentioned. Perhaps, he is even there as one of her accusers. I know from my own experience that the object of sexual temptation can often be simultaneously despised as an agent of moral sabotage.

There are a number of accusations here. Firstly, she is accused explicitly of immorality. Secondly, she is accused implicitly because of her gender. Thirdly, Jesus is set up for accusation. The *real* test here is for Jesus. The woman is a dispensable pawn pushed forward to checkmate Jesus in this game of moralistic chess. They challenge Him so that "...they might have some charge to bring against Him." (v.6),

Behind all of this, the Father is orchestrating events so that this woman will be a redemptive catalyst. She fully represents the fallenness and the victimisation of women and the spiritual feminine. However, her encounter with Jesus opens a way back to the Tree of Life. She (and Jesus) are in the court of the knowledge of good and evil. He is identified with her in the dock of accusation. The temple is the shrine of accusation; the nexus of moral perfectionism and condemnation.

The 'kangaroo court' convened by the Pharisees is intended to bring to bear the full weight of the knowledge of right and wrong, good and evil, not only upon the woman but upon Jesus. The religious leaders cite the law of Moses. Earlier (John 5:45,46) Jesus had told them that Moses was the one who accused *them*. They now turn 'Moses' back against the Son.

> *Jesus bent down and wrote on the ground. And as they continued to ask him, he stood up and said to them, "Let him who is without sin among you be the first to throw a stone at her." And once more he bent down and wrote on the ground."* — JOHN 8:6-8

Many have wondered and speculated about what Jesus writes. Let me suggest that He may have written symbolically to show a greater and more ancient law than the Law of Moses—the law of Love. The law of Moses was literally set in stone. It was encapsulated in the two tablets of stone carried from Sinai and placed within the Ark of the Covenant. It was immovable and non-negotiable. Jesus writes on a more malleable surface, the sandy dust of the ground. He writes a different commandment, which supersedes and underpins the law of Moses. He writes with the finger of God, not on stone but on dirt.

I do not know what words He wrote, but the symbolism of Him writing with His finger would not be lost on the Pharisees. They knew that the Two Tables of the Law were written with the finger of Yahweh.

The law of Moses had, because of sin, become the "law of sin and death" (Romans 8:2). Here we have, the "law of the Spirit of life" (Romans 8:2) being written on the ground.

Is it too big a stretch to imagine that the dusty ground is symbolic of the human heart? God formed Adam from the dust. The New

Covenant is written on the human heart (Jeremiah 31:33). The New Covenant is not a law-code external to the human person, but it is a principle of life internalised within the human person.

As Jesus writes on the ground, so He is writing on this woman's heart. Her heart becomes the tablet upon which the law of love is inscribed. She is becoming "a letter from Christ, written not with ink but with the Spirit of the living God, not on tablets of stone but on tablets of human hearts." (2 Corinthians 3:3)

FREEDOM FROM SIN IS A CONSEQUENCE OF FREEDOM FROM CONDEMNATION

The Son here is not governing from the Tree of Knowledge but in the government of the Tree of Life. He is executing judgement upon the law of sin and death. In other words, He is condemning condemnation. This poor woman would have been stoned to death under the law, but she is resurrected from that judgement into a place without condemnation.

To show that no-one is without sin removes a central plank from the religious construct. The religious construct subsists on condemnation. Those who have supposedly less sin exert leverage over those who sin more and they do so by means of condemnation. The religious system may concede that everyone is a sinner, but it also adheres to George Orwell's adage from the novel *Animal Farm*, "All animals are equal, but some animals are more equal than others." In the religious system, some are "more equal" than others and can exert control over the others. Jesus pulls the rug from under this culture.

After writing once more on the ground, Jesus stands up again. They have filed out, the oldest first. Those who are the most well-versed in legalism have led the way, leaving Jesus alone with the woman. The woman now stands on resurrection ground. She experiences what Romans 8 declares, "There is therefore now no condemnation to those who are in Christ Jesus." She has been snatched from the jaws of death to find herself suddenly and inexplicably "in Christ Jesus."

> *Jesus stood up and said to her, "Woman, where are they? Has no one condemned you?" She said, "No one, Lord." And Jesus said, "Neither do I condemn you; go and from now on sin no more."* — JOHN 8:10,11

Here is something astounding! Freedom from sin is inextricably linked to freedom from condemnation. Yes, it is! This is the master key that unlocks the prison door. While we are condemned within the knowledge of good and evil we can never be free from sin. It sounds somehow ironic but it is gloriously true!

This is how it works. Most of the sin we engage in is due to our need for affirmation and comfort. Sexual sin is a classic example of this. I was once caught in a trap of sexual sin. The trap had two pincers: one was condemnation, the other was false comfort. When I fell into the sinful activity, I immediately became condemned. My condemnation hindered me from coming to God to receive the comfort I so desperately needed so where did I get comfort? I had to revert back to the sexual sin to get comfort. I was caught in the revolving door and couldn't get out. The sinful act leads to condemnation, which leads to a need again for comfort. The Source of comfort is shut off. Comfort from God is completely inaccessible within the Tree of the Knowledge of Good and Evil. This is what Paul is talking about in 1 Corinthians 15:56, when he says that, "... The power of sin is the law."

Experiencing what it is to be loved by the Father breaks us out of this vicious cycle. Being loved by the Father, in Christ Jesus, immediately sets us free from condemnation. We can draw from His eternal and deep comfort. The need for the false comfort which sin offers then drops away.

By refusing to condemn this woman, Jesus set her free from the power of sin. His words carried the creative dynamism to allow her to "sin no more."

Like the woman in John 4, we do not know where she goes but her life is forever impacted by this encounter. She is a catalyst and a sign. Her experience breaks us out of the web of law and condemnation, of the assessment of good and evil. She catalyses the revelation of the law of the Spirit of life which sets us free in Christ Jesus from the law of sin and death (Romans 8:2). We have to wait for Paul to put words to what actually happened to her, but without doubt, this was her joyous experience.[19]

THE LIGHT OF THE WORLD

Again Jesus spoke to them, saying, "I am the light of the world. Whoever follows me will not walk in darkness, but

---

19. At this point, I need to recommend James Jordan's teaching entitled *The Third Law*, available either on CD/MP3 or as a chapter in his book, *The Ancient Road Rediscovered* published by Fatherheart Media, www.fatherheart.net. This teaching brings more depth and clarity to what I am saying here.

will have the light of life." So the Pharisees said to him, "You are bearing witness about yourself; your testimony is not true." Jesus answered, "Even if I do bear witness about myself, my testimony is true, for I know where I came from and where I am going, but you do not know where I come from or where I am going. You judge according to the flesh; I judge no one. Yet even if I do judge, my judgement is true, for it is not I alone who judge, but I and the Father who sent me." In your Law it is written that the testimony of two men is true. I am the one who bears witness about myself, and the Father who sent me bears witness about me. They said to him therefore, "Where is your Father?" Jesus answered, "You know neither me nor my Father. If you knew me you would know my Father also." These words he spoke in the treasury, as he taught in the temple; but no one arrested him, because his hour had not yet come. — JOHN 8:12-20

What is the light of the world? How is Jesus the light of the world? John has already told us that the True Light came into the world to enlighten everyone. The light has potential to enlighten the world but it is conditional upon having an open heart to receive the light. We are required to follow the light where the light leads us. Following the light will lead us inexorably into life; refusing to follow the light means that we continue to walk in the darkness without any revelation.

I have often heard people say that lighting a match dispenses with the darkness. That is true to a certain degree but lighting a match in a room does not light every cranny of the room. Jesus is, without doubt, the Light of the world, but that enlightenment is not automatic. Faith is needed to come to the Light and then follow the Light in order to become enlightened. God leaves us the choice to become enlightened by revelation or to remain in darkness. It is a question of our willingness to open our hearts.

It is clear that the Pharisees are not open-hearted enough to follow the Light. They resist the words of Jesus because they believe that He is His own witness. In their culture, every truth must be verified by other witnesses. This argument about 'witness' recurs again and again throughout this Gospel. The Pharisees are no more enlightened than before.

Jesus identifies their basic problem; they are judging *according to the flesh*. They cannot see spiritually with the eyes of the heart. Judging with the eyes of moral evaluation, they remain in the darkness of the knowledge of good and evil. The eyes which assess right and wrong cannot perceive sonship. They do not see Jesus as being sent from the Father. To know Jesus by revelation is to come to know the Father too.

John is intentional when he observes that Jesus spoke these words in the Temple treasury. What is so notable about the treasury? The Temple treasury was the place where people brought their offerings; sin-offerings, trespass-offerings and voluntary offerings. Put simply, the treasury is where you have to pay for transgressions. The worse your sin is, the more you have to pay. The more condemned you are, the more you are required to pay. The woman caught in adultery had an account which she could never pay financially. Her payment required her life by stoning.

Knowing the Father removes all condemnation. This is what the woman caught in adultery experienced. She discovered that she didn't owe anything to the treasury of the Temple; her debt had been paid and she was free to go. Becoming free from condemnation means that we do not give out of guilt or obligation, but we distribute the endless resources of the Father.

The words and actions of Jesus are inflammatory to the religious system. They are powerless to arrest Him, however, because 'His hour had not yet come." (v.20) The timing of Jesus' circumstances is determined by heaven and cannot be usurped by any human decision.

WHERE I AM, YOU CANNOT COME

So he said to them again, "I am going away, and you will seek me, and you will die in your sin. Where I am going, you cannot come." So the Jews said, "Will he kill himself, since he says, 'Where I am going, you cannot come?'" He said to them, "You are from below; I am from above. You are of this world; I am not of this world. I told you that you would die in your sins, for unless you believe that I am he you will die in your sins." — JOHN 8:21-24

There is a place that is inaccessible to those who insist on doing the right thing according to their judgement. This is not talking about those who are the wrong side of the moral divide. This is talking about those who are on the 'right' side of the moral divide. Those who are on the 'good' side will "die in their sin" because 'good' is as equally sin as 'evil' is. Sin is missing the mark. The mark is living in the intimate affections of the Father.

This is why Jesus says that they can never come to where He is going. He is returning to the Father's right hand. He came from 'above' and is soon to return there. He is of another world and His statement to them is that they are "of this world." Being "of the world" is not restricted to having secular and selfish motivations. Remember that Jesus is addressing this to the religious elite. Religion is *of the world*. The desire and effort to be good outside of relationship with the Father is *worldly*. The desire to become like God while still being independent from God is *worldly*.

I used to be deeply religious. I congratulated myself that I was not "of the world." When I came to know the love of the Father and my religious motivation was exposed, I was shocked to realise that, in actual fact, I had been extremely 'worldly.' It would horrify religious people to realise that they are as worldly as the people they label as being 'immoral,' but it *is* true. The only way to be free of the world (as a spiritual power) is to come to a realisation that we do not originate there. When we realise that our origin, like Jesus, is in the Father and (in Christ) we have our origin in heaven, we can then be free from what it is to be "of this world."

WHO ARE YOU?

So they said to him, "Who are you?" Jesus said to them, "Just what I have been telling you from the beginning. I have much to say about you and much to judge, but he who sent me is true, and I declare to the world what I have heard from him." They did not understand that he had been speaking to them about the Father. So Jesus said to them, "When you have lifted up the Son of Man, then you will know that I am

*he, and that I do nothing on my own authority, but speak
just as the Father taught me. And he who sent me is with
me. He has not left me alone, for I always do the things that
are pleasing to him." As he was saying these things, many
believed in him.* — JOHN 8:25-30

Jesus is a mystery to the people who are desperately trying to get a handle on Him. He confuses and confounds them; they are disturbed by Him. They keep looking for answers that will fit within their own paradigm. Jesus knows full well that His words can really only be grasped by revelation. It requires a shift in paradigm that can only be made by an opened heart.

"They did not understand that He had been speaking to them about the Father." The Father can only be known by revelation. In our orphan state, we do not even have a framework to understand who the Father is and what He is about. Outside of revelation, we can read many statements in the Scripture that speak of the Father but fail to realise what they mean. Jesus declares that a time will come when they will know who He is.

It is the lifting up of the Son of Man that will declare the Father. When Jesus is lifted onto the cross it will become clear who He is and what He is about. The cross will manifest who the Father really is and that the Father and the Son are one. This cuts against every worldly expectation. We would expect that Jesus will be revealed through power and glory. In our fallen perspective we want the persecutors of Jesus to get their comeuppance. That is not God's way.

Jesus' death on the cross will reveal the unity of the Father and the

Son. When the Son of Man hangs upon the cross in utter weakness, victimised by the orphan system, the Father will be declared. The cross will be the ultimate demonstration of the sacrificial nature of love; the true nature of the Father will be fully demonstrated in the Son. "He who sent me is with me," will be perfectly proclaimed when Jesus is crucified because then the Father's nature is demonstrated as outpoured love.

THE TRUTH WILL SET YOU FREE

So Jesus said to the Jews who had believed him, "If you abide in my word, you are truly my disciples, and you will know the truth, and the truth will set you free." They answered him, "We are offspring of Abraham and have never been enslaved to anyone. How is it that you say, 'You will become free?'"

Jesus answered them, "Truly, truly, I say to you, everyone who practices sin is a slave to sin. The slave does not remain in the house forever; the son remains forever. So if the Son sets you free, you will be free indeed. I know that you are offspring of Abraham; yet you seek to kill me because my word finds no place in you. I speak of what I have seen with my Father, and you do what you have heard from your father."
— JOHN 8:31-38

Everybody wants to be free. Throughout history, humanity has continually sought freedom. Freedom is a very popular word today. Wars are fought on the basis of different ideas about what freedom is. Western culture, in particular, has been built upon the values of freedom. But what is freedom and how can we be really free?

The word 'freedom' is actually a very subjective word. I can seek and insist upon my freedom but it will bring bondage to others. Similarly, the freedom of others may cause restriction and obligation in my life. One person's freedom can be another person's slavery. This definition of freedom cannot possibly be what Jesus is talking about when He speaks of being 'free indeed.'

Jesus promises that the knowledge of the truth will bring freedom. When He says this, the believing Jews have a predictable reaction. They think they are already free but their definition of freedom is not Jesus' definition of freedom.

True freedom is inextricably linked to knowing the Son. Knowing the Son cannot be separated from experiencing what it means for us to be in sonship. Freedom that is not subject to human definitions can only be experienced by connection to the Son. Abiding in the word that Jesus speaks brings us into truth, into fundamental reality. Reality can only be perceived through the eyes and ears of the heart. When Jesus speaks about 'truth' that brings freedom, He is not talking about doctrinal accuracy. He is talking about fundamental reality. The fundamental reality, by which all else makes sense, is that everything is based upon sonship.

The whole universe is geared towards living in love. The fabric of the cosmos is sustained by the love of its Source. When the universe is disconnected from the Source (as happened through the Fall) it comes into bondage. Returning to the reality of divine parenthood and creational childhood brings eternal freedom. There is no other alternative.

Being Abraham's physical offspring does not bring freedom. The problems of the Middle East are a tragic proof of that. To find true freedom we must trace our origin back to an earlier source than Abraham. Jesus calls out their claim to freedom and tells them to look at the symptoms of their life. The symptoms ("practising sin") are a dead giveaway of what the root cause is; the root cause is slavery. If they practise sin, they cannot possibly be free.

The woman caught in adultery found true freedom. She had practised sin because she was a slave to condemnation. Then she met the Son and experienced the truth. Meeting the Son set her free from condemnation. Sonship sets us free from condemnation because it is not conditional on good behaviour. Servants can never be free because servants are always bound by standards of behaviour. A son remains in the Father's house forever and his place is not conditional on anything. The removal of all conditions brings true freedom and actually sets us free from our propensity to sin.

How does the Son set us free? We are set free by being 'in Him,' in the place of no condemnation.

> *"I speak of what I have seen with my Father, and you do what you have heard from your father."* — JOHN 8:38

Our experience of freedom depends on who our father is. The Father of Jesus is the original father, and He is the only one who can bring true freedom. Throughout John's Gospel, Jesus meets people who look to fathers like Abraham, Jacob or Moses. These are the revered patriarchs and worthy of high honour, but it is a mistake to look to them as source. They did not even see themselves as being the source. When we settle for a source that is less than the Father of Jesus, the outcome is a loss of freedom.

I CAME FROM GOD AND I AM

They answered him, "Abraham is our father." Jesus said to them, "If you were Abraham's children, you would be doing the works Abraham did, but now you seek to kill me, a man who has told you the truth that I heard from God. This is not what Abraham did. You are doing the works your father did." They said to him, "We were not born of sexual immorality. We have one Father—even God." Jesus said to them, "If God were your Father, you would love me, for I came from God and I am here. I came not of my own accord, but he sent me. Why do you not understand what I say? It is because you cannot bear to hear my word. You are of your father the devil, and your will is to do your father's desires. He was a murderer from the beginning, and does not stand in the truth, because there is no truth in him. When he lies, he speaks out of his own character, for he is a liar and the father of lies. But because I tell the truth, you do not believe me. Which one of you convicts me of sin? If I tell the truth, why do you not believe me? Whoever is of God hears the words of God. The reason why you do not hear them is that you are not of God." — JOHN 8:39-47

The Pharisees are adamant that Abraham is their father. Jesus dismisses this claim outright. How can they come from Abraham and be trying to kill the One that Abraham foresaw? No! They are not Abraham's sons; they are the sons of disobedience. (Ephesians 2:2)

They are descended from none other than Satan, the original Orphan.

The Pharisees hurl the usual insults at Jesus; that He is "born of sexual immorality." (v.41) Presumably, Jesus would have had to endure these accusations a lot; the disrepute and gossip that He was an illegitimate child. The Pharisees claim that they have "one Father, even God." This does not mean that they have a revelation of God as 'Abba'; it means that they are justifying their behaviour as originating in God.

Jesus exposes the true source of their behaviour. The tree is known by its fruits. Murder and lies can only come from one place. This is learned behaviour from a parent. By looking at the behaviour of the children, you can see the ways they have been (or not been) nurtured. The lies of the religious leaders and their motivation to murder the Son of God has been put into them by the one who is their spiritual father, the devil.

"Whoever is of God hears the words of God. The reason why you do not hear them is that you are not of God." These people are created by God and loved by Him. There is never any doubt of God's pure love for human beings. When Jesus says to them that they "are not of God," He is referring to a religious persona. The legalistic identity which the Pharisees are hiding behind is not of God. They have become people without any ability to hear the words of God. In contrast to those who are not 'of God,' Jesus comes from His Father.

JESUS PRE-EXISTS ABRAHAM

The Jews answered him, "Are we not right in saying that

you are a Samaritan and have a demon?" Jesus answered, "I do not have a demon, but I honour my Father, and you dishonour me. Yet I do not seek my own glory; there is One who seeks it, and he is the judge. Truly, truly, I say to you, if anyone keeps my word, he will never see death." The Jews said to him, "Now we know that you have a demon! Abraham died, as did the prophets, yet you say, 'If anyone keeps my word, he will never taste death.' Are you greater than our father Abraham, who died? And the prophets died! Who do you make yourself out to be?" Jesus answered, "If I glorify myself, my glory is nothing. It is my Father who glorifies me, of whom you say, 'He is our God.' But you have not known him. I know him. If I were to say that I do not know him, I would be a liar like you, but I do know him and I keep his word. Your father Abraham rejoiced that he would see my day. He saw it and was glad." So the Jews said to him, "You are not yet fifty years old, and have you seen Abraham?" Jesus said to them, "Truly, truly, I say to you, before Abraham was, I am." So they picked up stones to throw at him, but Jesus hid himself and went out of the temple. — JOHN 8:48-59

The Son does not seek His own glory. True sonship has no interest in its own reputation; it is only interested in displaying who the Father is. However, the Father seeks the glory of the Son. The Father is very motivated to bring honour to the Son. It is no different for sons and daughters. The Father's 'culture of honour' flows from Him and when He is known we come increasingly into who we truly are.

The Jews stumble on Jesus' promise that whoever keeps His word will never taste death. If the greatest patriarch, Abraham, died, how can Jesus claim to escape death? Even the prophets died! Jesus' riposte is dumbfounding. He tells them that He *preceded* Abraham. What is more, Abraham saw by prophetic revelation that the Son would appear on the earth. The writer to Hebrews confirms this; that Abraham looked for a city that was built by God (Hebrews 11:10). Jesus declares unequivocally that He precedes Abraham. His statement includes the words "I am." The impact of these two little words would not be lost on the Jews, for this is the Divine Name by which God revealed Himself to Moses.

The real significance in this is that sonship precedes all the covenants. Relationship with God through sonship is a more primordial revelation than the Old Testament covenants. New Covenant revelation is more ancient than the Old Covenant. Paul brings this out in Galatians 3:16-18 when he declares that the promise of sonship came before the law. Our relationship with God is not based on law-observance. It is not even based on covenantal promise. Our relationship with God is based on sonship.

BLIND EYES OPENED

~

As he passed by, he saw a man blind from birth. And his disciples asked him, "Rabbi, who sinned, this man or his parents, that he was born blind?" Jesus answered, "It was not that this man sinned, or his parents, but that the works of God might be displayed in him." — JOHN 9:1-3

The healing of the blind man is another supernatural sign. This man is blind from birth, not as a direct result of his or his parents' sin. No, this man is blind because of a systemic disease in the human race. His physical blindness is symptomatic of a deeper, spiritual blindness. This man personifies what it is to be human without the Father. He cannot see reality as he is intended to see it. His sight-sense is irreversibly impaired.

Remarkably, Jesus doesn't highlight the cause of the man's blindness. Jesus doesn't attribute it as a punishment for any personal sin. Jesus, in His unassailable faith and authority, doesn't see the problem; He sees the solution. Following the impulse of the Father's compassion within Him, He sees this man as an opportunity for the miraculous outworking of God's love and power.

> *"We must work the works of him who sent me while it is day; night is coming, when no one can work. As long as I am in the world, I am the light of the world."* — JOHN 9:4,5

The works of the Father must be carried out in the season of faith and revelation. While Jesus is in the world it is a season when miraculous works can be done. A time is coming when the Light of the World will be absent. The works of the Father will be done again but they will be done in such a way that it takes revelation to apprehend them. When Jesus returns to heaven He will no longer be obvious to the world. The light can only enlighten when Jesus is received in the heart.

From one perspective, the night, when it comes, will not last very long. It will last no longer than the period between the crucifixion and Pentecost. After Pentecost, the works of the Father will be demonstrated again by the apostles. For the world, however, the night will begin when it crucifies Jesus. No longer will there be a location where Jesus can be physically seen. The works of the Father will be done in another way; by a community of faith scattered throughout nations. The night, too, will soon come for Israel. When Jesus is crucified, darkness will descend upon Israel. The hope of Israel will soon only be accessed through revelation and through repentance by faith. Paul is very clear about this when he writes:

> *"But their minds were hardened. For to this day, when they read the old covenant, that same veil remains*

unlisted, because only through Christ is it taken away.
But when one turns to the Lord, the veil is removed."
— 2 CORINTHIANS 3:14-16

SPIT AND MUD

Having said these things, he spit on the ground and made
mud with the saliva. Then he anointed the man's eyes with
the mud and said to him, "Go, wash in the pool of Siloam"
(which means Sent). So he went and washed and came back
seeing. — JOHN 9:6,7

Jesus then spits on the ground and makes mud with His saliva.
I love this. It is so robust, so unrefined and mucky. What a sign!
Divine DNA rubbed into earthy matter. This action encapsulates
the Incarnation. Saliva from the Son of the Father; a projectile of
moist DNA from the Word falls into the dry earth and is then
rubbed into the dust by the finger of God to make a substance that
can open blind eyes.

God's alchemy uses spit and earth to create a healing salve. That
in itself is worth pondering on. There are hints here of a reenactment
of the creation of Adam in Genesis, the action of the Word upon the
clay of the earth. Healing and freedom, restoration to new creation,
requires a synergy of the word from God with the imperfection of
the fallen creation.

What occurs when Jesus spits on the earth? A mixture of that
which is 'un-fallen' interacts with fallen creation and creates the
healing mud. God wants to meld Himself into the dirt of the fallen

earth and, as a result of that intermingling, the eyes of the blind will be opened.

It is not enough to anoint the man's eyes with mud. He needs to act out another precondition before he can *actually* see. He must go to the Pool of Siloam and wash, and then his eyes will function properly again. Why is John, the Gospel writer, so careful to tell us what Siloam means? I would like the offer the view that it is because the blind man needs to return to a place where he knows what it is to be *sent*. He needs to be reconnected to a sense of coming from a source. An orphan is a person who is essentially sourceless, but a son always knows that he is *sent* from a higher and deeper source.

Remember what John the Baptist said, "A person cannot receive even one thing unless it is given him from heaven." (John 3:27) To go and immerse yourself in that which is 'sent' is to return to the origin of all things. The eyes of our hearts became blinded when we became disconnected from the Sending Originator, the Father. To return to the pool called 'Sent' is to return to a place of eternal belonging and *in that place* blind eyes can see again.

"I DO NOT KNOW"

The neighbours and those who had seen him before as a beggar were saying, "Is this not the man who used to sit and beg?" Some said, "It is he." Others said, "No, but he is like him." He kept saying, "I am the man." So they said to him, "Then how were your eyes opened?" He answered, "The man called Jesus made mud and anointed my eyes and said to me, 'Go to Siloam and wash.' So I went and washed and received

my sight." They said to him, "Where is he?" He said, "I do
not know." — JOHN 9:8-12

The man becomes a witness. He is the sign. He cannot suppress the change that has happened in his life. All he needs to do is confirm that he was indeed the blind beggar. He has no theology, his communication is very simple. A man called Jesus made mud, anointed his eyes, told him to wash in Siloam and now he can see!

When they ask where Jesus is, the man says, "I do not know." Let me suggest that these words' "I do not know" are a more effective witness than we realise. Many Christians are afraid to admit that they do not know. Many leaders are *terrified* to say the words, "I do not know." We are uncomfortable with mystery and not knowing. I really like this man's candour. He speaks simply that he does not know where Jesus has gone. Jesus has performed the miracle and disappeared. I love it too that Jesus does not feel the need to stick around. He is supremely confident in what the Father is doing. So the man is brought before the Pharisees.

A SABBATH OF THE HEART

They brought to the Pharisees the man who had formerly
been blind. Now it was a Sabbath day when Jesus made
the mud and opened his eyes. So the Pharisees again asked
him how he had received his sight. And he said to them, "He
put mud on my eyes, and I washed, and I see." Some of the
Pharisees said, "This man is not from God, for he does not
keep the Sabbath." But others said, "How can a man who
is a sinner do such signs?" And there was a division among

them. So they said again to the blind man, "What do you
say about him, since he has opened your eyes?" He said, "He
is a prophet." — JOHN 9:13-17

John is very intentional in pointing out that Jesus has healed
the blind man on the Sabbath. When Jesus heals this man *on the*
Sabbath, He is firing a warning shot across the bows of the religious
system. The religious hierarchy immediately dismisses the fact that
Jesus can possibly be from God because He has apparently violated
the Sabbath. The truth is, by healing the man from his blindness,
Jesus *more than* fulfils the Sabbath. He invites the blind man into
a Sabbath of the heart.

When the man affirms his belief that Jesus is a prophet, we can
see that his inner eyes are beginning to see; not only to see physically
but to perceive *spiritual* realities. His previous statement, "I do not
know" is the perfect stimulus to receiving more revelation about
who Jesus really is. The best way to position ourselves for greater
revelation is to admit that we do not know. That humility leaves us
open to receive revelatory knowledge.

This man is on a revelatory curve similar to the Samaritan woman
in John 4. Like her, he affirms that Jesus is a prophet. It is the only
category that he can place Jesus in right now, but we will see that
his revelation (like the Samaritan woman's) progresses far beyond
seeing Jesus merely as a prophet.

The Jews did not believe that he had been blind and had
received his sight, until they called the parents of the man
who had received his sight and asked them, "Is this your son,

who you say was born blind? How then does he now see?" His parents answered, "We know that this is our son and that he was born blind. But how he now sees we do not know, nor do we know who opened his eyes. Ask him; he is of age. He will speak for himself." (His parents said these things because they feared the Jews, for the Jews had already agreed that if anyone should confess Jesus to be Christ, he was to be put out of the synagogue.) Therefore his parents said, "He is of age; ask him." — JOHN 9:18-23

The religious mindset is more resistant to God's supernatural working than the rationalist or atheistic mindset. The Jews refuse to believe that this man had even been born blind in the first place so they need to question his parents. His parents state the bald facts but push the focus of attention back to their son, "He is of age; ask him." His parents do not have a revelation of Jesus and are still afraid of possible excommunication from the synagogue so they do not make any commitment to affirming that Jesus is the Messiah. The man is left alone before the judgment of the Pharisees.

So for the second time they called the man who had been blind and said to him, "Give glory to God. We know that this man is a sinner." He answered, "Whether he is a sinner I do not know. One thing I do know, that though I was blind, now I see." They said to him, "What did he do to you? How did he open your eyes?" He answered them, "I have told you already, and you would not listen. Why do you want to hear it again? Do you also want to become his disciples?" And they reviled him, saying, "You are his disciple, but we are disciples of Moses. We know that God has spoken to Moses,

but as for this man, we do not know where he comes from."
The man answered, "Why, this is an amazing thing! You do
not know where he comes from, and yet he opened my eyes.
We know that God does not listen to sinners, but if anyone
is a worshipper of God and does his will, God listens to him.
Never since the world began has it been heard that anyone
opened the eyes of a man born blind. If this man were not
from God, he could do nothing." They answered him, "You
were born in utter sin, and would you teach us?" And they
cast him out. — JOHN 9:24-34

The spotlight of interrogation is swung back into the face of the man who had been blind. The Pharisees urge him to glorify God, and distance himself from the 'sinner' Jesus. How corrupt religion is! I do not really blame the Pharisees. The Tree of Knowledge defines Jesus as 'a sinner' because He does not fit its definition of being morally good. I lived my early life within an extremely religious culture but I cannot help loving the individual people that are within it. They, too, are victims of a deception. The Pharisees here cannot see that Jesus is sent from God. They are more blind than the man was who has now been healed.

The 'blind' man's witness is becoming bolder, sharper and more confrontational of the religious system. He is developing a cutting edge, challenging the Pharisees, "Do you also want to become disciples of Jesus?" If we read slowly through the narrative we can see a development in the confidence and skill of the man when he talks to the Pharisees. As his speaking becomes more spiritually insightful, it brings him increasingly on a collision course with the religious leaders. First he is interrogated, then his honesty is doubted, then he is reviled, and finally he is cast out. In many ways, this is how we know that we are speaking true revelation from God—by how the religious system reacts to it. The sharper the prophetic declaration, the more extreme will be the reaction from those who wish to maintain religion. It will ultimately come to the point where religion cannot abide the presence of those whose eyes have been opened.

The man's 'preaching' (from verse 30 to 33) lasts just a couple of seconds:

> ..."Why, this is an amazing thing! You do not know where he comes from, and yet he opened my eyes. We know that God does not listen to sinners, but if anyone is a worshipper of God and does his will, God listens to him. Never since the world began has it been heard that anyone opened the eyes of a man born blind. If this man were not from God, he could do nothing." — JOHN 9:30-33

The Pharisees claim to know that God had spoken to Moses but they had completely missed the point of Moses' ministry. Moses' ministry, like all God-anointed ministry throughout history, was to open blind eyes, the eyes of the heart.[20] Moses had summoned Israel and pronounced to them:

> "But to this day the LORD has not given you a heart to understand or eyes to see or ears to hear."
> — DEUTERONOMY 29:4

---

20. I am indebted to M. James Jordan for this revelatory observation. He brings this out very cogently in a chapter entitled 'Opening the Eyes of the Heart' in his book, *The Ancient Road Rediscovered* available on Amazon or from Fatherheart Media at www.fatherheart.net

Though they do not perceive it, Jesus is performing *par excellence* the ministry commission that had been given to Moses. Nothing has changed since the time of Moses, the ministry of giving 'eyes to see' is still needed. The man knows that the miracle is a supernatural attestation that Jesus is from God.

The healed man's words are few but they are potent enough to have him thrown out of the synagogue. The accusation against the man is precisely the opposite of what Jesus said about him. Jesus said that he had not sinned nor his parents (v. 3) but the judgement of the religious leaders is that he was "born in utter sin," (v.34) and he is excluded. The religious system has excluded him but Jesus *includes* him by seeking him out and finding him.

BANISHED BY RELIGION - FOUND BY JESUS

Jesus heard that they had cast him out, and having found him he said, "Do you believe in the Son of Man?" He answered, "And who is he, sir, that I may believe in him?" Jesus said to him, "You have seen him, and it is he who is speaking to you." He said, "Lord, I believe," and he worshipped him.
— JOHN 9:35-38

Jesus always seeks out and finds those who wish to know Him. It is only when the man has parted company with the structure of religion that he is ready to come into a deeper connection with Jesus. Jesus waits until the Pharisees throw the man out and then He finds him. We need never be afraid when we are rejected by what purports to serve God. If our eyes have been opened and we have a true revelation of who Jesus is as sent by the Father, we can be assured that He will seek us out and find us. There is a lot of talk about us seeking God, but the greater reality is that He is seeking us and makes decisive movements to find us.

Many people are afraid to leave what has become religious. Because they struggle under condemnation, they are afraid that they will lose all connection with God. But God looks at their hearts and He will always come looking for them and find them. God is much more proactive than we think but we miss this because of our fear and condemnation. I have known people (including myself) who have given up faith, but somehow Jesus comes to them where they are and finds them. It is only when our initiative ceases that we recognise God's initiative.

The healed man's revelation reaches its fullest point when he says, "Lord, I believe" and worships Jesus. At this point, his eyes are as fully opened as they can be, for he sees Jesus as God and as one with the Father. His eyes are fully open when he perceives Jesus as worthy to be worshipped. Essentially, he is now a 'Christian.' This man has truly departed from the strictures of his religious upbringing. He is an outcast from the synagogue, accused of blasphemy yet is now completely free to worship on the basis of revelation.

OPENING BLIND EYES - CLOSING SEEING EYES

Jesus said, "For judgment I came into this world, that those who do not see may see, and those who see may become blind." Some of the Pharisees near him heard these things, and said to him, "Are we also blind?" Jesus said to them, "If you were blind, you would have no guilt; but now that you say, 'We see,' your guilt remains. — JOHN 9:39-41

In these words, Jesus defines His ministry. Like the commission of Moses (Deuteronomy 29:4; like the sending of Isaiah (Isaiah 6:9,10); and later in the mandate given to Paul the apostle (Acts 26:12-18), the ministry of Jesus is to restore the sight of the heart. James Jordan puts it like this:

> *"From God's perspective, the singular goal of the Gospel is that the eyes of the hearts of people will be opened so that He will be known. God's heart is that every minister of the Gospel would have as their mandate to open the eyes that have become blind — the eyes of the heart."* [21]

Jesus comes to open the eyes which have been blinded through eating of the Tree of the Knowledge of Good and Evil. Opening the eyes of the heart is a *positive* judgement. But the judgement that Jesus executes is also a blinding of those who *think* they can see. He brings a shock of reality to those who are seeing with the eyes which assess good and evil. The ministry of Jesus will confuse and dim the knowledge and perception of good and evil. When revelation hits, those eyes actually become blind. Saul of Tarsus experienced this on the road to Damascus. He thought he could see but was struck blind.

Jesus' words to the Pharisees are: "But now you say, 'We see,' your guilt remains." Claiming to see without any revelation and without our eyes being anointed is to remain within the Tree of

---

21. M. James Jordan, *The Ancient Road Rediscovered*, Fatherheart Media, Taupo, 2014.

the Knowledge of Good and Evil. Most judgements are made from the wrong eyes. If we are not released from condemnation by the opening up of our heart-sight we remain under condemnation. The very fact that we see within the paradigm of the knowledge of good and evil means that we cannot be free from guilt.

With hardly a pause to catch His breath, Jesus continues addressing the Pharisees...

CHAPTER TEN

FALSE AND TRUE SHEPHERDS

~

We can only properly understand John 10 if we see it as a direct continuation of Jesus' speech to the Pharisees beginning in Chapter 9:39. This is one of the instances in which the chapter divisions added in the 13th Century have done us a disservice.

This chapter about the 'good shepherd' is not the fluffy, comforting speech of popular understanding. It is, in actual fact, a prophetic broadside against the Pharisees. It is primarily an indictment against religious leadership and those who are false shepherds. False shepherds are those who claim to see (John 9:41), but who are actually experts in the knowledge of good and evil.

THIEVES AND ROBBERS

"Truly, truly, I say to you, he who does not enter the sheepfold by the door but climbs in by another way, that man is a thief and a robber. But he who enters by the door is the shepherd

*of the sheep. To him the gatekeeper opens. The sheep hear his
voice, and he calls his own sheep by name and leads them
out. When he has brought out all his own, he goes before
them, and the sheep follow him, for they know his voice. A
stranger they will not follow, but they will flee from him,
for they do not know the voice of strangers." This figure of
speech Jesus used with them, but they did not understand
what he was saying to them.* — JOHN 10:1-6

Every time Jesus begins a speech with the words "Truly, truly, I say
to you" we know that we have to sit up and take notice. Here, Jesus
sharply contrasts the Good Shepherd with those who set themselves
up as 'shepherds' but who are not interested in the welfare of the
flock. Jesus is lambasting the false shepherds, the Pharisees, who
threw the blind man out of the synagogue because he was healed
on the Sabbath. That man was one of the sheep, as was the woman
caught in adultery in Chapter 8.

Before I get into the meat of *this* chapter, let me pick out a passage
from the Old Testament to provide a context for what Jesus is
saying here. Ezekiel 34 is a prophecy against the shepherds of Israel.
When we compare Ezekiel 34 and John 10, it will be self-evident
that Ezekiel 34 is in the back of Jesus' mind as He speaks to the
Pharisees. The Pharisees, I am convinced, are reminded of Ezekiel
34 too, which goes like this:

> *"The word of the LORD came to me: 'Son of man, prophesy
> against the shepherds of Israel; prophesy, and say to them, even
> to the shepherds, Thus says the Lord GOD: Ah, shepherds of
> Israel who have been feeding yourselves! Should not shepherds*

feed the sheep? You eat the fat, you clothe yourselves with the wool, you slaughter the fat ones, but you do not feed the sheep. The weak you have not strengthened, the sick you have not healed, the injured you have not bound up, the strayed you have not brought back, the lost you have not sought, and with force and harshness you have ruled them. So they were scattered, because there was no shepherd, and they became food for all the wild beasts. My sheep were scattered; they wandered over all the mountains and on every high hill. My sheep were scattered over all the face of the earth, with none to search or seek for them.

"Therefore, you shepherds, hear the word of the LORD: As I live, declares the Lord GOD, surely because my sheep have become a prey, and my sheep have become food for all the wild beasts, since there was no shepherd, and because my shepherds have not searched for my sheep, but the shepherds have fed themselves, and have not fed my sheep, therefore, you shepherds, hear the word of the LORD: Thus says the Lord GOD, Behold, I am against the shepherds, and I will require my sheep at their hand and put a stop to their feeding the sheep. No longer shall the shepherds feed themselves. I will rescue my sheep from their mouths, that they may not be food for them." — Ezekiel 34:1-10

This is the same context in which Jesus is speaking, 600 years later. The false shepherds in Jesus' day behave just like the false shepherds in Ezekiel's day. Throughout history every 'false shepherd' behaves the same. The difference now is that God is shepherding His own sheep if we have eyes to see it and the courage to ignore the voice of false shepherds and listen to the voice of the True Shepherd.

> *"For thus says the Lord GOD: Behold, I, I myself will search for my sheep and will seek them out. As a shepherd seeks out his flock when he is among his sheep that have been scattered, so will I seek out my sheep, and I will rescue them from all places where they have been scattered on a day of clouds and thick darkness. And I will bring them out from the peoples and gather them from the countries, and will bring them into their own land. And I will feed them on the mountains of Israel, by the ravines, and in all the inhabited places of the country. I will feed them with good pasture, and on the mountain heights of Israel shall be their grazing land. There they shall lie down in good grazing land, and on rich pasture they shall feed on the mountains of Israel. I myself will be the shepherd of my sheep, and I myself will make them lie down, declares the Lord GOD. I will seek the lost, and I will bring back the strayed, and I will bind up the injured, and I will strengthen the weak, and the fat and the strong I will destroy. I will feed them in justice."* — Ezekiel 34:11-16

The promise given through the prophet, Ezekiel, is now fulfilled. God has become the shepherd *Himself.* If you open your heart and live from your heart, the care of the Shepherd will be very evident to you.

Jesus is a Good Shepherd because He understands who the sheep are and how much they are valued by the owner, the Father. The Father does not view the sheep as a commodity; every sheep is called by name.

ENTERING BY THE DOOR

"Truly, truly, I say to you, he who does not enter the sheepfold by the door but climbs in by another way, that man is a thief and a robber. But he who enters by the door is the shepherd of the sheep. To him the gatekeeper opens." — JOHN 10:1-3

"So Jesus again said to them, 'Truly, truly, I say to you, I am the door of the sheep. All who came before me are thieves and robbers, but the sheep did not listen to them. I am the door. If anyone enters by me, he will be saved and will go in and out and find pasture. The thief comes only to steal and kill and destroy. I came that they may have life and have it abundantly. — JOHN 10:7-10

The true shepherd enters by the door. Jesus is the True Shepherd and He is also the Door. Since He is talking to leadership here, this must also apply to 'true shepherds' within the flock of God. Jesus Himself is the model for leadership. False shepherds try to circumvent the door to get to the sheep. False shepherds do not address the real needs of the sheep. They come by a way of legalism, not by a way of grace. False shepherds do not come by way of sonship. They do not shepherd through love. Leaders, who lead from their own orphan motivations, do not access the heart. They lead by false means, addressing issues that are not actually heart-issues.

"To him the gatekeeper opens." The gatekeeper is the guardian of all that is precious. I do not want to particularly identify the gatekeeper with a specific person because Jesus does not identify who the gatekeeper is. However, He makes it clear that the gatekeeper

recognises the true shepherd. The gatekeeper is the guardian of what belongs to the Father. It may even be that the gatekeeper is personified in John the Baptist. John the Baptist, representing the prophetic stream, opened the gate to let the Shepherd in.

The true shepherd does not drive the sheep. He calls them by name and they follow Him. The True Shepherd, who calls with the Father's voice, knows the unique identity of each individual sheep. When we are confident that we are known we are then free to follow. We lose confidence in following any leadership when we have a hunch that they do not really know us or value who we are.

As well as coming in through the door of the heart, Jesus says that *He Himself* is the Door. This is one of the glorious paradoxes that can only be spiritually understood. The Door, which leads to the Father, is Christ dwelling in the human heart. Sonship is experienced when we open our hearts for the Son to enter in. The heart is the interface between the human and the divine. This is much more than a mere intellectual assent to a creed. We have access to the Father through union with Christ.

True shepherding is that which brings the sheep through the Door into relationship with the Father. True shepherding leads a person by way of their heart to make heart-connection with the Son *and with the Father*. A Gospel which does not bring us home to the Father is, at best, incomplete and, at worst, robbery! That is a very strong statement but I believe it can be backed up by this passage in John 10. This passage makes the indictment clear; any 'shepherd' who does not use the door is a thief and a robber! Why?

Because they steal what belongs to the Father (the sheep) and they steal what belongs to the sheep (relationship with the Father). When the sheep (the children) have relationship with the Father they come into their true and unique identity.

If the Door is heart-relationship through Jesus with the Father, and thieves and robbers do not come through the Door, then:

- Those who insist on a literal Sabbath having priority over a Sabbath of the heart *are thieves and robbers.*

- Those who begrudge Jesus' healing power and freedom anointing, because it appears to break moral law and upset the status quo, *are thieves and robbers.*

- Those who promote a way of performance, leveraged through condemnation, *are thieves and robbers.*

- Those who perpetrate a ranking system based on ministry prestige *are thieves and robbers.*

- Those who operate a system which devalues the sheep and 'lords it over' the flock *are thieves and robbers.*

- Those who gather privilege to themselves at the expense of the sheep *are thieves and robbers*

- Those who portray God and represent Him as less than a loving Father *are thieves and robbers.*

In actual fact, those who lead and rule out of a paradigm that is less than the family of a loving Father are thieves and robbers. This is why Jesus says that all who came before Him were thieves and robbers. Because, without a revelation of the Father's love as the *modus operandi* of their leadership, they were only depriving the people of what truly belonged to them. Everything that belongs to the Father is the rightful inheritance of all God's children. There are different levels of maturity in accessing that inheritance but it nevertheless belongs to the children. The religious elite at the top of the edifice are not the true shepherds because they have no love for the sheep.

LIFE ABUNDANT

Then Jesus declares:

> *"I came that they might have life and have it abundantly"*
> — JOHN 10:10

True shepherding does not steal life away from people. It brings people into life in abundance. False shepherding, by micro-managing and controlling people and by keeping them herded within a servant-hearted mentality, robs abundant life from the people. When leadership is controlling, power-oriented and given to excessive management, the first casualty is *life*. Leadership in the paradigm of orphanness can only function by control, by monitoring and by drivenness. A lot of leadership in the Body of Christ functions like a cork in the bottle, stopping the free flow of the Spirit through the Body. False leadership requires people to ask for permission all the time; it does not govern with a free and open hand. When the hand of that type of leadership closes it chokes the life out of individuals as well as the corporate body.

True shepherding, which shepherds with the heart of the Father and with an open hand, grants permission wherever it goes. True shepherding *leads* the sheep, giving them the choice to follow or not. Someone has said that if you want to know whether you are a true leader or not, just look behind you and see if there is anyone following. That is so true! People will always follow what is life-giving and life-affirming. True shepherding will open its hand to allow life to flourish.

When you can go in and out and be fed, you will know that you are being shepherded by the Good Shepherd. The Good Shepherd is not insecure; He does not need to control access and egress. Good shepherding is not really concerned with membership lists or knowing who is on the inside and who is on the outside. Good shepherding is confident that the sheep can be relied on to choose who they will follow. The Good Shepherd is the Door. Through Him we have untrammelled access to the Father.

What is abundant life? Abundant life is having a heart connection with God. To be connected with God is to experience the full range of His emotions, His sorrow, His joy, His resolve. His creative life flows within us and flows through us. It flows for the sake of others but, before that, it flows for *our* sake. The pleasure of God's life flows primarily to bring Him expression through us. Abundant life does not seek to escape from the difficulties and the grief of life. Abundant life rises to the heights but it also plumbs the depths. When Jesus comes to give abundant life, He is not talking about a problem free life; He is talking about giving us *His* life.

THE ONE WHO WORKS FOR WAGES

"He who is a hired hand and not a shepherd, who does not own the sheep, sees the wolf coming and leaves the sheep and flees, and the wolf snatches them and scatters them. He flees because he is a hired hand and cares nothing for the sheep."
— JOHN 10:12,13

The 'hired hand' will never give his life to the wolf in order to preserve the life of the sheep because he serves for wages. The hired hand may not be as malevolent as robbers or wolves but he is of no benefit to the sheep. He is there to keep an eye on the sheep but is not a shepherd. The hired hand is not necessarily trying to steal the sheep but is only interested in earning money. He will not protect the sheep from their greatest threat, the wolf.

The ultimate personification of the wolf is Satan and Satan does his work through people. God's indictment against the rulers of Israel compared them to wolves:

"Her princes in her midst are like wolves tearing the prey, shedding blood, destroying lives to get dishonest gain."
— EZEKIEL 22:27

Jesus warns about 'wolves' when He says:

"Beware of false prophets, who come to you in sheep's clothing but inwardly are ravenous wolves." — MATTHEW 7:15

Paul's directive to the elders of Ephesus is also a warning to be on the lookout for wolves:

> *"Pay careful attention to yourselves and to all the flock, of which the Holy Spirit has made you overseers, to care for the church of God, which he obtained with his own blood. I know that after my departure fierce wolves will come in among you, not sparing the flock..."* — ACTS 20:28,29

The 'hired hand' is a person with an attitude of obligation, not the heart of a son. A servant who serves only out of duty and professionalism has no connection with the Father's love and cannot, therefore, be a conduit of the Father's love. In my life as a Christian and within ministry I have seen a fair amount of 'hired hands.' I have been a 'hired hand' myself, operating out of duty and for personal gain rather than love for others. I too have fled when the going became tough. When the wolf, Satan, broke in to scatter the sheep I lost interest and fled. However, as the Father's love fills my heart, I am being transformed into a person who genuinely loves the sheep. The greatest joy of my life is to see the sheep called by name and finding pasture. One of the major motivations of my ministry is to release others to be who they are meant to be, and to be free in their unique God-given identity. The Body of Christ will not come into maturity until every believer is set free to function in their God-given identity.

False shepherds, thieves and robbers, wolves and hired hands are all descriptions of an orphan-spirited approach to leadership. They are on a spectrum, no doubt, but they all contribute to the same result; harm, injury and death for the flock. They contrast utterly with the true shepherd.

THE TRUE SHEPHERD

In contrast to the corrupt and self-seeking leaders (thieves and hired hands), Jesus says twice "I am the *good* shepherd." What characterises the good shepherd is that he values the life of the sheep above his own life. That sounds absurd! A sheep is worth nothing compared to the life of the shepherd but that is exactly the point! The heart of the good shepherd is such that he is willing to die rather than let the sheep be harmed by the wolf.

The true shepherd lays down His life to bring abundant life to the sheep.

- He enters by the door.

- He calls the sheep by name and they recognise His voice.

- He leads (not drives) the sheep and they willingly follow Him.

- He leads the sheep to pasture.

- He brings abundant life to the sheep.

- He lays down his life for the sheep.

- He knows his own and they know Him.

- He unites the scattered sheep into one flock under Him.

In contrast to the thieves and robbers, the hired hand and the wolf, these are the characteristics of the Good Shepherd.

Jesus relationship with His own is parallel to His relationship with the Father. In the same way that the Father knows Jesus and Jesus knows the Father, Jesus knows and is known by those who belong to Him. When He says this, remember that He is *not* addressing the sheep. The sheep who belong to Jesus do not need reassurance of His care for them. It is enough for Him to call each one of them by name.

All true spiritual shepherding involves the use of both masculine and feminine attributes. True shepherds not only protect the flock from external dangers; they also nurture the flock and lead them toward lush pastures. True shepherds participate in the little known and often neglected vocation of spiritual midwifery. Spiritual midwifery has been one of God's main vocations since the beginning of time. The prophet describes Yahweh in this way:

> *"He will tend his flock like a shepherd; he will gather the lambs in his arms; he will carry them in his bosom, and gently lead those that are with young."* — ISAIAH 40:11

God is primarily concerned with safeguarding and fostering life and the continuity of life.

Jesus is both the Shepherd and the Door. By entering *into* Jesus we have access to the Father. He calls us by name and invites us into His heart, and in the heart of Jesus we find the Father. We realise the wonderful mystery that the Father is in Jesus, and Jesus is in the Father. We are caught forever into the swirling depths of that Father-Son relationship.

ONE FLOCK, ONE SHEPHERD

"And I have other sheep that are not of this fold. I must bring them also, and they will listen to my voice. So there will be one flock, one shepherd." — JOHN 10:16

This statement must have caught both the Pharisees and the disciples off guard. Who are these 'other sheep' from a different fold? Do they even realise that these 'other sheep,' who will become one flock with Israel under one Shepherd, are none other than the 'Gentile dogs'?

After Pentecost, it will take a major paradigm shift in the heart of Peter to make inroads into the Gentile fold. Peter's experience when he is on the roof and the great sheet full of unclean things descends (Acts 10) is to be the precursor for the gathering in of these 'strange' sheep.

The Gentiles are the sheep who are not of the fold of Israel. Jesus looks forward to the time when He will bring them in. Israel stumbled over the fact that the Gentiles were the sheep who also belonged to Jesus. When He calls the Gentiles by name and affirms to them that they are chosen on the basis that they are also the Father's family, they too will listen to His voice. The Gentiles are heirs of the promise on the same basis as the house of Israel; God's promise to Abraham (Galatians 3:14). The commission after the ascension of Jesus, will be that the Gentiles from another fold will hear the voice of the Shepherd calling them through the Door to the Father. The main spokesperson of this call will be the converted hyper-Pharisee, Paul of Tarsus.

Through an encounter with the comfort-love of God, Paul received a unique revelatory insight into what Jesus is talking about when He says, *"And I have other sheep that are not of this fold. I must bring them also, and they will listen to my voice. So there will be one flock, one shepherd."*

The mystery revealed to Paul was that the Gentiles were fellow-heirs with Israel:

> *"This mystery is that the Gentiles are fellow heirs, members of the same, and partakers of the promise in Christ Jesus through the gospel."* — EPHESIANS 3:6

> *"For he himself is our peace, who has made us both one and has broken down in his flesh the dividing wall of hostility…that he might create in himself one new man of the two, so making peace…and reconcile us both to God… For through him we both have access in one Spirit to the Father."* — EPHESIANS 2:14-17

God revealed to Paul that there was only *one* flock and *one* Shepherd. Through Jesus, Jew and Gentile are of one family. *Both* have access to the Father.

I LAY DOWN MY LIFE

> *"For this reason the Father loves me, because I lay down my life that I may take it up again. No one takes it from me, but I lay it down of my own accord. I have authority to lay it down, and I have authority to take it up again. This*

charge I have received from my Father."—John 10:17,18

When Jesus says, "For this reason the Father loves me, because I lay down my life for the sheep," it may appear at first glance that the Father's love for the Son is conditional. That is not the meaning of this statement, however. The English translation is slightly misleading here. The original language reads like this:

"Through this the Father is loving Me."

Strong's Concordance says that the word here "denotes the *channel* of an act." In other words, Jesus' act of laying down and taking up His life is a *channel* for the love of the Father. In the action of laying down His life, the Father is loving Him; the Father is also loving *through* Him. The word used here is *'agapa'* which denotes *unconditional* love.

True leadership knows that a life can only be laid down, by the willingness of the one who chooses to lay it down. The authority to lay one's life down is vested in the person who lays down his or her life. False shepherds expect *the sheep* to give their lives; they take life *away* from the sheep. Leadership that is not the shepherding leadership of Jesus operates on the basis of condemnation and obligation.

"This charge I have received from my Father" The Father has given Jesus a very specific mandate; to declare the Father's identity and manifest the Father's personality. The Father is overjoyed to see that His Son has the very same attitude as He, the Father. The eternal disposition of the Father is to lay down His life for those that He loves. I believe that the Godhead is in a perpetual motion of laying down Its life. The Father perpetually lays His life down for the Son

and the Spirit; the Son does so for the Father and the Spirit; the Spirit does so for the Father and the Son. They lay down their lives but their eternal life does not diminish. On the contrary, the laying down of life actually releases *more* life, because the flow of the life is an eternal fountain which never dries up.

NO ONE IS ABLE TO SNATCH THEM

There was again a division among the Jews because of these words. Many of them said, "He has a demon, and is insane; why listen to him?" Others said, "These are not the words of one who is oppressed by a demon. Can a demon open the eyes of the blind?"
At that time the Feast of Dedication took place at Jerusalem. It was winter, and Jesus was walking in the temple, in the colonnade of Solomon. So the Jews gathered around him and said to him, "How long will you keep us in suspense? If you are the Christ, tell us plainly." Jesus answered them, "I told you, and you do not believe. The works that I do in my Father's name bear witness about me, but you do not believe because you are not part of my flock. My sheep hear my voice, and I know them, and they follow me. I give them eternal life, and they will never perish, and no one will snatch them out of my hand. My Father, who has given them to me, is greater than all, and no one is able to snatch them out of the Father's hand."" — JOHN 10:19-29

He is either the Messiah or He is demonised; there is no middle ground. He is accused of blasphemy yet demons cannot open blind eyes. The Jews are desperate for answers yet the answers have been given to them all along. They cannot grasp the answer because their hearts are hard, their ears are closed and their eyes are blind. The reason they cannot believe is that they *are not part of the flock.*" (v. 26)

Being part of the flock is contingent upon being owned by the Father. Those who are owned by the Father, recognise the voice of the shepherd and follow Him. Inclusion in the flock is an issue of the heart. It is not about belonging to a particular 'in' group, neither is it on the basis of privilege. It is not a matter of being accepted or rejected by God. All who eat of the Tree of Life, who live in the Father's love in connection with Jesus, are *automatically* part of His sheep. If the heart is not in the flow of God's love, they are not part of the flock. Pharisees are not excluded from the flock; they exclude themselves because of a hardened heart. Nicodemus (one of the Sanhedrin) discovered that he was in the flock, as did Saul of Tarsus.

"No one will snatch them out of my hand…no one is able to snatch them out of my Father's hand." This is not really about an 'evangelical' understanding of eternal life or eternal damnation. The issue here is the choice between legalism and abundant life. The ones who would snatch the sheep from the hand of Jesus and the Father are the wolves and the robbers. They wish to rip the sheep away from the enclosure where life can be found. The false shepherds and the hired hands are equally complicit in putting the sheep at risk. What is clear is that love will always prevail.

THE ONENESS OF THE FATHER AND THE SON

"I and the Father are one." The Jews picked up stones again to stone him. Jesus answered them, "I have shown you many

> *good works from the Father; for which of them are you going to stone me?" The Jews answered him, "It is not for a good work that we are going to stone you but for blasphemy, because you, being a man, make yourself God." Jesus answered them, "Is it not written in your Law, 'I said, you are gods?' If he called them gods to whom the word of God came— and Scripture cannot be broken—do you say of him whom the Father consecrated and sent into the world, 'You are blaspheming,' because I said, 'I am the Son of God?' If I am not doing the works of my Father, then do not believe me; but if I do them, even though you do not believe me, believe the works, that you may know and understand that the Father is in me and I am in the Father." Again they sought to arrest him, but he escaped from their hands.* — JOHN 10:30-39*

In the eyes of those listening, Jesus is verbalising the ultimate blasphemy; He is stating that He is one with the Father. He is not the same person as the Father but He is one *with* the Father. He has the same DNA; there is no disconnect between the Father and the Son. What they see in Jesus is precisely who the Father is.

This 'blasphemy' evokes an immediate threat that He will be stoned to death. In the face of this, however, He is resolute. Jesus is overcoming the world through His internal peace. He is living in the continuous experiencing of His Father's love and He is not intimidated by the stones in their hands.

Jesus tells them that He has been sent into the world by the Father. What is more, He tells them that the Father *consecrated* Him for the mission to enter the world. This comment gives us a hint of what happened in heaven before the Son came to earth. The Father 'set Him apart,' commissioned Him, and gave Him a mandate to declare the Father's name. The Father entrusted the Son to fully reveal Him to the world.

The ability to fulfil the mandate given to Him by the Father is guaranteed for one reason; *the Father is in Jesus and Jesus is in the Father.* Jesus does not have to exert effort or plan a strategy to reveal the Father. He does not have to resort to marketing techniques. His union with the Father is enough to manifest the Father. It is the same for us; our witness for God is an automatic result of being united with God. The presence of the Father within sons and daughters will spill over and be manifested for all to see.

Jesus evades arrest because the time has not yet come for Him to be arrested. He has not completed His work of manifesting the Father. How does He escape from their hands? Do angels intervene and confuse them so that Jesus can get away from them? Whatever happens, we can be sure that Jesus was in peace because He knew that it was not time for Him to be seized. The will of heaven is being imposed upon the efforts of earth. Heaven only allows things to happen when they benefit the purposes of heaven. Jesus' arrest at this time will not benefit the greater strategy of heaven and so He escapes from danger to go across the Jordan

REVISITING THE PROPHETIC ENVIRONMENT

He went away again across the Jordan to the place where John had been baptising at first, and there he remained. And many came to him. And they said, "John did no sign, but

everything that John said about this man was true." And
many believed in him there. — JOHN 10:40-42

Jesus comes full circle to reconnect again with the legacy of John the Baptist. This is the last reference to John the Baptist in this Gospel. It is a final acknowledgement to the Baptist's role in pointing our attention to Jesus. John didn't do any sign but he was a sign himself. Everything he said about Jesus has been proved to be fully accurate. John, the Gospel writer, honours the Baptist, because the Baptist had successfully carried out his prophetic mandate.

Jesus intentionally crosses the Jordan and returns to the desert where John had been baptising. In doing so, He goes to a sacred space and recreates a prophetic environment. It is as if Jesus knows that the prophetic thread needs to continue; the true prophetic that will always operate from a place that is peripheral to what is popular. The desert place is a place of rupture, outside the status quo. It is also a place of spiritual abundance.

"And many believed in him there." The prophetic environment of the desert brings abundant fruit. What is arid in the natural is fecund in the spiritual. Without exception, the best spiritual fruit grows in an environment where there is little stimulation for the natural appetites. When I say this, I am not necessarily advocating some form of asceticism. What I *am* saying is that the more we add human 'mechanisms' the less the Spirit is able to function. There are so many resources available to us that we have lost the ability to live by our spiritual intuition. Many church programmes are so tightly organised that there is no room for any initiative that the Holy Spirit wants to take.

In the spiritual life, less is always more. Spiritual revelation comes much more readily and quickly when there is less, not more, information. Contemporary Christianity is addicted to giving and receiving information, to micro-management, and to technical excellence. Rather than enhancing our experience of spiritual realities, this has *diminished* our capacity to experience them.

As Jesus stays in the desert, He must be thinking about His cousin, John. It is very likely that He takes time to grieve over John and to remember him. In the hot days and the cold nights of the desert, Jesus is hearing the Father's voice. The Father is preparing His Son for another event, an event that will manifest who the Father is in an unprecedented way. That event will play itself out within a little family whom Jesus loves with warm affection. Very soon, Jesus must leave this desert area and go to a place called Bethany.

COMPASSION THAT BREAKS THROUGH DEATH

~

The tenth chapter of John's Gospel concludes with the observation that John the Baptist didn't perform any signs. He didn't need to. John's work was to direct attention away from himself and onto Jesus. The era of God speaking through prophets has ended and God is now communicating 'in Son.'[22] All signs from Yahweh under the Old Covenant have now ceased. The signs performed by Jesus are signs performed by the Father that manifest clearly who the Father is.

When a newer and more accurate revelation of God emerges it is always accompanied by signs. All signs associated with the previous revelation will discontinue. To put it more accurately, supernatural signs always accompany what the Spirit is currently doing. The Spirit of God does not give supernatural attestation to

---

22. Hebrews 1:1,2

an incomplete revelation of God when this has been superseded by a new revelation. The signs always accompany the fresh revelation to attest to the truth of that fresh revelation. Signs are used to lead us forward into a new understanding of who God is.

This chapter, John 11, unveils another sign, the most spectacular and supernatural sign yet; the raising of a dead person. The circumstances in which the death and resurrection of Lazarus occur are well worth considering. This man, Lazarus, is the brother of two sisters, Martha and Mary. It isn't entirely clear what the family set-up is but Jean Vanier has suggested that Lazarus may well have been chronically sickly or even disabled.[23] Within the culture of the time it would have been relatively unusual for three siblings to remain unmarried so it is quite possible that the sisters dedicated their lives to care for their brother Lazarus.

> Now a certain man was ill, Lazarus of Bethany, the village of Mary and her sister Martha. It was Mary who anointed the Lord with ointment and wiped his feet with her hair, whose brother Lazarus was ill. So the sisters sent to him, saying, "Lord, he whom you love is ill." But when Jesus heard it he said, "This illness does not lead to death. It is for the glory of God, so that the Son of God may be glorified through it." Now Jesus loved Martha and her sister and Lazarus. So, when he heard that Lazarus was ill, he stayed two days longer in the place where he was. — JOHN 11:1-6

---

23. "…Lazarus, who was sickly (*asthenes*). In the language of today, we would probably say "who was disabled. The Greek word '*asthenes*' can be translated as 'sick,' 'without strength,' 'feeble,' or 'insignificant'" from Jean Vanier, *Drawn into the Mystery of Jesus through the Gospel of John*, Paulist Press, New York, 1988.

Here we have a family who are affectionately loved by Jesus. They are not a successful family according to conventional standards; three siblings, all unmarried, without any children and presumably without parents still living. Jesus, however, loves them deeply. Their home in Bethany would be a place where Jesus could relax and put His feet up!

So the sisters sent to him, saying, "Lord, he whom you love is ill." (v.3) The word 'love' used here is *phileo*. It is the love of warm-hearted affection for a friend or family member. In other words, Jesus is particularly fond of Lazarus. He and Lazarus would have eaten and drunk together, swapped stories, laughed together, sat up talking late into the night. The deficit of parental love within this family, the love that gave protection, provision, and nurture, was made up to Martha, Mary and Lazarus by Jesus. Jesus manifested fathering and mothering love to them.

I have previously noted the way that John highlights women as catalysts for revelation. Martha and Mary are no exception. We will see how they catalyse the movement of the Trinity in the miracle of raising the dead. Here we have two single women, presumably having missed out on marriage and motherhood, dedicating their energies to care for their brother, Lazarus. I understand this situation well. I have two sisters who are unmarried, who have devoted themselves to the ongoing care of our elderly parents. This chapter shows that the Father is deeply compassionate and keenly interested in those who are in this sort of circumstance.

The sisters inform Jesus of the illness that had struck Lazarus. It is a critical situation and all hope of his recovery has faded away.

But when Jesus heard it he said, "This illness does not lead to death. It is for the glory of God, so that the Son of God may be glorified through it," — JOHN 11:4

In response to the hopeless news, Jesus immediately reveals *His* perspective. His perspective is the perspective of heaven, the perspective of the Father. This crisis has come, not to end in death, but so that the Father will again be manifested. Through this tragic happening the true personality of the Father will be declared. In addition, the true personality and status of the Son will be declared as the one who only does what He sees the Father doing. This situation will reveal what fatherhood and sonship really are. It will reveal that Jesus of Nazareth is not self-appointed and self-managed. It will demonstrate, rather, that the Father is working through Him to woo the human race.

Now Jesus loved Martha and her sister and Lazarus. (v.5) Perhaps surprisingly, the word for 'love' used here is *not* the affectionate *phileo* kind of love. The word used here is the unconditional, divine *agape* love. Jesus undoubtedly loves the three siblings with affection and He has a personal attachment of deep friendship with Lazarus. He cannot, however, operate from that when it comes to raising Lazarus from the dead. Jesus must go to a place beyond natural affection to a place of divine authority. Human affection, wonderful and God-given as it is, is often too subjective and too vulnerable to the rise and fall of emotions to be effective in making supernatural breakthrough. Jesus makes a very intentional movement away from being caught in a human perspective. A solely human perspective, based on human logic and human emotions, can never access the place from which supernatural authority is wielded.

I vividly remember receiving the dreadful news that a close friend's little boy was suddenly taken ill with viral meningitis. The child's life hung in the balance. I struggled to contain the feeling of dread which was rising in me. Somehow, by the grace of God, I was able to make a movement away from my natural reaction of grief and fear. I was able to go to a place where I perceived Jesus sitting on the Father's throne with authority and power. In my spirit I saw flashes of blue lightning coming out of His hands.

For a brief moment I came to a place that was beyond fear and doubt and I began to pray from that place. Then I saw a vision of a raptor-like demon stealing the child and running out of the room. Instinctively I shouted at the demon and commanded it to drop the child, which it did immediately. A few hours later I heard the happy news that the child was out of danger and would make a full recovery. If I had remained in my human response of grief and fear, I do not believe I would have been able to use any authority to see the child set free.

> *"So when he heard that Lazarus was ill, he stayed two days longer in the place where he was."* — JOHN 11:6

This two-day extension to stay away from Bethany is very important. In doing this, Jesus quells the surge of natural affection, an affection that would compel Him to rush to the bedside of His dying friend. This is an example of what the writer of Hebrews means in commenting about Jesus that:

> *"...although he was a son, he learned obedience through what he suffered. And being made perfect..."* — HEBREWS 5:8

By deliberately staying away from Lazarus' death-bed, Jesus is obeying the voice of the Father in His inner spirit. His emotions would readily compel Him to go straight away to Bethany but He grows in 'perfection' by living in His sonship to the Father. The two-day delay is a leaning back into the heavenly reality from which all the supernatural signs had come. For every sign that He performs, Jesus needs to make a movement of faith away from what the natural evidence was telling Him.

Maturity in sonship means that we are becoming more responsive to the Father's perspective and less ready to react to what the natural evidence is telling us. It means staying "two days longer."

"Two days longer" prepares the ground for resurrection life. "Two days longer" removes natural hope and human responses. The more hopeless the situation the more the glory of God will ultimately be seen.

ESTABLISHING FAITH'S ASCENDANCY

Then after this he said to the disciples, "Let us go to Judea again." The disciples said to him, "Rabbi, the Jews were just now seeking to stone you, and are you going there again?" Jesus answered, "Are there not twelve hours in the day? If anyone walks in the day, he does not stumble, because he sees the light of this world. But if anyone walks in the night, he stumbles, because the light is not in him." — JOHN 11:7-10

When Jesus decides, in harmony with the Father, to go to Bethany He is faced with the concerns of His disciples. Jesus then has to establish the ascendancy of His (and the Father's) perspective.

Even the Son of God needs an environment of faith to operate in. Mark 6:5 tells us that Jesus could not do any major miracles in His home town because of a pervasive culture of unbelief there. Here, in John 11, Jesus has to intentionally establish a culture of faith within the disciples. The forthcoming sign of raising Lazarus will be performed by Jesus and His Father but it will also belong to the believing community.

The disciples are understandably anxious for Jesus' safety. He is returning to the place where there are active death threats against Him. In establishing the culture of belief Jesus deals with the disciples' perspective. Having the right perspective is crucial in determining the effectiveness of our faith.

> *Jesus answered, "Are there not twelve hours in the day? If anyone walks in the day, he does not stumble, because he sees the light of this world. But if anyone walks in the night, he stumbles, because the light is not in him."* — JOHN 11:9,10

This statement is all-important in preparing the ground for faith to operate. What Jesus is saying here is that if we do not have the light of revelation, then our faith will waver and we will stumble. Faith is utterly dependent on and operates out of the revelation of who God really is. The 'daytime' is a state of bright and full understanding coming from the revelatory energy of the "light of this world." The light of the world is the very same light which John speaks of in the first chapter; it is the light "which enlightens everyone." It is in this light that the miracle will occur. It is the knowledge of God as compassionate Father that will work through the Son to restore this man back to his grieving sisters.

After saying these things, he said to them, "Our friend Lazarus has fallen asleep, but I go to awaken him." The disciples said to him, "Lord, if he has fallen asleep, he will recover." Now Jesus had spoken of his death, but they thought that he meant taking rest in sleep. Then Jesus told them plainly, "Lazarus has died, and for your sake I am glad that I was not there, so that you may believe. But let us go to him." So Thomas, called the Twin, said to his fellow disciples, "Let us also go, that we may die with him." — JOHN 11:11-16

Here we see a switching back and forth between the perspective of Jesus and the perspective of His disciples. Jesus, speaking from His vantage point of faith, His citadel of utter dependence upon the Father, sees Lazarus as merely having fallen asleep. Jesus has a perspective that death has no lasting hold on Lazarus. For Jesus, Lazarus' death is merely a deep sleep from which he can be awakened. The disciples (v.13) cannot see Jesus' perspective so He has to spell out plainly to them that Lazarus has literally died.

Jesus is glad that He was not present when Lazarus died. This gladness is not for His own sake but for the benefit of the disciples. Jesus is 'ring-fencing' the culture of belief. To be there to witness the literal evidence of death would have destabilised the disciples too much. Their faith could not have surmounted the overwhelming evidence that their senses fed to them, that Lazarus was very dead!

Jesus, the Son of the compassionate Father, summons the disciples with Him to witness and co-participate in the miracle of resurrection. He will call upon them to take away the stone and then to take the bindings off Lazarus. Thomas, obviously one of the spokesmen, has leadership gifting. He rallies the disciples forward to follow Jesus back into the imminent danger of being killed by the Jews. Thomas helps the others to face the reality that they may all be killed along with Jesus.

They will not die at the hand of the Jews this time. Maybe another death will be faced, however; a death of certainty, a death of their current mentality, and a death of their reputation. In Bethany, standing with Jesus outside the tomb of Lazarus, they will die a death to the limitations of human thinking and ways of being. This death is a letting go that will lead to the resurrection of Lazarus, and subsequently to the resurrection of a new experience of who Jesus is as the Son of the Father.

HE WAITS UNTIL DEATH IS RAMPANT

Now when Jesus came, he found that Lazarus had already been in the tomb four days. Bethany was near Jerusalem, about two miles off, and many of the Jews had come to Martha and Mary to console them concerning their brother. So when Martha heard that Jesus was coming, she went and met him, but Mary remained seated in the house. Martha said to Jesus, "Lord, if you had been here, my brother would not have died. But even now I know that whatever you ask from God, God will give you." Jesus said to her, "Your brother will rise again." Martha said to him, "I know that he will rise again in the resurrection on the last day." Jesus said to her, "I am the resurrection and the life. Whoever believes in me, though he die, yet shall he live, and everyone who lives and believes in me shall never die. Do you believe this?" She said

to him, "Yes, Lord; I believe that you are the Christ, the Son
of God, who is coming into the world." — JOHN 11:17-27

Jesus arrives at Bethany when all hope has gone. Lazarus is already in the tomb four days. Another writer has put it like this, "Jesus waits until death is rampant."[24] How true that is! How many times do we go beyond the place where there is any hope left and then, when we least expect it, we receive a breakthrough? It is because God waits until death is rampant. The more rampant death is, the more the glory of God will ultimately be seen. The word 'rampant' is used to describe something like a wildfire. It is unrestrained and beyond any control. In Lazarus' case, the decay of death is beyond control. His body is already decomposing. Death has established its claim on Lazarus. The mourning rituals are in full swing.

It is obvious that there is a contrast in personality between Martha and Mary. John, the writer, highlights the differences between the two sisters. Martha seems to be more active and pragmatic, while Mary is portrayed as being contemplative and devoted to Jesus. It appears that Martha is the older sister, and she goes to greet the arriving Jesus while Mary stays in the house with the mourners.

The steps of Jesus towards the house of mourning and the tomb are measured, even hesitant. Every step of the way He is leaning into the Father. His awareness is much more heaven-centred and heaven-focused than Bethany-focused. Every step closer to Bethany is a step deeper into the Father's heart. He will not be distracted from His focus on what the Father is doing.

---

24. This quote is from a writer called George Warnock. I cannot recall the title of the book in which it appears.

Martha meets Jesus and immediately shows that the family has confidence in Jesus' place of favour with God. "Lord, if you had been here, my brother would not have died." Martha and Mary have enough faith for the healing of their seriously ill brother but do they ever in their wildest dreams anticipate his return from death?

Martha tells Jesus that she is confident that God will grant Him whatever He asks. But is this a statement of forlorn hope and not really based on faith? Is she grasping at a straw? When Jesus tells her that her brother will rise again she gives a predicable answer, the same answer that we Christians often give in response to someone's death. Yes, they will rise again in the final resurrection, but they cannot possibly come back *now*.

Jesus' next words to Martha must have injected something into her that she has not grasped before. He pronounces to her that He is *the resurrection and the life,* and that everyone who believes in Him will *never die.* Jesus confronts Martha with a powerful challenge. Is she willing to take her normal, vague belief in the final resurrection and pull it into her present circumstance? Is she willing to focus her general belief into a specific belief in Jesus *right now*? He is a family friend, yes; they even know that He is the coming Messiah, but how will she handle this *new* claim that He is the personification of resurrection life?

THE RESURRECTION AND THE LIFE

How can Jesus be the resurrection and the life? The resurrection of Lazarus will be a demonstration of what Jesus had stated earlier:

"For as the Father raises the dead and gives them life, so also the Son gives life to whom he will." — JOHN 5:21

"For as the Father has life in himself, so he has granted the Son also to have life in himself." — JOHN 5:26

Resurrection life is innate in Jesus because of His divinity and because of His sonship in humanity. He is the creator of everything that exists and the sustainer of all life (John 1:3). The Father has also given Him the authority on earth to execute judgment over death. Sonship to the Father ultimately includes authority over death. Why? Because death is the greatest symptom of orphanness. Death is dislocation from the Source of life, the Father. Death is the judgment and consequence of living in the Tree of the Knowledge of Good and Evil. Death is inextricably linked with condemnation; therefore, resurrection life is inextricably linked with freedom from condemnation which can only be received through sonship.

Jesus is clothed in the authority of His sonship when He proclaims that He, the Son, *is* the personification of all that is resurrection life. He is the personification of the Tree of Life and He is about to demonstrate His mastery over death, the manifestation of the knowledge of good and evil.

MARTHA AND MARY AS
CATALYSTS FOR THE MIRACLE

When she had said this, she went and called her sister Mary, saying in private, "The Teacher is here and is calling for you." And when she heard it, she rose quickly and went to him.

Now Jesus had not yet come into the village, but was still in the place where Martha had met him. When the Jews who were with her in the house, consoling her, saw Mary rise quickly and go out, they followed her, supposing that she was going to the tomb to weep there. Now when Mary came to where Jesus was and saw him, she fell at his feet, saying to him, "Lord, if you had been here, my brother would not have died." When Jesus saw her weeping, and the Jews who had come with her also weeping, he was deeply moved in his spirit and greatly troubled. And he said, "Where have you laid him?" They said to him, "Lord, come and see." Jesus wept. So the Jews said, "See how he loved him!" But some of them said, "Could not he who opened the eyes of the blind man also have kept this man from dying?" — JOHN 11:28-37*

Martha is impacted by what Jesus says and goes to tell Mary that Jesus is calling for her. There is no record of Jesus actually asking for Mary but Martha senses that the time had come for something unprecedented. Like Mary, the mother of Jesus, at the wedding feast in Cana, Martha and Mary are catalysts to draw out the miracle. Martha knows that Mary has a particular revelation of Jesus and she summons her, sensing somehow that Mary will draw something more from Jesus. Martha is a catalyst for action in bringing Mary, but Mary is a catalyst for an upsurge of compassion in Jesus. Jesus is deeply moved when He sees Mary weeping.

Maybe Mary is sitting at home waiting for the right timing. Maybe she senses something that she cannot quite comprehend. Maybe Mary is waiting for a spark of faith in Martha. When she receives Martha's invitation she rises *quickly.* Mary is finely attuned to divine timing. Similar to Mary, the mother of Jesus, who said to the servants at the Cana wedding feast, "Do whatever He tells you," Mary of Bethany anticipates and is ready for the moment of faith. She moves with alacrity to be in the place where the miracle will occur.

To our human way of thinking, God often takes more time than we would like to prepare the ground for the miraculous. But when He moves, He moves very quickly. The waiting time is actually a time of preparing our hearts to be sensitive enough to the quickness of the Spirit's movement. The moment of faith comes quickly and must be grasped, for it passes quickly too. To move with the Spirit we need to be like surfers who wait for the right wave and then catch it and ride it. Mary waits for the wave to come towards the shore, then she catches it ("...rose quickly") and rides it the whole way to the shore. That wave is resurrection life and she rides it to the happy shore of receiving her brother back alive.

Jesus, deeply moved and troubled, is activated by Mary's weeping. He follows the pathway of compassion, engaging deeply with His emotions and identifying fully with the grief. This deep moving of His spirit is a groan of grief and compassion, but also of indignation and anger. He rages against Satan and the ravages of the law of sin and death. His groan is the groan of a birth pang. It is the groan, the contraction of the Spirit, that brings forth new creation.

Picture the scene. Jesus, deeply distressed and moved, asks them where the body of Lazarus is. They invite Him to come with them to see the cave. Jesus weeps again. This is the grief of Jesus, but it is also the grief of God the Father. The Son is weeping the tears of

God the Father. This miracle is a sign that God the Father weeps with sorrow over the grief of this family of two sisters and their brother. There is nothing particularly significant or important about Martha, Mary and Lazarus, but that is the whole point. "The love of God," says Denise Jordan "has *no point*. Love itself is the point."[25] Lazarus is not raised from the dead to accomplish anything other than restoring normal life and reconciling relationship with his two sisters. The Father's compassion has no hidden agenda; the Father loves for the sake of love.

HERE HE COMES!

Then Jesus, deeply moved again, came to the tomb. It was a cave, and a stone lay against it. Jesus said, "Take away the stone." Martha, the sister of the dead man, said to him, "Lord, by this time there will be an odour, for he has been dead four days." Jesus said to her, "Did I not tell you that if you believed you would see the glory of God?"
— JOHN 11:38-40

The writer, John, plays out a wonderful choreography as Jesus approaches the cave-vault. Jesus approaches the tomb in His third wave of emotion. He is now ready. The alignment of Jesus' spirit, soul and body is now 'perfected' to perform the wonder that the Father wants to do. The disciples and the mourners have a part to play in the choreography of the miracle. They are instructed to roll away the stone. Martha's response about the stench coming from the cave is understandable. Death *is* rampant. Jesus, however, rebukes Martha,

---

25. I think this was said at Inheriting the Nations School 2014.

"Did I not tell you that if you believed you would see the glory of God?"

Jesus' rebuke of Martha is less to do with her personally—He has deep compassion for her—and more to do with establishing the supremacy of God's perspective. He has to muzzle any protestations of unbelief, for He is operating from the paradigm of the Father's reality. The Father's reality does not recognise corruption or decay. Jesus' rebuke of Martha forcibly imposes the principle of life over the principle of knowledge. Martha's comment, understandable as it is, comes directly from her own observation of the natural law of death. It is based on the evidence of her senses and of her mind. Jesus' retort to her comes from the principle of spirit and life, and it carries that authority with it. So they roll away the stone.

CALLING FORTH AND UNBINDING

And Jesus lifted up his eyes and said, "Father, I thank you that you have heard me. I knew that you always hear me, but I said this on account of the people standing around, that they may believe that you sent me." When he had said these things, he cried out with a loud voice, "Lazarus, come out." The man who had died came out, his hands and feet bound with linen strips, and his face wrapped with a cloth. Jesus said to them, "Unbind him, and let him go." — JOHN 11:41-44

Jesus' prayer to His Father is the central part of the miracle. It is the pivot upon which the whole action moves. This is the sign which points to somewhere. Jesus acknowledges publicly in front of the gathered crowd that the miracle of dead-raising, which is

226

about to happen, is actually the work of His Father. The Father's compassion and motivation is communicated through the Son. The 'executive action' of calling Lazarus forth is the Father's speech in the mouth of the Son.

Jesus does not doubt that the Father always hears Him and responds to Him. The Son follows the Father's leading, but the Father also hears and responds to the Son's request. Sonship is fully confident of the Father's understanding and sympathetic ear. Jesus, the Son, is always confident of the Father's willingness to act on behalf of the Son and to fully attest to the Son's faith. Jesus speaks out loud to the Father, not to address the Father but to declare to those standing around that this imminent miracle is actually a miracle rooted in the relationship between the Father and the Son. Eternal life, according to John 17:3, is the knowledge of the Father *and* the Son. The Father-Son relationship generates a life-energy that always overcomes death.

Having established beyond dispute the central role of His Father in the raising of Lazarus, Jesus stands resolute in His sonship and cries out loudly, "Lazarus, come out." This is a command roared aloud with 'executive' authority, with the authority that comes from standing with and on behalf of the Father. He shouts out *from* the Father. The working of miracles is not a request *to* the Father; rather, it is a declaration *from* the Father. For sons and daughters, prayer is less a request than it is speaking from a place of unconditional love. Sonship is a life in harmony with the Father and this harmony brings with it a guarantee of answered prayer. In commanding Lazarus to come out, Jesus, the Son, is in full harmony with His Father.

Jesus then instructs them to unbind Lazarus and let him go from the winding sheets that restrict his body. Who unbinds him? Is it the disciples? Is it the two sisters, Martha and Mary?

I like to think it was Martha and Mary who remove the binding cloths from Lazarus. The final co-participation with Jesus in this miracle is reserved for the two sisters who had loved and lost so much. The miracle becomes a miracle owned by them all—Jesus, the disciples, the mourners, and the sisters. I love to imagine that Martha and Mary, with trembling hands and tears of joy, lovingly unwind the strips of cloth from Lazarus. Surely the first sight that Lazarus sees is the eyes of his two sisters.

The more that I come to know who the Father is, who Jesus is, and who the Holy Spirit is, the more it does not surprise me that Jesus stands aside while others release Lazarus. It is so typical of Jesus, so typical of the Godhead, to stand back and not take the central place, but to reunite the family as quickly as possible. Jesus has no self-interest at all, and He follows the Father in that. He leaves that final loving act of tenderly unwrapping the gift of the re-vivified Lazarus to the two sisters.

The Father's love breaks death to restore our own humanity back to us, but it also restores relationships with others back to us. It restores the whole human race back to us. Sonship, the continuous experiencing of the Father's love, allows us to see others with the Father's gaze of love, enables us to free them from death, and unbind them from the grave clothes of judgment for free relationship once again.

THE WIDENING SHOCKWAVE

Many of the Jews therefore, who had come with Mary and had seen what he did, believed in him, but some of them went to the Pharisees and told them what Jesus had done. So the chief priests and the Pharisees gathered the council and said, "What are we to do? For this man performs many signs. If we let him go on like this, everyone will believe in him, and the Romans will come and take away both our place and our nation." But one of them, Caiaphas, who was high priest that year, said to them, "You know nothing at all. Nor do you understand that it is better for you that one man should die for the people, not that the whole nation should perish." He did not say this of his own accord, but being high priest that year he prophesied that Jesus would die for the nation, and not for the nation only, but also to gather into one the children of God who are scattered abroad. So from that day on they made plans to put him to death. — JOHN 11:45-53

The ripple-effect from the raising of Lazarus is inevitable. It is more like a nuclear fallout, if the truth be told. The Jews are split between those who believe in Jesus (whatever that actually entailed) and those who are so entrenched in their positions that they are deeply threatened.

The shockwaves of the blast carry as far as the Sanhedrin, the religious 'Supreme Court.' This sign of Lazarus' resurrection has implications that are now *political*. It rocks the power-structures of the religious system and begins to threaten the political structures. Power structures are always threatened by the reality of the Father's love expressed in the Spirit through sonship. That is why so many church leaders have closed down the movement of the Spirit. The new wine *must* burst the old wineskins. The new wine of the Spirit cannot be contained by old structures.

This miracle of Lazarus' resurrection takes the notoriety of Jesus beyond the crowds to shake the religious and political power base. The Pharisees now fear that the Romans will step in and exercise tighter controls on this part of the Roman Empire. They are afraid because their power is dependent on the political patronage of the Roman Empire. The great fear among them is that the Romans "will take away our place." (v. 48)

The intervention by Caiaphas is very interesting. Caiaphas is *not* defending Jesus. When Caiaphas predicts that Jesus is going to die for the nation, he is actually identifying Jesus as a scapegoat. According to Caiaphas, the presence and preaching of Jesus is so divisive and so disruptive to the political and religious status quo that killing him will bring a much needed unity. Caiaphas' prediction is that the death of Jesus will be politically expedient and save the Jews from Roman reprisals. In other words, if they put Jesus to death, there will no longer be a threat of political instability. Executing Jesus will unite the nation residing in the land but it will also unite those of the Diaspora, scattered among the nations. Caiaphas is persuasive and consequently, "…from that day on they made plans to put him (Jesus) to death."

The prophecy of Caiaphas is not intended for good. It is intended as a measure to keep the Roman authorities from getting too upset. Unbeknownst to Caiaphas, however, the prophecy has a deeper, redemptive meaning. The death of Jesus *will* unite the children of God who were scattered abroad, but not in the way that Caiaphas predicted. It will unite the children of God as follows:

> *"For he himself is our peace, who has made us both one and has broken down in his flesh the dividing wall of hostility, by abolishing the law of commandments and ordinances, that he create in himself one new man....and he came and preached peace to you who were far off and peace to those who were near. For through him we both have access in one Spirit to the Father."* — EPHESIANS 2:14-18

JESUS GOES UNDERGROUND

> *Jesus therefore no longer walked openly among the Jews, but went from there to the region near the wilderness, to a town called Ephraim, and there he stayed with the disciples. Now the Passover of the Jews was at hand, and many went up from the country to Jerusalem before the Passover to purify themselves. They were looking for Jesus and saying to one another as they stood in the temple, "What do you think? That he will not come to the feast at all?" Now the chief priests and the Pharisees had given orders that if anyone knew where he was, he should let them know, so that they might arrest him.* — JOHN 11:54-57

With plans afoot to kill Jesus, He is constrained to avoid the Jews. He knows that it is not the right time for His life to end and so slips away with His disciples to the town, Ephraim. His actions are not actions of fear; Jesus is being deliberately subversive. Spiritual resistance takes place away from the arena of physical combat and political protest. Spiritual combat takes place in a theatre of war that is not obvious to human observation. The will of the Father cannot be thwarted or pre-empted but must be discerned and waited upon. It is not yet time for Jesus' life to be given up.

As I said before, the ministry of Jesus is taking a turn in a different direction. In terms of human contact, His profile is diminishing. Many of His disciples have given up following Him, and the crowds no longer swarm around Him to witness signs and wonders. The large crowd will only reappear again when He enters Jerusalem on the way to the cross. Speculation is rife about what Jesus will do; will He make an appearance at the Passover feast or will He completely avoid it? Jesus has become an enigma to the people and a threat to the structure of organised religion. His purpose is now to meet the principalities and powers head on. He is about to wrestle demonic hands away from the controls.

THE FOOLISHNESS OF LOVE

~

Jesus returns to the place where He feels most at home, Bethany. This is where He raised His friend Lazarus from death and reunited him with his two sisters, Martha and Mary. By now, Jesus is well known in Bethany, as one who raises the dead. The people of the town may be afraid to look at Him yet they have seen something in Him that is deeply compelling. They have witnessed, either directly or indirectly, the compassion of the Father flowing through Jesus that is powerful enough to raise Lazarus.

Six days before the Passover, Jesus therefore came to Bethany, where Lazarus was, whom Jesus had raised from the dead. So they gave a dinner for him there. Martha served, and Lazarus was one of those reclining with him at table. Mary therefore took a pound of expensive ointment made from pure nard, and anointed the feet of Jesus and wiped his feet with her hair. The house was filled with the fragrance of the perfume. But Judas Iscariot, one of his disciples (he who was

about to betray him), said, "Why was this ointment not sold
for three hundred denarii and given to the poor?" He said
this, not because he cared about the poor, but because he
was a thief, and having charge of the moneybag he used to
help himself to what was put into it. Jesus said, "Leave her
alone, so that she may keep it for the day of my burial. For
the poor you always have with you, but you do not always
have me." [26] — JOHN 12:1-8

Presumably, the meal is given to honour Jesus and celebrate
Lazarus returning to life. They are all in awe of Jesus and the
atmosphere crackles with tension; they now see Him as someone
who has the ability to raise the dead. Imagine how Martha, Mary
and Lazarus feel. A dear friend they thought of as a prophetic teacher
has turned out to be something entirely different. What would *you*
say to a friend who now claims to be 'The resurrection and the life'
and backs up His claim with a spectacular demonstration which
He attributes to God His Father?

Lazarus is there, doubtless talking about *his* experience of being
raised from the dead. What was it like to be dead? Where did he
go? Was he in the bosom of Abraham? What was it like to wake up
in the tomb by a voice that shattered his 'sleep'? How did he hear,
"Lazarus, come out?" What did it feel like to find himself fully
alive yet bound in grave clothes, and to stumble towards the light
at the mouth of the cave to be greeted by his hysterical sisters? He
has become a witness to his own resurrection; a powerful enough

---

26. Biblical commentators are divided as to how many times Jesus is anointed by a woman in the
Gospels. That debate is not my focus in this writing so I will not enter into it. I have decided
to refrain from cross-referencing with other accounts in the Synoptic Gospels and just deal
with John's account at face value.

witness to rattle the cage of those who cling onto religious and structural power.

In the midst of this scenario, John turns his attention to two individuals, Mary and Judas, and deliberately highlights the contrast between the two. Firstly, let us consider Mary.

MARY'S ACT OF DEVOTION

Everyone is eating and talking while Martha is busy serving food and wine to the guests. Suddenly, there is a movement and a rustling and everyone turns around as Mary enters the room. What is she holding in her hands? She carries a receptacle and, with trembling hands, she breaks it open. Dropping to her knees she pours the amber liquid over the feet of Jesus and uses her hair to massage His feet. Mary is motivated by a powerful inner compulsion. The sacred well of love within her heart is overflowing and it moves her to this act of abandon. The fragrance of the aromatic oil permeates the house.

Mary expresses her heart in an outpouring of indulgent devotion to Jesus. Her offering is both wasteful and scandalous. She squanders a huge amount to anoint the body of Jesus. Incredibly, the value of this ointment is estimated at something like $25,000 US in today's currency. It is spikenard, a viscous and intensely aromatic essential oil, reminiscent of lavender.

This is devotion bordering on folly. It is wasteful and sensual. Carried out in full view of the guests, it may well have been misunderstood and caused embarrassment and scandal. But Mary is undeterred by this. Her focus is on Jesus alone. As she anoints

Him, she repays Him for what He has done by giving Lazarus back to her. Mary has an extravagant, even profligate, response to Jesus. She is like King David, who danced with abandonment before the ark (2 Samuel 6:14). True holiness is easily misunderstood because it regularly challenges religious and social norms.

As he watches this, Judas struggles to suppress the rage and indignation boiling within him until he speaks out and accuses her:

> *"Why was this ointment not sold for three hundred denarii and given to the poor?"*

THE INDIGNATION OF JUDAS ISCARIOT

Judas calls Mary's action into question as being a colossal waste of resources. According to him, the money should have been spent on the poor and needy. John, the writer, gives us an insight, however, into Judas' true motivation. Judas is the treasurer and his hands frequently stray into the bag containing the money.

Judas, in the depths of his heart, is full of the characteristics of an orphan. His stealing from the money bag is symptomatic of his fear and lack of trust. Everything that Jesus had said about not laying up treasures on earth, about not being anxious, about asking and it will be given, is lost on Judas. Judas has not really gained any greater level of trust in Jesus and the Father so he has to take the money matters (literally and metaphorically) into his own hands. He is still trapped in the fear of not having enough and having to provide for himself. Stealing is simply an orphan form of getting our needs met. I know what this temptation feels like.

Consider for a moment what motivates Judas Iscariot. Has he always been someone who has stolen the money? Has he always planned to betray Jesus?

Martin Scott has pointed out something about Judas; a crucial insight which has been largely missed but nonetheless rings true. His assessment is that Judas Iscariot is not essentially a bad person. On the contrary, Judas may actually have been one of the *best* disciples. Therein lies the big problem. Why? Here's what Martin Scott says:

> *"I think Judas had a great heart to see Jesus succeed. But there came a point where his agenda for Jesus was stronger than Jesus' agenda for the Kingdom. Judas says, "We know what it will take to make you successful, Lord." The path that Jesus was going on was not the path of success. Judas did not need a high IQ to realise that the way Jesus was going was towards trouble. He could see it coming, it was on the horizon….*
>
> *Judas got to the point where he knew better than Jesus what the way forward was. He thought that he could make this thing (Jesus' ministry) successful. He has seen Jesus heal the sick, he has seen Jesus minister to the crowds. He has seen Him raise the dead! We get to Jerusalem, and if He does not get His act together, it's going to be the disappearance of Jesus! The One we had our hope in is going to disappear and everything will be lost!*
>
> *Does this make sense of Scripture? Why is Judas one of the Twelve? Because, I think Judas is the model that we follow! That's why! Is there a Judas spirit that has to be rooted out*

of the Church that has betrayed Jesus? Is there something in us that wants Jesus to get His act together?

I think Judas goes to the high priest, because if he can set something up it will shake Jesus into getting His act together. Because if Jesus doesn't get His act together they will take Him captive and probably crucify Him. What is Judas' expectation? His expectation is that Jesus will see sense, deal with the issues, and take power.

What happened to Judas? He committed suicide, because he had lived so much to make Jesus successful, but ended up distraught because all his efforts to make Jesus who he thought Jesus should be had come to nothing.

How many people start out and give up? I can commit spiritual suicide today by disconnecting from the life of God. Sometimes we have to discover that all our efforts to make Jesus successful have ended up in nothing.

The Judas spirit is a spirit of betrayal. 'But Lord, if we do so and so, look how good You could be. Look how far You could go.' That is the Judas spirit, but I believe God is going to take the Judas spirit out of the Church."[27]

This is a compelling and persuasive insight. Judas may well be one of the most dedicated disciples but his dedication is misplaced. Judas wants to control and make successful the ministry of Jesus. The 'Judas

---

27. This was taken from a talk by Martin Scott called 'Empire is Over.' With his permission I have adapted it for written media.

spirit' wants to treat the life of God as a marketable commodity. Somewhere along the line, Judas begins to realise that his agenda for Jesus and the kingdom is not succeeding and disillusionment overwhelms him. Judas cannot see beyond a political solution. He has no idea that the kingdom of God is predicated on the spiritual dynamic of death and resurrection.

MARY'S INVESTMENT IN RESURRECTION

In contrast to Judas, Mary has no intention of helping Jesus get His act together. She is motivated by a deeper spiritual discernment. Jesus recognises this and springs to her defence. He chides Judas:

> *"Leave her alone, so that she may keep it for the day of my burial. The poor you always have with you, but you do not always have me."* — JOHN 12:7,8

What Judas sees as a tremendous waste, Jesus sees as an investment. Mary is anointing Him for His burial. She has prophetic revelation, seeing what others do not see. She knows that Jesus will die and be buried. Is it possible that she has a growing hunch that He will also be resurrected by the Father? I believe she does. After all, He revealed Himself in her own, personal experience as 'The Resurrection and the Life.' She knows too, that Jesus is living out what His Father wants.

Judas has carried his own misplaced agenda to see Jesus build the kingdom of God on earth but Mary does not have an agenda. Her anointing is not for success; it is for burial. Mary knows that the ministry of Jesus can never succeed on earth until it has passed through death and resurrection.

By anointing Jesus for His burial, Mary is making an investment of faith. To the natural way of thinking she has just wasted a huge amount of money. To the spiritual way of thinking, however, she has made a wise investment. She has sown a seed of faith by anointing Jesus for burial. She knows that she will get a return when He is raised from the dead. She lost Lazarus and received him back. She will lose Jesus but will receive Him back too. This is a wonderful story to give us hope that nothing is wasted. What may *appear* to human wisdom to be wasted will pay a dividend in resurrection that we cannot even begin to imagine.

Mary's foolishness is wiser than the wisdom of Judas. She has become like God in this, for God, too, is 'foolish.' Paul says:

> *"For the foolishness of God is wiser than men, and the weakness of God is stronger than men."* — 1 CORINTHIANS 1:25

The reason why God seems 'foolish' and 'weak' is because His wisdom and power work along entirely different lines. They work on the principle of resurrection, and the criteria for resurrection is the letting go of every orphan instinct of self-determination. We can only participate in the foolishness and weakness of God by being secure in our identity as sons and daughters. I believe that Mary is discovering sonship, identifying with Jesus in His sonship to the Father, and responding by acting in the 'wise foolishness' of being a true daughter of God.

THE HUMBLE ENTRY INTO JERUSALEM

When the large crowd of the Jews learned that Jesus was

there, they came, not only on account of him but also to see Lazarus, whom he had raised from the dead. So the chief priests made plans to put Lazarus to death as well, because on account of him many of the Jews were going away and believing in Jesus.

The next day the large crowd that had come to the feast heard that Jesus was coming to Jerusalem. So they took branches of palm trees and went out to meet him, crying out, "Hosanna! Blessed is he who comes in the name of the Lord, even the King of Israel!" And Jesus found a young donkey and sat on it, just as it is written,

> *"Fear not, daughter of Zion;*
> *behold, your king is coming,*
> *sitting on a donkey's colt!"*

His disciples did not understand these things at first, but when Jesus was glorified, then they remembered that these things had been written about him and had been done to him. The crowd that had been with him when he called Lazarus out of the tomb and raised him from the dead continued to bear witness. The reason why the crowd went to meet him was that they heard he had done this sign. So the Pharisees said to one another, "You see that you are gaining nothing. Look, the world has gone after him." — JOHN 12:9-19

The scene shifts outside the confines of the house. News has spread that Jesus and Lazarus are in the house in Bethany and a large crowd gathers. They are clamouring to see Jesus and also to see Lazarus. Lazarus is a dangerous man. He is an 'insider' to what the Father and Jesus are about. He is the prime witness to his own resurrection and he is a marked man. The religious authorities have signed a death warrant for Lazarus because they are losing power over the people.

The people, who John identifies as 'the large crowd,' are, for the moment, on the side of Jesus. For them, Jesus has a certain celebrity status. As we have noted before, however, their appreciation of Jesus is not informed by revelation. The palm-waving crowd completely misunderstand Jesus and the nature of the heavenly kingdom that His Father has given to Him. As a result, they try to make Him a king.

We need to be cautious about 'the large crowd' for it is not much different from Judas Iscariot. The crowd is looking for a king and this is what orphans default to. In our orphan mentality we look to be in the presence of and follow someone who will tell us what to do and instruct us how to live our lives. Humans always look for a defender, a protector and a provider. In our orphanness, we cannot see this as coming from the Father. A king is really a substitute for the Father. When we lose connection with the Father, we lose our awareness that fathering is what we need so we look for a ruler. This is apparent in 1 Samuel 8: 7-18 when the people asked for a king and God warns Samuel what kind of king they would actually get. The king will not rule in the dominion of love; he will rule in the domination of power.

The crowd believes that the time has come, at last, for Jesus to enter triumphantly into Jerusalem and set them free from Roman occupation. They are carried on the momentum of His reputation as one who performs mighty deeds. They pin their expectations on

Him as the longed-for Messiah. If He can go to Jerusalem and set up His kingdom, then all will be well. They cry out in jubilation that the fulfilment of the Messianic prophecies is at hand.

Jesus, however, does not ride in triumph into the city. Jesus chooses a young donkey and rides upon it. He does not ride a war horse but sits upon a young beast of burden. He chooses a humble means of transport, demonstrating the method of His rule. Jesus' rule will extend the Father's heavenly kingdom. The Father rules in humility and love, and His Anointed One is transported in meekness and lowliness.

John draws upon the prophecy of Zechariah to verify what Jesus is doing:

> *"Rejoice greatly, O daughter of Zion!*
> *Shout aloud, O daughter of Jerusalem!*
> *behold, your king is coming to you;*
> *righteous and having salvation is he,*
> *humble and mounted on a donkey,*
> *on a colt, the foal of a donkey."* — ZECHARIAH 9:9

This has become a familiar passage but we are less familiar with what follows it:

> *"I will cut off the chariot from Ephraim*
> *and the war horse from Jerusalem;*
> *and the battle bow shall be cut off,*
> *and he shall speak peace to the nations."* — ZECHARIAH 9:10

Zechariah prophesies that the kingdom of God will not be instituted by chariot and war horse. It will not come in demonstration of strength but it will come in humility. For many years I exerted power and strength to try and bring in the kingdom of God. I found, to my surprise, that when my power diminished and humility emerged, then the power of the kingdom was much more obvious because it came in humility and compassion. The prophecy of Zechariah is fulfilled; the true King has been revealed as a Son and the Kingdom is a dominion of love.

"GREEKS SEEK WISDOM… BUT WE PREACH CHRIST CRUCIFED."

Now among those who went up to worship at the feast were some Greeks. So these came to Philip, who was from Bethsaida in Galilee, and asked him, "Sir, we wish to see Jesus." Philip went and told Andrew; Andrew and Philip went and told Jesus. And Jesus answered them, "The hour has come for the Son of Man to be glorified. Truly, truly, I say to you, unless a grain of wheat falls into the earth and dies, it remains alone; but if it dies, it bears much fruit. Whoever loves his life loses it, and whoever hates his life in this world will keep it for eternal life. — JOHN 12:20-25

The next thing we read is that some Greeks seek out Jesus. The consensus among scholars is that these Greeks are wanting to become disciples of Jesus and that the influence of Jesus is now crossing the frontiers of Israel. That may well be true but something else springs to mind when I read these verses.

I am reminded of Paul's comment in 1 Corinthians 1:22:

"For Jews demand signs and Greeks seek wisdom…"

I believe that these Greeks are seeking to understand Jesus on the basis of intellectual wisdom. They approach Philip and request to be introduced to Jesus because they want to discover the idealistic wisdom that they think Jesus possesses. The text is not entirely clear whether Jesus actually agrees to meet the Greek enquirers. Regardless of whether He does or not, what He says next directly contradicts their perspective.

"The hour has come for the Son of Man to be glorified. Truly, truly, I say to you, unless a grain of wheat falls into the earth and dies, it remains alone; but if it dies, it bears much fruit. Whoever loves his life loses it, and whoever hates his life in this world will keep it for eternal life." — JOHN 12:23-25

This is not Greek wisdom. It is not a sign that will satisfy the Jews. This is the wisdom of God and the sign from heaven. This sign is the falling into the ground of the grain of wheat. Jesus' answer to the seeking of the whole world, both Jew and Gentile, is to unite signs and wisdom within His dying on the cross. I cannot put this better than Paul does in Corinthians:

"Where is the one who is wise? Where is the scribe? Where is the debater of this age? Has not God made foolish the wisdom of the world?…For Jews demand signs and Greeks seek wisdom, but we preach Christ crucified, a stumbling block to Jews and folly to Gentiles, but to those who are

called, both Jews and Greeks, Christ the power of God
and the wisdom of God. For the foolishness of God is wiser
than men, and the weakness of God is stronger than men."
— 1 CORINTHIANS 1:20-25

Paul's statement is an articulate commentary on the enquiry of
the Greeks and how Jesus responds to it.

The wisdom that Jesus gives to the Greeks is not the high and
idealistic wisdom that the Greek mind is seeking from Him. Rather,
it is a paradoxical and 'foolish' wisdom, a wisdom that advocates
death before effectuality. The wisdom that Jesus offers to the Greeks
is a wisdom which is not of this world. The grain of wheat has no
interest in saving its own life; there is no hint of self-preservation. Its
life is propagated through death. The kernel of wheat is swallowed
up by the dark and moist earth and lies there. When spring comes,
the new shoots poke through the earth.

Jesus has intimate knowledge of how the grain of wheat propagates.
He, too, will go the way of the wheat-germ. He is already falling
into the earth, falling from the Father's outstretched hand. Before
long, He will be swallowed up in burial so that He will not remain
alone. The Trinity does not want to be alone for the precise reason
that the Godhead *is* love. Love cannot possibly remain alone so it
has to fall into the earth and die in order to have the fruit of love.

Jesus calls us to go the way that He goes. The way of sonship is
a way of falling into the earth and dying. This is neither morbid
or morose, however. When we are loved we can let go of the need
to preserve ourselves or fight our own corner. We can let go of

selfishness knowing that the Father will take care of our needs and desires. The one who loves their own life will lose it because they are completely self-absorbed. The one who lives in love will not seek to preserve what belongs to them but in giving out for others, will experience eternal life. This expression "whoever hates his life" must be understood as the Biblical readers would have understood it. In Biblical parlance, the word 'hate' is not as malevolent as we understand it to mean today. Rather, it is a comparative word to describe "loving less than."[28] Put simply, if we love our lives in this world to the detriment of growing in the love of God, we will not experience eternal life. To love our lives, in this context, is to remain in the state of being an orphan. It is to be totally self-absorbed which brings spiritual and psychological death.

> *"If anyone serves me, he must follow me; and where I am, there will my servant be also. If anyone serves me, the Father will honour him."* — JOHN 12:26

Following Jesus as a disciple means to become like Him. Following Jesus will lead us inevitably to the Father. Serving Jesus from a heart of love will lead us to sonship. Following Jesus does not mean that we are to copy what He does; it means that we are to become what He is. The pursuit of intimacy with Jesus will not leave us absorbed with Jesus. No! Intimacy with Jesus will absorb us with who He is absorbed with, the Father! The disciple of Jesus, who becomes like Jesus will be honoured by the Father, not as a servant but as a son or daughter.

---

28. "Biblical Hebrew lacks the necessary language to exactly define the comparative sense, *i.e.*, 'more than' or 'less than'. Instead it tends to express two things which may be comparatively of different degree like 'first' and 'second' as extremes such as 'first' and 'last'. In this way love and hate whilst appearing as opposites may in fact be related but lesser terms such as 'love more' and 'love less'." taken from www.biblicalhebrew.com

THE FATHER GLORIFIES HIS NAME

"Now is my soul troubled. And what shall I say? 'Father, save me from this hour'? But for this purpose I have come to this hour. Father, glorify your name." Then a voice came from heaven: "I have glorified it, and I will glorify it again." The crowd that stood there and heard it said that it had thundered. Others said, "An angel has spoken to him." Jesus answered, "This voice has come for your sake, not mine.
— JOHN 12:27-30

Jesus is feeling intense pressure, and His emotions are agitated. His soul is troubled. He is shrinking at the thought of what lies ahead of Him. In His spirit, however, He is resolute. In His spirit, there is the peace of knowing that He has reached the time appointed for Him.

There is no contradiction here. The human emotions of Jesus are just like ours. He feels trepidation and wants to cry out to the Father to rescue Him from the ordeal. But is He going to allow His soul to determine what He does? He gives expression to the consternation of His soul but He is resolute in the purpose for which He has come to 'this hour.' The time has finally come to surrender to the inevitability of going to the cross.

As the Son, He orientates Himself fully to the purpose of His sonship. The purpose of His sonship is to glorify the Father's name. The Son lives to see the full expression of who the Father is. It makes no difference where the Son is, whether He is on earth or in heaven. His sole and entire purpose is the declaring of the Father's name. It is to manifest who the Father really and truly is.

When we look at Jesus, we see the outshining of the Father's glory. When we see the Father in Jesus, the Father's purpose is accomplished. When we see the Father in Jesus, the mission of the Son is also accomplished. It is the Spirit in us who makes this real in our experience.

A voice like a thunder clap comes from heaven and shakes the atmosphere. What a supernatural moment! What a sign! A voice that declares, "I have glorified My name, and I will glorify it again!" The Father affirms that Jesus, the Son, has fulfilled the mandate given to Him. The Father is happy to announce that His name has been glorified by the Son. Everything that the Son has said and done has effectively declared who the Father is.

What is more, the Father has not finished manifesting Himself through the Son. What happens from now on, as Jesus approaches the cross, will continue to express the fulness of who the Father is. Jesus does not need to hear this voice from heaven. He needs no assurance since He already knows within Himself that He is pleasing to the Father; He already has the Father's seal of approval in His heart. The Father has spoken to reiterate to the people that this Jesus of Nazareth is indeed the Son of God. Just as at His baptism, the heavens are torn open and the Father's affirmation for the Son is announced from heaven.

THE CROSS IS JUDGEMENT TO THE WORLD

"Now is the judgment of this world; now will the ruler of this world be cast out. And I, when I am lifted up from the earth, will draw all people to myself." He said this to show

*by what kind of death he was going to die. So the crowd
answered him, "We have heard from the Law that the Christ
remains forever. How can you say that the Son of Man must
be lifted up? Who is this Son of Man?"* — JOHN 12:31-34

Jesus pronounces that the judgement of the world is at hand. The
time is *now* for the judgement of the world to be meted out. The
word 'judgement' here is better translated as 'crisis,' a turning point,
a watershed. When Jesus pronounces the immediate judgement of
the world, He is declaring that the world is at a watershed, and what
happens to Jesus when He is crucified on the cross will provoke the
greatest crisis in cosmic history. Jesus will be lifted up on the cross
and, in that act, the ruler of the world will be cast out.

The judgement of the world and of Satan is not a judgement of
military dominance. What casts Satan out and provokes a crisis
for the world is the Son of God hanging on a cross. The weakness
and foolishness of God is a direct riposte to the fallen wisdom and
strength of the Orphan Spirit and his system.

In Christianity, there is an abiding principle which has been
largely missed. Like the crowd, we have an inbuilt tendency to
believe that, "…the Christ remains forever." We cling to what we
know and are afraid of it dying. But the only way to actually 'remain
forever' is to let our present reality die so that we will come into a
life *beyond* our present reality. Life beyond our present reality is a
life in resurrection. The Christ *does* remain forever but not in the
way that the world wants Him to remain.

"Who is this Son of Man?" He is not what we expected. He does not behave the way the Messiah should behave. He is not going to vindicate us and humiliate the Romans. He is going to submit Himself to the indictment of the religious and secular courts and end up dying on the cross. How can this be? What sort of Anointed One would behave like this?

SONS OF LIGHT

So Jesus said to them, "The light is among you for a little while longer. Walk while you have the light, lest darkness overtake you. The one who walks in the darkness does not know where he is going. While you have the light, believe in the light, that you may become sons of light."
— JOHN 12:35,36

To really perceive who this Son of Man is we need to remain within the light. If we do not walk in the light of revelation, we will be overtaken by darkness. The only way to keep walking in the right direction and arrive at the destination is to walk by the light. Jesus is unequivocally stating that knowing Him is to walk in the light. To believe in the light is to be in relationship with the light and to allow ourselves to be transformed by the light. In actual fact, we cannot live without the transformative power of revelation. To be without revelation is to walk in darkness. To live by our own human power of deduction and our own judgements is to walk in darkness.

Who Jesus is and who the Father is cannot be perceived without having a revelation. To resist that revelation is to let the darkness overtake. Revelation is much more than supernatural knowledge. Revelation is a matter of seeing things differently as they are illuminated in the light of love. Love illuminates. Love opens our eyes to see and, when we see with the eyes of love, we know that love must ultimately embrace the cross for love gives itself wholly for those it loves. It is only in the light of love that we can perceive that the Son of Man must be lifted up to die.

As we believe in the light, we become sons of light. In other words, we take on the characteristics of the light. We ourselves become channels of revelation and agents of enlightenment to others. As we adhere to and put our trust in the light of Christ's sonship, we will become transformed by the light into His image. The light of love acting upon the surface of our humanity will bring forth an image that is reflective of the Father.

GLORY FROM MAN OR GLORY FROM GOD?

When Jesus had said these things, he departed and hid himself from them. Though he had done so many signs before them, they still did not believe in him, so that the word spoken by the prophet Isaiah might be fulfilled:

> *"Lord, who has believed what he heard from us,*
> *and to whom has the arm of the Lord been revealed?"*

Therefore they could not believe. For again Isaiah said,

> *"He has blinded their eyes*
> *and hardened their heart,*
> *lest they see with their eyes,*
> *and understand with their heart, and turn,*

and I would heal them."

Isaiah said these things because he saw his glory and spoke of him. Nevertheless, many even of the authorities believed in him, but for fear of the Pharisees they did not confess it, so that they would not be put out of the synagogue; for they loved the glory that comes from man more than the glory that comes from God. — JOHN 12:36-43

Jesus leaves the people and hides from them. These are the people who hailed Him as the king of Israel. He has not fulfilled their expectations of kingship. He is a king but not one by worldly definitions. Jesus will be crowned with thorns and enthroned on a cross. His kingdom will not be obvious to them since they refuse to walk in the light of heart-belief. He has performed many signs but while the people are inebriated with demonstrations of power, they remain immune to what the signs are actually designed to achieve. The signs are only revelatory if the heart is open. When the heart is open the signs will be seen for what they are; as manifestations of the Father's name.

James and Denise Jordan have reintroduced a very significant revelation to the Body of Christ today. It is precisely what John states here when he quotes from the prophet Isaiah. It is the revelation that the eyes of the heart need to be reopened. The eyes of the heart closed when the man and his wife ate of the Tree of the Knowledge of Good and Evil. When they did so, according to Genesis 3:7, the eyes that could perceive good and evil were opened but the eyes of the heart became blind.

In a chapter called 'Opening the Eyes of the Heart,' in his book *The Ancient Road Rediscovered*, James Jordan recounts the commissioning of the prophet Isaiah. Isaiah was given an impossible mandate, to preach to blind eyes, deaf ears and hardened hearts. There was to be no success for Isaiah, as James Jordan writes, "The ministry of the prophet will bear no fruit. Quite the opposite—it will drive people further away."

Jesus has been given the same mandate as Isaiah the prophet: a mandate to open the eyes of the heart to perceive who the Father is. James Jordan defines this mandate as being the only real mandate of ministry throughout all history:

> *"This is what all ministry really boils down to…the issue of ministry throughout all time since the Garden of Eden is that the eyes of our hearts will be enlightened. From God's perspective, the singular goal of the Gospel is that the eyes of the hearts of people will be opened so that He will be known. God's heart is that every minister of the Gospel would have as their mandate to open the eyes that have become blind—the eyes of the heart."[29]*

Even those who believe in Jesus are afraid to confess their belief. Like the parents of the blind man in John 9:18-23, they are afraid of the consequences of following Jesus. Following Jesus will inevitably involve a confrontation with the structural power of religion. Fear of man and the need for glory from man are two sides of the same coin. When we do not have God's approval we seek approval from

---

29. M. James Jordan, *The Ancient Road Rediscovered*, Fatherheart Media, Taupo, 2014, p 69

human sources, and this is conditional upon submitting to human rules and expectations. Even those who see who Jesus is cannot surmount their need for approval from a source other than God. When God glorifies us, He glorifies us in the likeness of His Son. That glory is contrary to the swelling of our orphan ego. We need the eyes of our hearts opened to truly see the value of the glory that comes from God.

WHOEVER SEES ME SEES HIM WHO SENT ME

And Jesus cried out and said, "Whoever believes in me, believes not in me but in him who sent me. And whoever sees me sees him who sent me. I have come into the world as light, so that whoever believes in me may not remain in darkness. If anyone hears my words and does not keep them, I do not judge him; for I did not come to judge the world but to save the world. The one who rejects me and does not receive my words has a judge; the word that I have spoken will judge him on the last day. For I have not spoken on my own authority, but the Father who sent me has himself given me a commandment—what to say and what to speak. And I know that his commandment is eternal life. What I say, therefore, I say as the Father has told me."— JOHN 12:44-50

As this turbulent phase in the ministry of Jesus comes to an end, Jesus concludes everything by speaking about the Father. He cries aloud that to believe in Him is to believe in the Father. Perceiving who Jesus really is means knowing that He has been sent by His source, the Father. Belief in and knowledge of the Son cannot be separated from knowing His Father. To have revelation is also to see *how* Jesus sees. Jesus, like the Father, is love itself and love *sees*. When we embrace the Son and enter into His sonship, we can experience the radiance of the Father's smile and the approving glint in the Father's eyes.

The world is under judgement. This judgement is not so much a direct judgement from God. After all, Jesus declares that He does not judge but that He has come to save the world. The judgement reserved for the one who rejects the Son is that they will remain trapped in the snare of the knowledge of good and evil. The problem with religion is that it can hear the words of God spoken through Jesus but it has no capacity to keep them. There is a huge credibility gap between hearing the words and doing what the words say. Many Christians mistakenly try to do what Jesus says without experiencing the Father's love. The only way to do what the words of Jesus say is to experience what He is talking about.

Hear the words of Jesus as if the Father is speaking them to you, because life is found in relationship with the Father. The commandment of the Father for a son is very different to the commandment of God for a servant. A son obeys the Father's command out of love, not out of dutiful obligation. A son knows that the Father's instruction has inherent life within it. It comes from the Father's heart and therein is eternal life.

CLOSING REFLECTION

As Chapter 12 closes out, we come to the end of the active public ministry of Jesus. He is about to seclude Himself in the Upper Room with His disciples. He has performed miracles, remonstrated with the Pharisees and evaded the attempts to make Him a king. Condemnation has been condemned and the woman caught in adultery liberated. The eyes of the blind man have been opened and the false shepherds of Israel indicted. The Father has asserted with confidence that the Son has succeeded in glorifying the Father's name.

Mary of Bethany has shown, again, that women are seen as catalysts for revelation in this Gospel. Perhaps more than anyone else, she has insight into the true mission of Jesus. She knows that He must die, be buried, and rise again. She rejoices as she watches the grain of wheat falling into the earth. She prepares it for burial in the earth. She sees the kingdom of weakness and foolishness, the kingdom of love, having dominion over excellence and power.

The way of love is humble and gentle; it stoops lower and lower reaching to every place where the ravages of orphanness have been extended. The paradoxical wisdom of God is there for those who have ears to hear, and the upside-down kingdom of God is at hand for those who have eyes to see. The way of love chooses to wash feet. It chooses the donkey rather than the warhorse. It chooses the way of descent to the cross. This is the way of the Son. Most importantly, it is the way of the Father, too. God *is* Love and God is Light and in Him no darkness dwells. This is the hope of the world.

PART THREE

A NEW FAMILY

LOVE'S CONTINUOUS DESCENT

~

HE LOVED THEM TO THE END

Now before the Feast of the Passover, when Jesus knew that his hour had come to depart out of the world to the Father, having loved his own who were in the world, he loved them to the end. During supper, when the devil had already put it into the heart of Judas Iscariot, Simon's son, to betray him, Jesus, knowing that the Father had given all things into his hands, and that he had come from God and was going back to God, rose from supper. He laid aside his outer garments, and taking a towel, tied it around his waist. Then he poured water into a basin and began to wash the disciples' feet and to wipe them with the towel that was wrapped around him.
— JOHN 13:1-5

And so begins the final part of the narrative on the eve of Jesus' crucifixion. This is the closing phase of Jesus' ministry on earth. However, to paraphrase a famous quote, it is not so much the beginning of the end, but rather the end of the beginning.[30] Jesus knows that His hour has come, for He carries with Him an intricate sense of the timing of the Father. A sense of timing is vital to maturity in ministry. To be effective in manifesting the Father involves moving in a nuanced sense of the timing of the Spirit. When our hearts and spirits are dull to the inner pulses of the Holy Spirit, our spiritual timing is out of kilter. We revert to either aggression (moving too quickly) or to passivity (moving too slowly or not at all).

The keys to good timing are to recognise what is actually on our hearts to do, to be without condemnation (which paralyses us), and then to move in faith. We see here, in John 13, that Jesus operates out of a deep inner knowing that leads Him to taking decisive actions. He acts out of rest. Acting from rest will invariably ensure the right timing.

Jesus knows that the time has come to depart to the Father. The entirety of His mission here on earth is an orchestration of the Father. It is a sending *from* the Father, a manifesting *of* the Father, and returning *to* the Father. Returning to the Father is not a completion of Jesus' mandate but it is, nevertheless, a completion of this particular phase of sonship.

"Having loved his own who were in the world, he loved them to the end." This statement is loaded with significance. It is a summation of the life of Jesus: to love His own, and to love them *to the end*. His 'own' are those who have been given to Him by the Father. They are a group of people, loved intentionally and intimately by Jesus.

---

30. Winston Churchill after the Battle of El Alamein: "Now this is not the end. It is not even the beginning of the end. But it is, perhaps, the end of the beginning."

He loves them with a parental love, the Father's love. He loves them by comforting them, by giving them identity, by teaching them, by modelling to them the life of sonship. He loves them utterly. He loves them and will love them to the conclusion of everything that they will ever have to experience.

Because He is fully human, Jesus can only love a select group "to the end" while here on earth. In His humanity, Jesus is limited in full expression in communicating love to others. The love of the Father will only be made available to all through the indwelling Spirit. Of course He can intercede; of course He can convey revelation, but the Spirit who cries out "Abba, Father" has not, as yet, come to live within the human heart. He cannot fully express love to the entire population of the earth because He is limited to living within human parameters.

In order to fully release and manifest the love of the Father throughout all time and eternity, the Son needs to return to the Father so that the Spirit (of the Father and the Son) can be poured out. The Father's love was manifested externally by the Son here on earth. But the Son in resurrection, through the Spirit, manifests the Father's love *internally,* a love surging up from the innermost being. The heart is now the connection point to the Father's essence. The Father loves and communicates heart to heart. The Father's love is a love "to the end." It is a love which outlasts everything that anyone endures on earth.

THE PERFECT HUMILITY OF GOD

He laid aside his outer garments, and taking a towel, tied it around his waist. Then he poured water into a basin and

began to wash the disciples' feet and to wipe them with the
towel that was wrapped around him. — JOHN 13:4,5

This action of humility, of washing the feet of the disciples, is a manifestation of sonship. More than that, it is a manifestation of God's parenthood. It is a demonstration of the divine love that eternally stoops to minister. The Father's love pours itself out to refresh and cleanse, to comfort and adorn. In seeing Jesus divest Himself of His outer clothes and move resolutely into action, we see Him taking a *lower* level than the disciples. He takes, in front of them, the stance of a slave. It is astonishing to us that Judas is included in the washing, but it only *seems* astonishing because we are immature in love. Jesus washes the feet of Judas Iscariot with a full heart, with a heart that loves Judas without hesitancy or qualification. I am confident of saying this, because otherwise Jesus would be a hypocrite. Jesus washes the feet of Judas without the slightest hint of cynicism.

Fully aware that Judas is about to betray Him, Jesus manifests the humility of the Father to the betrayer. What is increasingly opening up to us in this revelation of the Father's love is the *perfect humility* of God. Love is humble, always esteeming the other as better than itself. God is love, therefore, God is the most humble being in existence. God the Father is supreme over all, yet somehow esteems the other as better than Himself. This is a staggering paradox which is scandalous to the orphan mind; the persons of the Godhead somehow esteem others as better than themselves. It almost sounds sacrilegious but Paul gives credence to this reality in Philippians 2:3-11:

"Do nothing from selfish ambition or conceit, but in humility
count others more significant than yourselves. Let each of you

look not only to his own interests, but also to the interests of others. Have this mind among yourselves, which is yours in Christ Jesus, who, though he was in the form of God, did not count equality with God a thing to be grasped, but emptied himself, by taking the form of a servant, being born in the likeness of men. And being found in human form, he humbled himself by becoming obedient to the point of death, even death on a cross. Therefore God has highly exalted him and bestowed on him the name that is above every name, so that at the name of Jesus every knee should bow, in heaven and on earth and under the earth, and every tongue confess that Jesus Christ is Lord, to the glory of God the Father."

As the truth of who God really is dawns on us, we discover that it is actually a misrepresentation of God to say that He is *anything other* than humble, meek, and ready to lay down His life. Jesus' washing of the disciples' feet demonstrates this reality.

The essential characteristic of Trinitarian love is that it is continually being poured out. The essential characteristic of Trinitarian *life* is that it is continually being laid down. As a bubbling spring continually pours out of itself but is not diminished, so the love of the Trinity continually pours out. A bubbling spring is in a constant movement of laying down its essence, but the essence is never lost. The essence moves away from the source but simultaneously remains with the source. This is what the love of God is like.

What is the motive for this action of Jesus? Simply stated, it is *sonship*. Jesus is deeply centred here, deeply ingrained in His sonship, expressing His full maturity in the human dimension of His sonship to the Father. We need to understand that Jesus Himself grew in maturity in His *human* expression of sonship. This is what Hebrews 5:8 means when it says:

> *"Although he was a son, he learned obedience through what he suffered."*

How did Jesus learn obedience? Did He *need* to learn obedience? It goes without saying that He did not need to learn obedience to correct some sort of rebellion to the Father's will. He did, however, need to learn to align His human body and soul to perfectly express the Spirit of the Father within Him. As the Son in human form, He needed to progressively learn to express the Father.

THE SERVANT-GOD

> *He came to Simon Peter, who said to him, "Lord, do you wash my feet?" Jesus answered him, "What I am doing you do not understand now, but afterwards you will understand." Peter said to him, "You shall never wash my feet." Jesus answered him, "If I do not wash you, you have no share with me." Simon Peter said to him, "Lord, not my feet only but also my hands and my head!"* — JOHN 13:6-9

Simon Peter's reaction is, as always, very instructive; he often expresses what we wish to express and Peter's reactions help to draw out the teaching of Jesus. He is often spoken of in a disparaging way by preachers and commentators as if they have more faith than he does, but that is naive and somewhat arrogant. Peter expresses freely what is on his heart and he is typically Jewish in his interactions with his rabbi, Jesus. Peter engages in open discussion and is not afraid of the cut and thrust of debate. The Holy Spirt honours and gives profile to Peter. God uses those who are less restrained to draw specific truths from Jesus. If Peter hadn't worn his heart on his sleeve and given vent to his fears and doubts, the responses from Jesus would be lost to us. It is often the persistent questioning of those that we might dismiss as being "awkward" or "difficult" that draw forth more revelation. As we grow more secure in love, we will see that God works in everything to bring forth His wisdom.

Simon Peter's reaction exposes our misperception of the true nature of God. Peter is still in a religious mindset, believing that he is not worthy to be served by God. Jesus retorts to Peter, "If I do not wash you, you have no share with me." In other words, if Peter does not learn how to receive the free gift of outpoured love through the servant-heart of God, he cannot be united with Jesus. To come into all that God has for us, we need to learn how to receive the Father's servanthood.

I have begun to realise something that is utterly scandalous yet wonderful. It is this: As we come to know the Father and His love, we leave behind servant-hearted Christianity. Then we discover to our amazement that the direction of servanthood has been reversed. We no longer serve God as we did before but we discover that the Father *Himself* is the ultimate Servant. In wide-eyed amazement we find that servanthood flows from the Father, who serves *us*. In Him, service and offering flows through us to others.

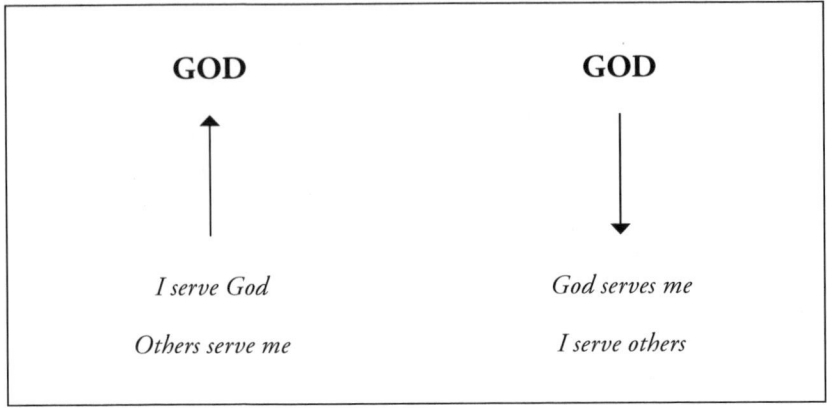

To *not* receive this is to remain an orphan. Little children are able to receive. They know how to receive the serving of their parents, washing them, clothing them, feeding them, protecting and supporting their lives.

Jesus then says to Peter, "What I am doing you do not understand now, but afterwards you will understand." You will understand when you see Me die on the cross, and when you see Me in resurrection life. You will understand, Peter, when the Spirit of sonship cries "Abba, Father!" from within your heart. Then you will understand who God is. Then you will understanding how far-reaching is the extent of the Father's love.

THE TOWEL AS SCEPTRE OF THE KINGDOM

Jesus knows that the Father had given all things into His hands. He knows that He had come from God, His Source, and that He is going back to God, His Destination. The circle of sonship here on earth is almost complete. It is already complete for Jesus in His own heart, for He knows everything now. He knows the eternal beginning, He knows the middle, and He knows the eternal end. He knows what the conception was, and He knows what the consummation will be. Jesus knows that the Father has given *everything* to Him. This is full maturity of sonship.

Knowing Source and knowing Destination determines the quality of the mission. When we know what Jesus knows, our *modus operandi* will be like His. The methodology of full, centred, and mature sonship is to stoop lower and lower. It is to take the towel and to wield it. It is to go to the cross.

The towel becomes the sceptre of the kingdom. Jesus is ruling here, not by domination but in dominion by washing the feet of the disciples *including* Judas. Jesus has full confidence in the alternative kingdom, the *true* kingdom that operates differently to every other kingdom.

> *Jesus said to him, "The one who has bathed does not need to wash, except for his feet, but is completely clean. And you are clean, but not every one of you." For he knew who was to betray him; that was why he said, "Not all of you are clean." When he had washed their feet and put on his outer garments and resumed his place, he said to them, "Do you understand what I have done to you? You call me Teacher and Lord, and you are right, for so I am. If I then, your Lord and Teacher, have washed your feet, you also ought to wash one another's feet. For I have given you an example, that you also should do just as I have done to you. Truly, truly, I say to you, a servant is not greater than his master, nor is a messenger greater than the one who sent him. If you know these things, blessed are you*

if you do them. I am not speaking of all of you; I know whom
I have chosen. But the Scripture will be fulfilled, 'He who ate
my bread has lifted his heel against me.' I am telling you this
now, before it takes place, that when it does take place you
may believe that I am he. Truly, truly, I say to you, whoever
receives the one I send receives me, and whoever receives me
receives the one who sent me." — JOHN 13:10-20

He communicates to them the downward movement of love. Washing their feet is the overflow of His and the Father's heart-reality. This is what He wants the disciples to emulate. Children do what they see parents do, out of a heart that is connected to the parents. In telling the disciples to follow His example, Jesus is not talking about a merely external gesture. He is talking about action that springs from the heart. A purely external action of servitude (feet-washing or anything else) that is not heart-inspired can never be sustained in the long-term.

James Jordan has pointed out that Jesus being "Teacher and Lord" (v.13) is not primarily about relating to Him by rote and command. Rather, making Jesus lord and following His teaching means that we are to become *everything that He is.* His life is to have dominion in our hearts. The life of sonship is to surge beyond our natural life. It takes faith to perceive and live from this reality.

BETRAYAL AND GLORIFICATION

After saying these things, Jesus was troubled in his spirit, and
testified, "Truly, truly, I say to you, one of you will betray me."
The disciples looked at one another, uncertain of whom he

spoke. One of his disciples, whom Jesus loved, was reclining at table at Jesus' side, so Simon Peter motioned to him to ask Jesus of whom he was speaking. So that disciple, leaning back against Jesus, said to him, "Lord, who is it?" Jesus answered, "It is he to whom I will give this morsel of bread when I have dipped it." So when he had dipped the morsel, he gave it to Judas, the son of Simon Iscariot. Then after he had taken the morsel, Satan entered into him. Jesus said to him, "What you are going to do, do quickly." Now no one at the table knew why he said this to him. Some thought that, because Judas had the moneybag, Jesus was telling him, "Buy what we need for the feast," or that he should give something to the poor. So, after receiving the morsel of bread, he immediately went out. And it was night. — JOHN 13:21-30

When Judas leaves the room it is night. Any flickering light or warmth of revelation and belonging has died out for Judas; he is oblivious to the True Light. Judas has reached the zenith of orphanness, and Satan has entered into him. From now on, Judas will exemplify what orphanness really is. For the orphan, it is night, a darkness without any revelation, where one can only stumble and only rely on self to find a way.

When Judas goes out, the atmosphere in the room changes. The disciples gathered are deeply shocked and reeling from the fact that one of the most prominent in the group, one who had leadership responsibility, is identified as a betrayer. They had wondered who it would be and John had asked Jesus (v. 25) who it was. Now, the sense of shock in the room is palpable. I sense a mix of sadness, relief and inevitability in Jesus as He says:

"Now is the Son of Man glorified, and God is glorified in him. If God is glorified in him, God will also glorify him in himself, and glorify him at once."— JOHN 13:31,32

For Jesus, the time is *now*. Throughout John we have heard the repeated phrase that "…the time is coming and now is." Here the time is no longer *coming*; it *has come*. What is "at once?" What is the immediate? The *immediate* for sonship is when the Father glorifies Himself in the Son.

Note that it is Son of *Man* who is glorified, not the Son of God. The eternal purpose of God is not to retain glory 'trapped' within the Godhead, but to be glorified in sonship within *humanity*. Jesus is the trailblazer, the forerunner who of unites of heaven with earth, and divinity with humanity.

Poised between foot-washing and the cross, the Son of Man is glorified and God is glorified in Him. This is the total antithesis of all religion and of all empire-mentality, the double-headed totem of the Orphan Spirit. The spirit of religion and the spirit of empire are glorified in an upward movement of becoming more powerful and more excellent. Contrary to this, *God* is glorified in a downward movement of becoming *less*. The glory of God is most fully manifested in its condescension in the human condition.

On the cusp of ultimate weakness, having manifested the Servant-Father to the disciples, Jesus is glorified "at once." This is a wake-up call to us. Why? Because glory is not in exaltation, glory is seen most fully in the outpouring of love. Glory is displayed in descending lower, not climbing higher. The time for glory is *now* and *at once*.

Jesus is telling us, "Watch me, as I become humiliated and powerless. If you have eyes to see, you will see the manifestation of my glory and the Father's glory!"

A NEW COMMANDMENT

"Little children, yet a little while I am with you. You will seek me, and just as I said to the Jews, so now I also say to you, Where I am going you cannot come. A new commandment I give to you, that you love one another: just as I have loved you, you are also to love one another. By this all people will know that you are my disciples, if you have love for one another." — JOHN 13:33-35

This is the new commandment — "Love one another: just as I have loved you." This new commandment supersedes and subsumes the previous commandment. The previous commandment was to "love the Lord your God with all your heart, soul and strength." This commandment was not possible to fulfil. It is only possible to love God back with the same love that He loves us with. Loving God is reciprocal; it is in response to being loved by Him.

In the new commandment the loving is initiated by God - "Just as I have loved you, you also are to love one another" (v. 34). This new commandment is contained within the New Covenant. The essence of the New Covenant is that all loving and all righteousness (right relationship) is initiated, energised and sustained by *God.* The generative power of the commandment is from heaven and by heaven, in the Father's love.

"By this all people will know that you are my disciples, if
you have love for one another." — JOHN 13:35

Love is evident to others. To love another, truly, fully and
consistently is evidence of having love. We love because we have
received love. Love is a substance. Love produces fruit and fruit is
obvious. Lush fruit weighing down the branches of a tree is clear
evidence of good soil quality and favourable weather conditions.
Fruit is evidence of both nature and nurture. Love for one another
is evidence of an underlying cause, of being loved.

YOU CANNOT FOLLOW ME NOW…
BUT YOU WILL FOLLOW ME AFTER.

"Simon Peter said to him, "Lord, where are you going?"
Jesus answered him, "Where I am going you cannot follow
me now, but you will follow afterward." Peter said to him,
"Lord, why can I not follow you now? I will lay down my
life for you." Jesus answered, "Will you lay down your life
for me? Truly, truly, I say to you, the rooster will not crow
till you have denied me three times." — JOHN 13:36-38

I love Simon Peter's personality. He 'shoots off his mouth' easily
and vocalises without thinking too much about what he is going
to say. His heart is worn firmly on his sleeve as he asks where Jesus
is going but Jesus does not answer him directly. Jesus does not
specifically mention the cross or His death; instead Jesus merely
tells Simon Peter that He must go there alone and that He cannot
be followed there now.

Peter's enthusiasm is bigger and more blustering than his actual commitment to what he says. He has a grandiose idea of what *he* can do for Jesus and the kingdom of God. Peter's confidence is based on his own energy. He believes that his own zeal and enthusiasm can carry him all the way to laying down his life for Jesus, but Jesus tells him that it is not enough. The emotion of the moment is not sufficient to make Peter lay down his life. The passion and commitment of the last three years is not enough to make Peter become like Jesus.

Jesus pinpoints where Peter's heart is really at. "The rooster will not crow till you have denied me three times." The impending trauma of Jesus' arrest, trial and crucifixion will be too much for Peter's current level of faith. It is only what happens to Peter *after* the resurrection that will enable him to go all the way to laying down his life in crucifixion. The big difference in Peter being able to 'follow Jesus afterwards' will be the comforting presence of the indwelling Spirit. When the Spirit comes to live inside Simon Peter he will have what is required to go all the way to martyrdom.

It is not so much that the Spirit will *empower* Peter's commitment to lay down his life for Jesus. Rather, it is the Father's love poured out internally within his heart that will overcome what stops him giving his life. Christ formed within Peter will allow him to be led to the inverted cross on which he is said to have been crucified. Historical tradition tells us that Peter chose to be crucified upside down. When the Spirit enters him, Peter will become "a partaker of the divine nature" (2 Peter 1:4). The divine nature is the only nature that can lay down its own life. But for now, Peter will deny Jesus three times. Then the rooster will crow…

ORPHANS NO MORE

~

PREPARATION FOR CATACLYSMIC TRANSITION

John 14 to 16 narrate the final words of Jesus to His immediate group of friends. Judas has gone out into the night and leaving the remainder of the Twelve, as well as Jesus' mother, Mary Magdalene, and a few other women. Jesus gives them a final impartation, a communication of intimacy. Chapters 14 to 17 are a hoard of rare jewels, gems of priceless value. These words are spoken literally on the eve of the crucifixion. Writing this, I pause and sense a surge of anticipation in my chest. My breath shortens in the silence and the only noise I can hear is my pen scratching the paper. I know that revelation will flow and the words on the page of the opened Bible will explode in front of me as I read them. I have no fear of getting writer's block in these chapters. My only concern is being able to keep up. Will my hands and fingers get cramped as I struggle to keep up with the revelatory flow of the Spirit?

Jesus emerges in the full bloom of His human sonship here and it will be fully seen as He hangs on the cross. As a human being, He has learnt what it is to overcome the limitations of the human soul and body. He has learnt to channel His emotions, set His will and align His mind. He allows His spirit freedom to inhabit His body fully as a temple for the fulness of the Godhead to live through. Jesus needs faith to live from a place of burgeoning revelation about who He is, with a growing realisation of His mission on earth. He has learned to mature in relationships with other people around Him, and in taking responsibility for the redemption of the human race and the orphaned cosmos. This cosmic redemption is truly, in the words of James Jordan, a "son-sized task."

Jesus sits with His loved ones and comforts them with these words:

> *"Let not your hearts be troubled. Believe in God; believe also in me. In my Father's house are many rooms. If it were not so, would I have told you that I go to prepare a place for you? And if I go and prepare a place for you, I will come again and take you to myself, that where I am you may be also. And you know the way to where I going."* — JOHN 14:1-4

Jesus speaks to hearts that are confused, troubled and apprehensive. He is preparing them for transition. The transition period will last, at least, until the Day of Pentecost, until the new Comforter comes to live inside them. If any of them retain any residual hope that His kingdom is "of this world," that hope will soon be in tatters. In addition to the shattered Messianic expectation, they are about to witness His arrest, trial and execution. A few of the gathered group will be witnesses to His dying throes on the cross.

John's Gospel deals with spiritual transition, and Jesus' final words to His disciples are to prepare them for the final transition. As the transition draws closer, through the deconstruction of their current paradigm, Jesus tells them to believe in God and believe also in Him.

The God that they must believe in is revealed to be different to the one that they have believed in all their lives. Their belief is about to undergo a radical transition, shifting from knowing God as Yahweh to knowing Him as Abba, Father. To make that transition they must adhere to Jesus. There is a real need to have confidence in the God who is inextricably connected to Jesus. This is the God (familiar to them as Yahweh) but revealed and incarnated before them as "Abba, Father."

Jesus is pressing upon them that Yahweh is really to be known intimately as "Papa." If it were not so, He would not have told them. They trust Him now. They need to trust the fact that He is going to the Father to prepare a place for them.

"In my Father's house there are many rooms." Other versions use the term "abiding places." The Father's house is our home and Jesus is going to the Father so that we will live with Him in the place where He lives, in the centre of the Father's affections.

There are many abiding places in the Father's love. Each one of us has our own unique place in the Father's affections. There is enough space for our individuality, our history, even our idiosyncrasies. The Father loves us as we are and anything that is not who we really are will fall away as we learn to relax in our place of eternal belonging. To have a room in the Father's house is to be relaxed and at rest in who we are, without need for striving and struggling to change ourselves.

It is to live from an innate sense of our worthiness to the Father.

THE WAY AND THE DESTINATION

"And you know the way to where I am going." Thomas said to him, "Lord, we do not know where you are going. How can we know the way?" Jesus said to him, "I am the way, and the truth, and the life. No one comes to the Father except through me. If you had known me, you would have known my Father also. From now on you do know him and have seen him." — JOHN 14:4-7

This is a well-known passage and for that very reason, it must not be overlooked. It is the overly familiar verses that must be looked at again to find the revelatory gems contained therein. Evangelical Christians are, in many ways, *too* familiar with the Bible. The Bible needs to be approached with fresh eyes every time we read it. It needs to be read with openness of heart, with suspended thoughts, so that it can be revealed by the Spirit. The unrevealed text brings only death (2 Corinthians 3:6).

Like Simon Peter, Thomas's interjection is used by the Holy Spirit to bring forth a potent revelation. Our tendency has often been to view with suspicion every person in the Gospel who questions what Jesus is saying; however, these interjections are devices used by the Spirit to draw out fresh revelation. This is a well-known method of teaching used by Jewish rabbis. Rabbinical teaching doesn't use a lecture style such as we are used to. The lecture style is a predominantly Greek model of teaching. Rabbinical instruction uses the to and fro of question and response and is more polemical.

Often the rabbi will put a question to his students to illicit their responses and thus draw out the wisdom of the rabbi. Reading through the Gospels we can see this dynamic methodology used by Jesus with His disciples.

Thomas' question, "How can we know the way?" draws out a response from Jesus.

> *"I am the way, and the truth, and the life. No one comes to the Father except through me."*

The true meaning of these words have been obscured behind what has become an Evangelical cliché. As Derek Prince pointed out, this verse is about a way and a destination; Jesus is the way, but *the Father* is the destination. Derek Prince made the further observation that the Church has become "stuck on the way."

Jesus does not show the way or point the way. He Himself *is* the Way to the destination, just as He is the Door (John 10:9). These are different descriptions of the same reality that Jesus *must be entered into* so that we may come to the Father.

How does this happen? How do we come to the Father by entering into and coming through Jesus? It happens through forgiving our natural parents from the heart and restoring the heart of sonship. When we open our hearts to Jesus, receive forgiveness of sins (including "good" sins as well as "bad" sins), He comes to indwell our hearts. By faith we realise that Christ indwells us and that we are in Christ.

One of the things that has caused us to become "stuck on the way," is that we have not had a sufficient revelation that we are united with Jesus in His sonship to the Father. When the truth is revealed to us that Jesus' core identity is in His sonship to the Father, we can begin to travel along 'the Way' towards 'the Destination.'

Similarly, the Church has become stuck at the *Mediator*. The Church, through lack of revelation, has failed to allow the Mediator to effectively do His mediatorial work. The work of the Mediator, as Son, is to reconcile us to the Father.

Now it is Philip's turn to speak:

> *Philip said to him, "Lord, show us the Father, and it is enough for us." Jesus said to him, "Have I been with you so long, and you still do not know me, Philip? Whoever has seen me has seen the Father. How can you say, 'Show us the Father'? Do you not believe that I am in the Father and the Father is in me? The words that I say to you I do not speak on my own authority, but the Father who dwells in me does his works. Believe me that I am in the Father and the Father is in me, or else believe on account of the works themselves.*
> — JOHN 14:8-11

The point of Jesus' response to both Thomas and Philip is to declare that there is *no disharmony* between the Son and the Father. It is to invite us to have confidence in the Way, that *this* Way (Jesus) will inevitably lead us to the Destination. Thomas and Philip are wavering about trusting the Way because they are hesitant to believe that Jesus had been sent by the Father. They are reluctant to fully commit in faith to Jesus' revelation that the one they had known as 'Yahweh' is actually 'Papa.' They are disorientated because Jesus is telling them plainly that Yahweh is fully represented and expressed in Him.

Jesus is saying to Philip, "Philip, have you missed the point entirely? Has it not dawned on you, after all this time, that I am here to reveal the Father?" When Jesus says, "Whoever has seen me has seen the Father," this has been generally misrepresented to mean that it is sufficient to have relationship with Jesus without any need to relate to the Father. However, the opposite is true. Knowing who Jesus is gives confidence to access the Father through Him, because He (Jesus) perfectly reveals what the Father is like. To know Jesus is to have access to the Father for "I am in the Father, and the Father is in me." Yes, they mutually indwell each other, yet they are never indistinguishable. The words and the works, spoken and performed by Jesus, are not His own but originate in the Father. All the signs, the wonders, and the demonstrations of miraculous power that had so often crossed the religious rubicon, and challenged social and political stratification (based on who was deserving and who was undeserving) actually showed what God was truly like! Would Yahweh the Lord of Hosts actually disrobe and wash their feet? The resounding and unequivocal answer of Jesus is, "Yes!"

GREATER WORKS THAN THESE

"Truly, truly, I say to you, whoever believes in me will also do the works that I do; and greater works than these will he do, because I am going to the Father. Whatever you ask in my name, this I will do, that the Father may be glorified in

the Son. If you ask me anything in my name, I will do it."
— JOHN 14:12-14

For those of us who are familiar with the Pentecostal/Charismatic tradition, the phrase "greater works than these" is very familiar. But what are the greater works and how are they to be done? I am reluctant to make much comment here because I really doubt whether I personally have done any 'greater works' myself. I have not yet sufficiently entered the experience of 'greater works' to make authoritative comment on it. However, I am approaching this verse without any preconceptions so I will just write as it appears to me. Make no mistake about it, I do hope to see and move in the realm of greater works.

My conviction is that greater works are only available for sons and daughters. They are only accessible through sonship to "whoever believes in Me." To believe in Jesus is not to offer some form of intellectual assent nor is it an effort of the will in positive thinking. To believe is to open our hearts to enter within His heart. To believe is to have the heart of a son towards the Father. As we continue to operate more in the heart of sonship, we will enter deeper into belief in the Son. The Son receives everything from the Father.

This statement about the greater works is an *hors d'ouvre* for what Jesus is about to introduce. He is about to tell them about the Holy Spirit and He attracts them by promising that the one who believes in Him will do greater works. The 'greater works' will become possible because Jesus is returning to the Father.

What does Jesus' return to the Father have to do with being

able to perform greater works than He Himself did? Because the Father will answer Jesus' request to send another Comforter! The other Comforter (the Holy Spirit) will continue the work of the first Comforter (Jesus) in manifesting the Father. The works that Jesus performs and the greater works are all the Father's works. When Jesus was on earth, the Father could only manifest Himself through the singular person of the human Jesus. What the Father actually wants, however, is to manifest Himself through a many-membered body, a body comprised of sons and daughters. To achieve this, Jesus will return to heaven and the Spirit, the Helper, the Comforter, will be poured out.

GUARANTEED ANSWERS TO PRAYER

"Whatever you ask in my name, this I will do, that the Father may be glorified in the Son. If you ask for anything in my name, I will do it." — JOHN 14:13,14

This undertaking given by Jesus, to do anything that is asked in His name, is huge. To highlight its importance, He repeats his promise to do *anything* that is asked in His name. The ramifications of this statement are massive, yet in the experience of many Christians there is a colossal credibility gap between what Jesus promises and what our life experience is. How many people can really say that they know what it is to ask something of Jesus, and to see it consistently accomplished? How many of us can match the answer exactly to the prayer that we have prayed? How many times do we settle for a compromise and our hearts are disappointed? If the words that Jesus says are really true in our experience we would be overwhelmed and overjoyed. If we promise others that they would receive exactly what they ask for in His name, how easy it would be to lead them to Christ. So what is the problem? How do we close this credibility gap?

The effectiveness of requesting and getting positive results is, without exception, conditional upon one thing: asking in His name. Asking in His name is an ironclad guarantee of getting Him to do it.

As you and I well know, there is no phrase which has been used more than, "…and we ask this in the name of Jesus." It is the most repeated phrase in Christendom. Yet the evidence of 'anything' being done in answer to requests in Jesus' name is not really there to prove it.

What then is asking "in my name?" What does it really mean to ask in the name of Jesus? It cannot be, and clearly is not, a formula or a mantra. Yes, we have all be patronised by the 'wise' who tell us that we must ask "within the perfect will of God." But what is the perfect will of God? Why is it so elusive? In my own life I have been deeply frustrated because I could never find the perfect will of God enough to have my prayers answered. I asked for many things "in Jesus' name" but did not receive definitive answers. However, my experience has shifted. I am now living increasingly of getting what I ask for. What has changed?

Asking in Jesus' name and receiving answers is for one purpose— so that the that the Father may be glorified in the Son. This promise of Jesus to His disciples is to give inarguable proof that the Father is just like Jesus. The disciples need to know that the Father is exactly who Jesus claims that He (the Father) is. Is Jesus really in the Father, and is the Father in Jesus? Here is how it can be proved; by getting whatever we ask for.

When we begin to receive revelation that connects Jesus to the Father, we will come to the reality of seeing prayer answered. The whole purpose of Jesus' life, on earth and in eternity, is to reveal the Father. He lives to reconnect us to the Father. When we look to Jesus as the Way to the Father, Jesus will give us what we ask Him. Why? Because He wants to reveal to us that the Father is a kind and generous Parent who loves us eternally in our humanity. Jesus' mandate is to reveal a compassionate Father to us. This promise to ask for whatever we wish and it will be done is repeated again, so that we will have confidence that the Father is *just like* Jesus. I have met so many people who lived in a 'Jesus only' Christianity, with no revelation of the Father, and who prayed futilely in the name of Jesus. Once they began to connect Jesus back to the Father, answered prayer began to flow. The barren tree of praying began to produce abundant fruit. This is because the Father is to be glorified in the Son.

The principle of flow and generosity in the universe comes from a Father who is a loving and compassionate Source. When we pray in Jesus' name but have a dissonance in our hearts as regards the Father, we cannot receive answers to prayer. Praying without a revelation of the Father cannot access the generosity that flows from heaven. Praying without a revelation of the Father is the prayer of a servant-orphan and there are no guarantees of getting exactly what we ask for. Disconnecting Jesus and the Father actually short-circuits the flow of blessing that is available to us.

Jesus answers prayer in order to manifest the Father. My counsel to you, my reader, is this; make requests of Jesus on the basis of Him revealing the Father to you. I am willing to wager that you will see increasing evidence of answered prayer in your life.

KEEPING THE COMMANDMENT OF LOVE

"If you love me, you will keep my commandments. And I will ask the Father, and he will give you another Helper, to be with you forever, even the Spirit of truth, whom the world cannot receive, because it neither sees him nor knows him. You know him, for he dwells with you and will be in you." — JOHN 14:15-17

Loving the Son and keeping His commandments is a consequence of being already loved by the Father. This statement must be read in context, in the underlying assumption of all that has been said previously. The principle of "first love" and "source love" has been established; therefore, loving the Son is a responsive and reciprocal love. The truth is, love *always* keeps commandments. The person who loves cannot fail to do the will of the lover. Love does not require obedience, love *precipitates* obedience. The commandment is the new commandment from John 13:34, to "love one another as I have loved you."

The power (*dunamis*) to keep the commandment of loving others is by the empowering Spirit, who is given from the Father. The indwelling Spirit who abides inside the heart is the conduit of the love that springs from Source. The Spirit is continually pouring this love out within our hearts (Romans 5:5). He is the Spirit of truth, the Spirit of full reality. His truth is expressed in the cry inside the human heart—Abba, Father! The commandment is not a command to a servant, but a command to a son that carries with it the creative energy of its own fulfilment.

The Spirit is not apparent to the world, to the orphan system. The world only sees the obvious and it only perceives the external. The Spirit, however, is unseen and internal, known primarily in the sanctuary of the heart. The heart receives the revelation that we are loved and lived in by the Father and the Son.

FATHER COMES TO US

"I will not leave you as orphans; I will come to you. Yet a little while and the world will see me no more, but you will see me. Because I live, you also will live. In that day you will know that I am in my Father, and you in me, and I in you. Whoever has my commandments and keeps them, he it is who loves me. And he who loves me will be loved by my Father, and I will love him and manifest myself to him. Judas (not Iscariot) said to him, "Lord, how is it that you will manifest yourself to us, and not to the world?" Jesus answered him, "If anyone loves me, he will keep my word, and my Father will love him, and we will come to him and make our home with him. Whoever does not love me does not keep my words. And the word that you hear is not mine but the Father's who sent me. — John 14:18-24

James Jordan has introduced the paradigm-shifting revelation that this statement, "I will not leave you as orphans; I will come to you," is a statement which sums up the entire history of the cosmos. What appears to be a little throwaway line is, in reality, the underpinning and overarching truth of the Gospel. James Jordan has preached and written eloquently on 'the Orphan Spirit,' so I will not linger on it. To really understand my perspective in this book, it is essential to grasp this paradigm.[31]

My only comment on this verse is that it contains God's analysis of, and answer to, the problem of the entire universe. The cosmic crisis can be summed up in the word 'parent-less-ness.' When Jesus says, "I will come to you," He is emphasising that the answer to the rootlessness of the universe is to be found in the Father. The Father has taken the initiative to come to the human race and to creation. God has made and continues to make a downward movement towards orphaned creation.

In sending the Son, the Father has taken the initiative. The Father has manifested Himself through the Son on earth. But that was never intended to be the limit of the Father's revelation. The Father cannot be limited in His expression to a single Event in human history. The Son must depart to another realm so that He and the Father can indwell human history, not through a single Event but through an ongoing Event. Jesus must leave the world, which will no longer see Him and go to a place where He can dispense the life that He lives by. While He remains on earth, Jesus cannot give eternal life to us. The quality of life that He lives by is eternal life and that can only be instilled by the presence of the Holy Spirit *inside* us. The life of the Father and the Son becomes resident in us by the Holy Spirit.

---

31. James Jordan's teaching is available from <u>www.fatherheart.net</u>

The Holy Spirit within us brings this eternal life into us. It is the intertwined life-force of the Father and the Son within our life. The Son is in the Father, we are in the Son, and the Son is in us. In Christ, we inhabit the Father. The Father is our home. Our natural habitat is within the Father. When we live naturally and easily within the Father, we will keep the love-commandments of the Son. The life of sonship will be manifested to us and through us.

> *"These things I have spoken to you while I am still with you. But the Helper, the Holy Spirit, whom the Father will send in my name, he will teach you all things and bring to your remembrance all that I have said to you. Peace I leave with you; my peace I give to you. Not as the world gives do I give to you. Let not your hearts be troubled, neither let them be afraid. You heard me say to you, 'I am going away, and I will come to you.' If you loved me, you would have rejoiced, because I am going to the Father, for the Father is greater than I. And now I have told you before it takes place, so that when it does take place you may believe. I will no longer talk much with you, for the ruler of this world is coming. He has no claim on me, but I do as the Father has commanded me, so that the world may know that I love the Father. Rise, let us go from here."* — JOHN 14:25-31

The Holy Spirit is the doorway into everything in the New Covenant. He holds the key to everything. The New Covenant is internal, within the housing of humanness. Since Jesus died, was buried, then raised up and went to heaven, the entire means of access to God is *spiritual,* through the heart. It is now by means of 'spirit' that we connect with God. Jesus is telling the disciples this now because a time will come soon when they will not have his literal, audible voice to tell them. They will have the inner witness of the Spirit.

Why is the New Testament so much shorter than the Old Testament? Because, Christianity, unlike Judaism (or even Islam), is *not* a religion of the book. Christianity is a 'religion' of the heart and the indwelling Spirit. In Christianity, the Torah, the Writings and the Prophets have all become internalised within the human receptacle. Therefore, the New Testament is very much shorter than the Old, because there is less need for a written corpus.

One of the reasons why we do not experience the Holy Spirit bringing things to our remembrance is because we tend to rely too much on external memory aids. Many Christians rely on external stimuli to keep faith and hope buoyant. There has never been such an abundance of resources available to tell us how to live the Christian life. Resources are to be appreciated, and they have been very useful to me. However, I offer this thought; Why don't you experiment with taking a break from reading Christian books and listening to Christian teaching for a while? Look within, listen to the voice coming from your own heart. Could it be that it is the Holy Spirit bringing things to you? The Holy Spirit teaches us, not by informing the mind, but by bringing revelation in our spirit *through* our minds. Revelation does not come *to* the mind, but it does come from the spirit *through* the mind, otherwise we would not be able to receive it.

Jesus speaks peace to the disciples to prepare them for the transition which is bearing down upon them, a transition from the physical and external presence of Jesus to the spiritual and internal presence of Jesus. But not only Jesus, they will also receive the spiritual and internal presence of His Father as well. The 'ruler of this world' is, almost literally, at the door. He is "the prince of the prince of the power of the air, the spirit that is now at work in the sons of disobedience." (Ephesians 2:2) This ruler will judge Jesus as not fit to live, will torture Him and put Him to death on the cross. The ruler of the world believes that he is getting the upper hand but he has no claim on Jesus. Jesus is doing as the Father has commanded. Even when it seems that everything is going against the will of God, the initiative in the unseen realm is with the Father.

Peace that the world gives is on the basis of external harmony. I am very familiar with the efforts of peacemaking to a situation where there is political conflict. In my home country of Northern Ireland, peacemaking has been relatively successful. However, it is only the peace that the world gives. It is a hammered-out agreement based on a lot of bargaining and compromise. The peace that Jesus promises is a deeply seated peace on the inside that no external circumstance can shift. It is a peace that comes because the heart is no longer troubled or afraid. This peace is contingent upon the indwelling presence of the Father.

FRUITFUL ABUNDANCE

~

The fourteenth chapter of John concluded with Jesus and the disciples leaving the Upper Room where they had just taken the Passover meal. They now go to another location, moving across the Kidron Valley towards the garden at the foot of the Mount of Olives. During this transition Jesus communicates some of the most revelatory and potent words in the entire Gospel.

As Jesus begins His soliloquy, He uses the metaphor of the vine and the branches. They have just partaken of wine at the supper and the Holy Spirit quickens the metaphor to Jesus so that He can communicate effectively to His disciples.

The metaphor runs like this: the Father is tending His vine; the Father's vine is Jesus the Son, and the branches of the vine are the disciples. This is the immediate meaning to those who hear it directly. The meaning can be extended, of course, to include you and I as the branches.

"I am the true vine, and my Father is the vinedresser. Every branch in me that does not bear fruit he takes away, and every branch that does bear fruit he prunes, that it may bear more fruit. Already you are clean because of the word that I have spoken to you. Abide in me, and I in you. As the branch cannot bear fruit by itself, unless it abides in the vine, neither can you, unless you abide in me. I am the vine; you are the branches. Whoever abides in me and I in him, he it is that bears much fruit, for apart from me you can do nothing. If anyone does not abide in me he is thrown away like a branch and withers; and the branches are gathered, thrown into the fire, and burned." — JOHN 15:1-6

MAXIMISING FRUITFULNESS

In the Vine, there are branches that receive life and branches that do not receive life. The branches that receive the flow of sap bear fruit and the branches that cannot receive the sap wither and die. The sap that runs through both Vine and branches is the love that comes from the Father. The sap is the spirit-energy of the life of God. Connection to the life of God in Jesus is what produces fruit. However, the best crop is produced in branches that are pruned.

Every branch in me that does not bear fruit he takes away, and every branch that does bear fruit he prunes, that it may bear more fruit. — JOHN 15:2

If anyone does not abide in me he is thrown away like a branch and withers; and the branches are gathered, thrown into the fire, and burned. — JOHN 15:6

When He talks about the withered branch, I suspect that Jesus is, first and foremost, giving an explanation of why Judas Iscariot left the disciples and was about to betray Jesus. The disciples would have been hurt and confused when Judas fled into the night. Judas Iscariot did not bear any fruit even though he was attached, to some degree, to the Vine. Detachment from the Life Source causes withering because there is no supply of life-giving sap. Judas Iscariot had been withering on the Vine since the day he joined the disciples. The atmosphere of love among Jesus' circle was so free of judgement that the Twelve didn't realise that Judas was withering on the Vine.

When Jesus says that the withered branches are gathered and burnt, He is making an observation of what happens in everyday life. The withered branches have no life in them and are only useful for lighting fires. The point is not the withered branch; the point is the branches which remain in the Vine and let the sap flow through them. The branches that bear fruit cannot wither because they are 'already clean.' They are clean because they have received life-generating words from the Son. Reading back through John's Gospel, the text is proliferated with life-generating revelation. When Jesus speaks, His words have inherent life within them. Those, like Judas, who wither and die on the Vine, must shut their ears and be hardened to the words which cleanse and bring life. There is no other explanation, for very word uttered by Jesus fizzes and sparks with life.

The ability to bear fruit is contingent upon abiding in the Vine. The Vine is lush and fecund, because He, the Vine, continually draws the nourishment that comes from His Source and feeds it to the branches. Every branch that remains in Jesus is simultaneously connected in sonship to the Father. Every branch that is not in Jesus is simultaneously cut off from the life of the Vine and disconnected from the root system. In other words, it is orphaned. The Vine grows in the soil of the eternal love of the communion of the Godhead. The branch which bears fruit abides in the Vine. This means that it is permanently attached to and of the same substance as the Vine. The branch that abides is the branch that has sprouted from the root of the Vine.

We need to understand that Jesus Himself was pruned by the Father. Pruning the branches causes 'pain' to the Vine. The writer of Hebrews describes this pruning:

> *"Although he was a son, he learned obedience through what he suffered."* — HEBREWS 5:8

Jesus suffered when His followers left Him and went away (John 6:66). Jesus suffered when He saw Judas withering on the Vine and departing into the night to betray Him. The suffering of the Son is the pruning of the Father. In pruning the Vine and the branches the Father suffers too, because He has compassion and does not inflict suffering willingly. Yet He knows that the pruning will ultimately produce heavy and juicy fruit. When the branches are pruned, they draw more effectively from the Vine.

All pruning involves death. It involves the removal of something that is actually receiving life. The Father needs to prune what is merely 'good' in order to produce the best. The experience of sons and daughters is intended to parallel the experience of the Son. It is a similar journey towards a cross and a death which is redemptive, through to a resurrection which is fruitful and abundant. The only way to bear spiritual fruit is to go through the same process that Jesus went through in order for Him to bear eternal fruit. That process is weakness, death and resurrection. All seeds must fall into the ground and die before they can bear fruit. Why do people think that they can bear the fruit of the kingdom and bypass falling into the ground? No death equals no fruit. The grain of wheat must fall into the ground and die in order to bring forth the fruit of the many sons and daughters.

ABIDING IN LOVE

"If you abide in me, and my words abide in you, ask whatever you wish and it will be done for you. By this my Father is glorified, that you bear much fruit and so prove to be my disciples. As the Father has loved me, so I have loved you. Abide in my love." — JOHN 15:7-9

One of my favourite biblical words is the word 'abide.' It is a word that is outdated semantically but it is a rich word and much more meaningful to me than the word 'remain.' The word 'abide' has resonances of 'love,' 'rest,' and even 'pleasure' in it. Abiding in Jesus is not spasmodic, nor is it precarious. To abide is to relax deeply into something greater that holds us and surrounds us. The proof of discipleship is not in a 'disciplined' life; the proof of discipleship is to abide in the same way as the Son abides. Out of this comes fruitfulness.

Fruitfulness is not to be confused with productivity. Productivity is what we are engaged in when we are *not* abiding. Productivity is essentially self-generated whereas fruitfulness is generated from another Source. The Father is glorified by fruitfulness because the fruit is a manifestation of who the Father is. In the same way that a lemon tree is 'glorified' by its lush fruit, or a rose bush is 'glorified' by its fragrant flowers, so the Father is glorified by the fruit of discipleship. The fruit of discipleship is to be a son like Jesus.

Abundant fruit within the Vine is also demonstrated by asking what we wish and having it done for us. I have written about this in a previous chapter, but here it is mentioned again. One of the major proofs of true discipleship, of becoming like Jesus, is to have what we wish granted to us by the Father. Answered requests from the Father are the evidence of sonship.

Answered requests have a very specific prerequisite. The prerequisite to "asking whatever you want and it will be done for you" is this: "If you abide in Me and My words abide in you." One of my primary desires is to experience the fulfilled promise of asking what I want and see it being done for me. This may sound selfish but I do not apologise for it. It is vital to know when I am abiding and when I am not abiding. When I get what I ask for from the Father it is evidence that I am abiding in Him and when the contrary happens, it is evidence that I am *not* abiding.

Knowing God as Father changes everything about Christianity. We are guaranteed things with the Father that we are not guaranteed as the servant of the Master or a subject of the Kingdom. The level of confidence we have in getting requests answered is infinitely greater in sonship. In fact, confidence grows exponentially when we start to make requests from *our Father*. Father supplies our daily bread because it is in His nature to do so, not because it is our reward. The supply of our daily bread is not conditional upon our obedience. It is conditional upon His fatherhood, which is the perfect fatherhood.

THE COMMANDMENTS OF LOVE

"As the Father has loved me, so have I loved you. Abide in my love. If you keep my commandments, you will abide in my love, just as I have kept my Father's commandments and abide in his love. These things I have spoken to you, that my joy may be in you, and that your joy may be full. This is my commandment, that you love one another as I have loved you. — JOHN 15:9-12

Jesus is taking the metaphor of the fruit-bearing branch right back to its source, that of the Father loving the Son. The source of the Vine is the Father's love for the Son. That love flowing through the branches produces the fruit of answered requests. If the Son is the Vine, then the Father is the taproot of the Vine, or even the soil in which the Vine is planted and from which it is nourished. And the sap, the life-energy which flows through the Son and produces fruit on the branches, is the Father's love!

Jesus states that He abides in the Father's love by keeping the Father's commandments. Then, by extension, He says that we can abide in *His* love by keeping *His* commandments. Initially, this feels like an obligation. It feels like we *have to* do something in our strength until we realise that the 'commandment' is to let the love flow from the Source, through the Vine, to the branches. "Love one another as I have loved you." What comes first here is, "As I have loved you," *and then,* only after we have received, we can "love one another." The Father's commandment to Jesus is to be a conduit for the Father's love. It is the same for us. Our joy is complete when we are filled with the Father's love and when that love overflows to others.

> *Greater love has no one than this, that someone lay down his life for his friends. You are my friends if you do what I command you. No longer do I call you servants, for the servant does not know what his master is doing; but I have called you friends, for all that I have heard from my Father I have made known to you.* — JOHN 15:13-15

Love is fully demonstrated in the laying down of life. Life can be laid down either in living or in death. The motivation and the result is the same. The friendship that Jesus talks about here is much more than the back-slapping of mates. It is a friendship based on carrying out His commands. These commands, however, are *not* the servile commands given to servants. Now they are friends with whom He can share His heart. These commands are the commands of love, to love others as they have been loved by Him and the Father.

They are no longer servants; they are now His friends. He doesn't call them brothers, however, until after the resurrection. Jesus tells Mary Magdalene, "Go tell my brothers." (John 20:17) Co-sonship with Christ can only be realised on the other side of death. He can only give the Spirit of sonship when He is risen from the dead. He can only take them from being servants to being friends this side of the cross, because sonship is only possible by the Spirit who cries out "Abba Father" within our hearts.

THE FRUIT OF ABIDING IS ANSWERED PRAYER

"You did not choose me, but I chose you and appointed you that you should go and bear fruit and that your fruit should abide, so that whatever you ask the Father in my name, he may give it to you. These things I command you, so that you may love one another." — JOHN 15:16,17

The incredible thing about this saying of Jesus is that the fruit He speaks of is *not* good Christian character. Neither is it holy living. Nor is it even the 'fruit of the Spirit' of Galatians 5. The fruit spoken of here, by which the Father is glorified, is the proven results of having whatever we ask done for us! The object of the Father's love gets everything he or she asks for. In verse 16, Jesus again repeats "You did not choose me but I chose you." He is establishing that the initiative does not come from us. "I appointed you to bear fruit that abides, so that whatever you ask the Father in my name, He may give it to you."

James Jordan once said that we should never make a prayer request until we have basked in the experience of being the Father's beloved child. The only way for us to enter in and experience asking whatever we wish and having it done for us is to receive the Father's love and rest in that love.

When I read these verses, I am both bewildered and excited. I am bewildered because I see a credibility gap in my own personal experience. I am bewildered because I do not always perceive my prayers to be effectual and it seems that all my successes are equally shot through with failure. But I am also deeply excited because I am slowly learning to abide in the Father's love. In the environment of the Father's love, my desires and His desires become intermingled. As I am loved by Him, I can ask Him whatever I wish for. The receiving of the answer is merely a matter of time. The answer will come to me within my lifetime, either on this earth or beyond.

The evidence of loving one another is seen in asking from the Father in Jesus' name. To truly ask in Jesus' name is to understand that we are co-participators in His sonship. For that reason, we are to see others as our brothers and sisters of the same heavenly DNA. When we love each other with the love that comes from the Father, we are then able to ask in Jesus' name. We are asking not only on our own behalf but on behalf of our spiritual siblings. The family grows together in a bond of love.

THE WORLD HATES SONSHIP

"If the world hates you, know that it has hated me before it hated you. If you were of the world, the world would love you as its own; but because you are not of the world, but I chose you out of the world, therefore the world hates you. Remember the word that I said to you: 'A servant is not greater than his master.' If they persecuted me, they will also persecute you. If they kept my word, they will also keep yours. But all these things they will do to you on account of my name, because they do not know him who sent me. If I had not come and spoken to them, they would not have been guilty of sin, but now they have no excuse for their sin. Whoever hates me hates my Father also. If I had not done among them the works that no one else did, they would

not be guilty of sin, but now they have seen and hated both
me and my Father. But the word that is written in their
Law must be fulfilled: 'They hated me without a cause.'"
— JOHN 15:18-25

The word 'hate' is a heart-word, an instinctive reaction to something. Children use the phrase, "I hate that" quite often. The intellectual mind is oftentimes too cultured, controlled and sophisticated to hate. Hatred is not logical. In Biblical understanding, hatred is the primary emotion that fear gives expression to. The world is afraid of sonship and, as a result, it *hates* sonship. The world is the system which is controlled by Satan, a system that is built upon orphanness. The world does not know or depend on the Father. The world has developed a very sophisticated system of independence from the Father; it is a system that is built upwards to reach increasingly higher heights. It is the same system whether it is religious or secular.

The orphan system (the 'world') has hated Jesus long before it has hated those who are in His image. The world system has always hated the Son of the Father. The Orphan Spirit, whose ambition is to become as God, loathes the One who lives in continual dependence upon the Father. Satan is deeply disturbed and horrified at the presence of the Beloved who abides in the bosom of the Father.

Another reason why the orphan system hates the sons and daughters is because they are "not of the world." Sons and daughters do not look to the world for identity and security and, as a result, can never fit into the structures that the world has created. The 'world' is a regime which perpetuates the state of orphanness. Jesus chooses His disciples out of the world to live by another 'system' which is entirely free from orphan ways and methods.

"Remember the word that I said to you: 'A servant is not greater than his master.' If they persecuted me, they will also persecute you." — JOHN 15:20

Jesus' definition of the servant-master relationship here is not so much about obeying commands. The emphasis is on the servant *becoming like* the master. The servant cannot expect to avoid what the master must go through because the life of the servant is inextricably tied to the life of the master. The disciples of Jesus are on a journey towards becoming like Him. That journey will take them through the cross to the far shore of resurrection. In becoming like their Master, they will ultimately arrive at sharing in His sonship to the Father. As part of that package, they *will* be persecuted.

The world persecutes sons because it does not know the Father. The world persecutes because it feels threatened and confused by those who are living in true sonship. True sonship exacerbates the feelings of the orphaned world. Sonship exposes the world in its orphanness, driving it back into its insecurity and fear. Its reaction is to go on the offensive and resort to persecution.

Sons and daughters, born of the Spirit, are like the wind. They appear and then disappear as moved by the Spirit within them. They cannot, and will not, be boxed into a system. They cannot, and will not, fit the categories and expectations placed upon them. Paul describes this life in his letter to the church in Corinth:

"We are afflicted in every way, but not crushed; perplexed, but not driven to despair; persecuted, but not forsaken; struck down, but not destroyed..." — 2 CORINTHIANS 4:8,9

"...by great endurance, in afflictions, hardships, calamities, beatings, imprisonments, riots, labours, sleepless nights, hunger,...through honour and dishonour, through slander and praise. We are treated as impostors, and yet are true; as unknown and yet well known; as dying and behold we live; as punished and yet not killed; as sorrowful, yet always rejoicing; as poor, yet making many rich; as having nothing, yet possessing everything." — 2 CORINTHIANS 6:4-10

Sons and daughters will, of course, thrive within professions, within the arts, within business. But they thrive and succeed, *in spite* of the world's systems, not because of them. They succeed because of their sonship to the Father, their Christlikeness, and their following of the Spirit.

"If I had not come and spoken to them, they would not have been guilty of sin, but now they have no excuse for their sin. Whoever hates me hates my Father also. If I had not done among them the works that no one else did, they would not be guilty of sin, but now they have seen and hated both me and my Father. But the word that is written in their Law must be fulfilled: 'They hated me without a cause.'" — JOHN 15:22-25

The world system is guilty of sin. It is guilty of sin *because it lives by* the Tree of the Knowledge of Good and Evil. The world is guilty of sin because it has rejected the true revelation of God the Father. This is not a contradiction of John 3:16 that says God loves the world. This statement here is an indictment of the system that remains in the ways of disobedience and independence from the Father.

There is no excuse for that sin because the Father's love has been manifested right in front of them. Their response to the manifestation of the Father is to put a price on the head of the Son of the Father's love. The Father sent His Son into the world and the world crucified Him. When the Absolute Incarnation of Pure Love is rejected nothing is left but a self-imposed judgement. The world hates sonship because it feels, thinks and decides within the principle of right and wrong. Sonship in the Tree of Life cannot measure up to the standards of good in the other Tree so it is feared, then hated.

"They have hated me without a cause" is a quotation from Psalm 35:19 and Psalm 69:4. Their hatred of Jesus has no direct cause; there is no logical reason for it. It is because of orphanness and because Satan has hated the Son from the very beginning. In John 8:44, Jesus says, "You are of your father the devil, and your will is to do your father's desires. He was a murderer from the beginning and has nothing to do with the truth, because there is no truth in him." The real cause of the world's hatred of sonship is located in the origin of Satan becoming the ultimate orphan.

Jesus is fully confident now that His work is well-nigh accomplished. The world has now seen the Father. The world has seen the full manifestation of the Father and the Son and it has *hated* the Father and the Son. In order to save the world which He loves, God must call people out of the world that hates Him. The Father loves the people of the world, and He loves His creation but the institution that is built upon orphanness always hates Him and His children.

THE COMFORTER IS THE ANSWER
TO THE ACCUSER

"But when the Helper comes, whom I will send to you from the Father, the Spirit of truth, who proceeds from the Father, he will bear witness about me. And you also will bear witness, because you have been with me from the beginning.
— JOHN 15:26,27

The answer to everything that the world throws at us is at hand. All the hatred, rejection, and persecution from the world will be met by the arrival of the Spirit from the Father. The solution to being outcast from the world system is beyond what we can imagine or begin to hope for. The answer is to be found in the new Comforter, the Helper, who will live *inside* us. Everything that we ever need is to be found in the Gift that is sent from the Father.

The Comforter comes to replace Jesus and continue His work of manifesting the Father. Jesus returns to heaven after death and He sends the Spirit who issues from His Father, to live eternally inside us. The Father Himself, in Spirit, comes to abide in the core of our beings. The Spirit of Truth "proceeds from the Father." (v.26). This is an ever-present reality. There is never a time or situation when the Sprit is withdrawn or shrinks back into the Father. The Spirit gushes forth the Father's personality. The Father's mind, will and emotions are expressed in the Spirit who emerges from Him. The Spirit of truth that gushes from the Father's heart declares who He really is by crying out, "Abba! Father!" (Galatians 4:6).

In addition to all this, the Parakletos is the ever-victorious opponent of the Accuser. The Spirit comforts us at the core of our being. The death of Jesus, thought of as a victory for Satan, only served to internalise comfort and love without condemnation. With the Spirit of the Father continually pouring out comfort-love within our hearts, the Accuser is silenced. With Paul we can then cry out, "There is therefore now no condemnation to those who are in Christ Jesus." (Romans 8:1) The Spirit of life sets us free from the principle of sin and death by removing accusation from our hearts.

The Spirit of Truth also bears witness about Jesus, the Son of God. When the Parakletos comes, He brings knowledge which is irreversible. The Spirit of Truth brings revelation and opens the eyes that have been closed. The opened eyes of the heart can now perceive what was imperceptible. What we now see cannot be unseen.

As the Spirit witnesses within us, the spontaneous outflow is that *we* bear witness. What is inside must ultimately overflow and be seen on the outside. The witness of the Spirit about the Father and the Son bubbles up as living water.

Jesus says to the disciples, *"You will bear witness, because you have been with me from the beginning."* (v.27) The disciples may well have taken this at face value, assuming that Jesus was talking about the beginning of His ministry, some three years earlier. There is a deeper meaning, however, which they will realise when the Spirit comes. They will realise that they have been with Jesus, the Son, from the beginning of *everything*.

When the Spirit comes to them and cries out within them, "Abba! Father!", the realisation will come that they have been chosen in Christ before the world existed. Here is what they will say:

> "...the Father of lights with whom there is no variation or shadow due to change. Of His own will he brought us forth by the word of truth that we should be a kind of first fruits of his creatures." — JAMES 1:17,18

> "...so that...you may become partakers of the divine nature." — 2 PETER 1:4

> "In this is love, not that we loved God, but that He loved us and sent His Son...: — 1 JOHN 4:10

Then Paul, not from the original Twelve but appointed by the resurrected Christ, writes:

> "Blessed be the God and Father of our Lord Jesus Christ, who has blessed us in Christ with every spiritual blessing in the heavenly places, even as he chose us in him before the foundation of the world that we should be holy and blameless before him in love." — EPHESIANS 1:3,4

As they listen to Jesus, reeling from the revelation that pours from Him, comforted with a peace that surpasses all understanding, He continues to speak the words of life...

THE FATHER HIMSELF LOVES YOU

~

THE MAELSTROM OF TRANSITION

The coming storm will be very severe for the disciples. They will be propelled through a colossal transition, from sight to faith, from the physical to the spiritual. They will lose the physical presence of Jesus but they will gain so much more for they will gain not only the spiritual presence of Jesus but His Father too. Jesus and the Father will come and live within them in the person of the Holy Spirit.

At this point they have no idea what this will be like so they are apprehensive and fearful. There is a very real chance, if fear gets hold of them, that they will not be able to endure the greatest disruption and turbulence of their lives.

This is the way of spiritual transition. To leave the present reality and go to a future, greater reality always involves pushing through the 'unknown.' The most stressful thing that our human hearts cope with is, without doubt, the uncertainty of the unknown.

These words that Jesus speaks after the departure of Judas are the only anchor they have to hold onto as they enter the maelstrom of transition.

PERSECUTED BY THE SERVANT-HEARTED

"I have said all these things to you to keep you from falling away. They will put you out of the synagogues. Indeed, the hour is coming when whoever kills you will think he is offering service to God. And they will do these things because they have not known the Father, nor me. But I have said these things to you, that when their hour comes you may remember that I told them to you." — JOHN 16:1-4

One thing is guaranteed; they will experience persecution. Sonship is always persecuted by the orphan-hearted. Persecution can be anything from mild to severe. It can involve actions such as censorship, sidelining, disempowering, and a lot more besides. Ultimately, persecution involves actual murder.

This persecution will inevitably be religious, carried out in the 'name' of God. Those who persecute and kill will believe they are doing so as a service to God. Religiously motivated sacrifice offers human life *to* God. In contrast, the sacrifice of sonship offers the life of God to others. The orphan-hearted person believes in a God who requires the killing of self and others in order to be appeased. To serve God by killing another is to believe in a God other than the One whom Jesus reveals.

They will kill as an act of service to God because they do not know the Father. The Father's way of serving is the laying down of one's life for one's friends. The chasm of difference between religion and the Gospel is this: Religion takes a life to serve God, whereas God the Father lays down His life to serve His children.

"That when their hour comes..." While orphanness remains, sons and daughters will invariably suffer some form of persecution. We will not escape the coming of the 'hour.' The orphan system will, without exception, pit itself against sonship. Whether by marginalisation or murder, or something in between, authentic sonship will be chased down by those whose motivation is to render service to God.

THE SPIRIT OF TRUTH

I did not say these things to you from the beginning, because I was with you. But now I am going to him who sent me, and none of you asks me, 'Where are you going?' But because I have said these things to you, sorrow has filled your heart.

Nevertheless, I tell you the truth: it is to your advantage that I go away, for if I do not go away, the Helper will not come to you. But if I go, I will send him to you. And when he comes, he will convict the world concerning sin and righteousness and judgment: concerning sin, because they do not believe in me; concerning righteousness, because I go to the Father, and you will see me no longer; concerning judgment, because the ruler of this world is judged.

"I still have many things to say to you, but you cannot bear them now. When the Spirit of truth comes, he will guide you into all the truth, for he will not speak on his own authority, but whatever he hears he will speak, and he will declare to you the things that are to come. He will glorify me, for he will take what is mine and declare it to you. All that the Father has is mine; therefore I said that he will take what is mine and declare it to you." — JOHN 16:4-15

Transition always involves temporary disorientation. This will be the experience of the disciples. In transition, we can easily lose sight of what the Lord is doing. We cannot see the future and do not know what lies on the other side of transition. The dominant emotions at the beginning of transition are anxiety and grief. Like the disciples, we forget to ask the Lord what *He* is doing. The disciples are so absorbed (understandably) in the apparent collapse of all that is familiar that they do not think to ask Jesus where He is going. The truth is, Jesus is returning to the Father, and from that place He will dispense the new era.

"Nevertheless, I tell you the truth: it is to your advantage that I go away, for if I do not go away, the Helper will not come to you. But if I go, I will send him to you." — JOHN 16:7

The disciples in their turmoil find it almost impossible to believe that the return of Jesus to the Father will actually make things better. They have no idea of the superiority of the life that awaits them on the other side. There are times when the mainstays of our spiritual life, our spiritual fathers and mothers, go away. The time comes when the people that we look to for security can no longer provide that security but they themselves would tell us that this is to our advantage.

When our 'parents' in the Christian life can no longer be our North Star, we have to look within ourselves. When there is no one left externally to look to, we are driven to look within our hearts. The wonderful reality is that the Spirit of the Father and the Son is already within us waiting to be discovered.

Our spiritual life is rejuvenated when we are left alone without external props to lift us up and keep us secure. While we grieve the loss of the external structures, something new is born within our hearts. What is newly growing within the heart is infinitely more powerful to the things that we have clung to.

Jesus *will* leave them, and they *will* be afraid and grieve. But He will come to them again in resurrection, and then by the Spirit who will bring His and the Father's presence permanently inside them.

> *"And when he comes, he will convict the world concerning sin and righteousness and judgment: concerning sin, because they do not believe in me; concerning righteousness, because I go to the Father, and you will see me no longer; concerning judgment, because the ruler of this world is judged."* — JOHN 16:8-11

The arrival of the Holy Spirit will convict the world in a three-pronged thrust; of sin, of righteousness, and of judgement. These three convictions will highlight the orphan condition of the world, showing it for what it really is. The presence of the Comforter (the

Helper) will clearly accentuate the difference between the world system that hates God and the created world which God loves.

This three-pronged attack of conviction is nothing other than a display of divine love. It is through the Holy Spirit's ministry of love that the world is convicted. Love is the only thing that really convicts of sin; it is only the manifestation of divine love that highlights how much we have missed the mark. Jesus tells the disciples that the Holy Spirit will convict the world about three things:

Firstly, He will convict the world about sin. The sin of the world is to reject the Son who came to reveal the Father. To reject the Son is to reject the Father and remain in orphaned self-reliance. The world system chooses to believe in no God or to believe in a distant and vengeful God rather than a loving and compassionate Father. Once the belief is established that God is our loving Source, the world system cannot survive.

Then, the Holy Spirit will convict the world about righteousness. Biblical righteousness is wholeness of relationship rather than moral excellence. Biblical righteousness is to live in harmony with God, with self, with others, and with creation. The basis of righteous is found in the love between the Father and the Son. The centre of the universe is a relationship of love without conditions. In contrast, the world system is built on the disruption of harmonious relationship. True relationship with God can only flourish when God Himself inhabits the human heart. When we relate to God at a distance, or to a God who only exists outside of ourselves, we are in caught in the estrangement of religion.

Finally, the Spirit will convict the world about judgement. The presence of the Comforter inside us brings an indictment to the ruler of the world. The more deeply we are comforted by the Abba-crying Spirit in our hearts, the less orphan ways have a grip on us. Comfort on the inside closes up the void that the world attempts to fill. The world cannot fill the vacuum of comfort at the core of the human heart. That is why the presence of the Comforter is the only antidote to the world. The Comforter judges the ruler of the world. By His very presence, the Comforter overcomes the "prince of the power of the air…at work in the sons of disobedience." (Ephesians 2:2)

> *"I still have many things to say to you, but you cannot bear them now. When the Spirit of truth comes, he will guide you into all the truth, for he will not speak on his own authority, but whatever he hears he will speak, and he will declare to you the things that are to come. He will glorify me, for he will take what is mine and declare it to you. All that the Father has is mine; therefore I said that he will take what is mine and declare it to you."* — JOHN 16:12-15

Jesus cannot tell the disciples everything because the Holy Spirit is not yet in them so that they can receive what Jesus has to say. When revelation comes it not only needs to come by the Holy Spirit, it also needs to be *received* by the Holy Spirit. The human person without the Spirit does not have the capacity to receive the revelation of the mysteries of God. Our spirits need to be supernaturally equipped to receive the generous gift from God.

Paul wrote to the church in Corinth:

"What no eye has seen, nor ear heard, nor the heart of man imagined, what God has prepared for those who love Him."
— 1 CORINTHIANS 2:9

The problem is that we latch on to these words and neglect to read the next line, which says:

"...these things God has revealed to us through the Spirit. For the Spirit searches everything, even the depths of God"
— 1 CORINTHIANS 2:10

The promise of the departing Jesus is that the Spirit of truth will *reveal* what cannot possibly be imagined. He will guide us into *all* truth. The promise to be led into *all* truth is staggering. Imagine for a moment what it would be like to be led into *complete* truth. What does this mean? It is to have full knowledge of *everything*. Mind-boggling, isn't it?

Paul, the apostle, discovered how to come into *all* the truth. He could foresee the way ahead of him into the fulness of knowledge:

"Now I know in part; then I shall know fully, even as I have been fully known." — 1 CORINTHIANS 13:12

We are guided into *all* truth as the love of God is increasingly poured out within our hearts. Truth is not the opposite of love, it is a *product* of love. It is only love which sees the truth and which can apprehend the truth; it is only the love of God which sees everything as it truly is. Fulness of love brings fulness of understanding. As the love of God is poured out within the heart it will bring an ever-brightening dawn of revelation.

We need to realise that coming into all truth is not to be seen as an individual experience. It is a shared experience; an experience of being united *together* in Christ. It is not really possible to know the fulness of all truth outside of our connection with the Body of Christ. Paul speaks of this when he asserts:

> *"For who has understood the mind of the Lord so as to instruct him? But we have the mind of Christ."*
> — 1 CORINTHIANS 2:16

In other words, it is not possible for any single individual to know the full mind of the Lord. But the mind of the Lord, known as 'all truth,' is to be found within the community of the Body of Christ. The Spirit is contained in His fulness, not in a single individual but in the fellowship of many unique individuals within the Body of Christ.

The Spirit only speaks what He hears. He listens to the conversation between the Father and the Son, and conveys that to us through our spirits. The Spirit has the authority of the Father and the Son because He is sent by them. The foremost and foundational work of the Spirit is to pour the love of God out within our hearts. Then His words and revelations land upon that fertile ground. This is the only way we can receive truth; it must be received within an environment of the outpoured love of the Father or else it will be distorted. The Spirit takes the substance of a loving Father-Son relationship and communicates it to us.

"...he will not speak on his own authority, but whatever
he hears he will speak, and he will declare to you the things
that are to come." — JOHN 16:13

The speech of the Holy Spirit comes directly from the Father and
the Son. He speaks with their authority. If you really desire to hear
the conversation that is going on in heaven, look inwards into your
own heart. The speech of heaven is heard within our hearts. The
heart is the organ by which we perceive the realm of heaven. To
access the mysteries of heaven, don't look upwards to the sky; look
inward to the depths of your heart. Inside the human heart lives
the One who hears and who speaks what He hears. The portal to
heaven is in the core of my being and your being.

The Spirit of truth will declare *the things that are to come.* This does
not mean that He gives us an understanding of eschatology. Rather,
it means that the Spirit declares the things that Jesus wanted to say
but they couldn't bear them. The time will come for the disciples
when the Spirit of truth will reveal to them what Jesus had to hold
back from telling them.

He will glorify me, for he will take what is mine and
declare it to you. All that the Father has is mine; therefore
I said that he will take what is mine and declare it to you."
— JOHN 16:14,15

The Holy Spirit will manifest the full personality of Jesus. He
will manifest the sonship of Jesus inside us. He manifests sonship
individually and corporately, within the body of believers. The next
line sums up the experience of full sonship - *All that the Father has*

is mine. The Son is the legitimate possessor of all that the Father has. Self-confident and mature sons and daughters know that the full inheritance belongs to them.

The full meaning of Jesus' words here needs revelation in order to be understood. The Holy Spirit "will take what is mine and declare it." What belongs to Jesus is nothing less than "all that the Father has." The Son possesses *everything* that is in the Father.

A LITTLE WHILE

> *"A little while, and you will see me no longer; and again a little while, and you will see me." So some of his disciples said to one another, "What is this that he says to us, 'A little while, and you will not see me, and again a little while, and you will see me'; and, 'because I am going to the Father'?" So they were saying, "What does he mean by 'a little while'? We do not know what he is talking about." Jesus knew that they wanted to ask him, so he said to them, "Is this what you are asking yourselves, what I meant by saying, 'A little while and you will not see me, and again a little while and you will see me'?"* — JOHN 16:16-19

The return of Jesus to the Father is imminent. Soon He will disappear from the world's view, buried in a tomb. After hanging naked and helpless on a cross, He will diminish and fade from sight. That is the view of Jesus the world system has been left with. We know, of course, that that is not the whole story. However, from the perspective of orphan values Jesus is seen as a failure and something to be laughed at. That perception of Jesus is fixed; it can never change.

If Jesus the Son is perceived through the paradigm of excellence, of success in terms of ministry, His life on earth has been futile. The world rejoices because Jesus appears to have been neutralised.

Paul writes to the community in Corinth that Christ "...*was crucified in weakness, but lives by the power of God.*" (2 Corinthians 13:4). This is the paradox of the life of sonship. Looking through the eyes of the world Christ has indeed been crucified in weakness. His pain-wracked body has been removed from sight. The world can continue in orphan ways. But the mega-shift has already happened because the Crucified One is living in the power of God in another dimension called resurrection life. To the eyes of the heart, which see a perspective on the other side of Jesus' death on the cross, Jesus lives in an entirely different dimension, of the power of God in resurrection.

> *"Truly, truly, I say to you, you will weep and lament, but the world will rejoice. You will be sorrowful, but your sorrow will turn into joy. When a woman is giving birth, she has sorrow because her hour has come, but when she has delivered the baby, she no longer remembers the anguish, for joy that a human being has been born into the world. So also you have sorrow now, but I will see you again, and your hearts will rejoice, and no one will take your joy from you."* — JOHN 16:20-22

Jesus evokes the image of a woman giving birth. No human event brings so much stress and pain followed by relief and joy as a mother giving birth. The strain of the birth itself may last for hours but it is forgotten when the baby comes. Jesus uses this metaphor of a woman giving birth to reassure the disciples about His death. The disciples are now caught in the pain and the stress of the impending birth. They are focused on the contractions. From their perspective, they have no idea that new life will be born safely and what the 'baby' will look like. They have no choice but to allow the 'baby' to transition through the birth canal. Being with Jesus has been exciting and confirming, but the time has now come to hover between life and death, and to enter death itself. The 'baby' will be born on the other side of the death experience, in resurrection life.

Losing control and being rejected by the world can often cause considerable grief and anguish. But these feelings turn to joy when we feel the pulsations of the power of God within us. Crucifixion opens up a new life source that is available to us. This newly discovered source is resurrection life! If we could only realise that much of our stress and anxiety in life are the symptoms of impending birth, we would have more hope. When times of stress arrive and intensify they are contractions which lead to the emergence of a new life in the Father's love.

THE FATHER *HIMSELF* LOVES YOU

"In that day you will ask nothing of me. Truly, truly, I say to you, whatever you ask of the Father in my name, he will give it to you. Until now you have asked nothing in my name. Ask, and you will receive, that your joy may be full. I have said these things to you in figures of speech. The hour is coming when I will no longer speak to you in figures of speech but will tell you plainly about the Father. In that day you will ask in my name, and I do not say to you that

I will ask the Father on your behalf; for the Father himself
loves you, because you have loved me and have believed that
I came from God. I came from the Father and have come
into the world, and now I am leaving the world and going
to the Father. — JOHN 16:23-28

When Jesus speaks these words to His disciples, He is uttering some of the most important statements He will ever make. He tells them that the day is soon coming when He will hand them over to have their own relationship with the Father. When the Spirit of sonship comes to live inside them, they will have untrammelled access to the Father. They will not need to access the Father through the Mediator, in the sense of connecting with Jesus who will then ask the Father on their behalf. The power of this declaration changes how we understand the mediation of Jesus.

Many Christians remain in the position of asking everything from Jesus, expecting Him to plead on their behalf before a reluctant Father. That is not how it is meant to be. Jesus actively and intentionally moves us away from that belief. "No!" He says, "I will no longer ask on your behalf. You can now ask the Father directly." That day was imminent for the disciples, but it is immediate for us. We are now living in the time of direct and unimpeded access to the Father. We are fully 'in Christ' and we are the Father's *own* sons and daughters.

The 'name of Jesus' is not a mantra or a formula that moves the Father to answer prayer. Praying and asking in the name of Jesus is to see ourselves as being united with Him. Being 'in the name of Jesus' is to identify ourselves as being in the Son; we know full well that the Son receives from the Father all that He asks. Therefore, to pray from a place of full identity with Jesus is to be confident of being heard by the Father. Asking from within the identity of Jesus carries an ironclad guarantee of being answered. Jesus promises that we will ask and *we will receive.*

For much of my life, I asked but I could not say that I always received. Receiving is a privilege only granted in sonship. In servanthood we can ask but there is no guarantee of receiving. The Old Covenant is a covenant of asking, seeking and knocking; but New Covenant is a covenant of being answered, of receiving, and of the door being flung wide open. While I was locked in Old Covenant mentality my joy was only partial. Joy becomes full when we receive what we ask for. Sonship is intended to be like this.

Jesus also anticipates a time when He will no longer talk about the Father in figures of speech. This day will be the day when the Spirit of truth resides inside the human heart. We are now living in the day of clear and plain speaking about who the Father is. Regrettably, it has taken the Church many centuries to catch on to this reality. Figures of speech are only necessary when the eyes of the heart are dim. Jesus explained:

> *"This is why I speak to them in parables, because seeing they do not see; and hearing they do not hear, nor do they understand."* — MATTHEW 13:13

Then comes the all-important statement, the culmination of everything that Jesus has spoken and manifested in His life on earth to this point:

"...for the Father himself loves you..." — JOHN 16:27

The Son declares unequivocally that we are loved personally by the Father *Himself.* We are loved with *phileo* love, which is the warm affection of family relationship.

This warm, familial affection of the Father can be experienced because "...you have loved me and have believed that I came from God." This is not to say that the Father's love is conditional. It does, however, mean that the *experiencing* of it is conditional. When we come to love the Son with affectionate love (*phileo*) and know by revelation that He is sent from the Father, we experience what it is to be reconciled with the Father. Jesus's work, as Mediator, is to draw us into loving Him. Then He shows us that He is the Firstborn of the Father's family. As our eyes are opened to see the Son living downstream from the Father's love, we begin to experience the continuous flow of the Father's fondness for us. Feeling the warmth of the Father's affection gives us a burgeoning confidence to ask and receive from Him.

In order for the disciples to experience all this, Jesus must return to the Father. His return to the Father will bring them, through the Spirit, fully into union with His sonship.

> *His disciples said, "Ah, now you are speaking plainly and not using figurative speech! Now we know that you know all things and do not need anyone to question you; this is why we believe that you came from God."* — JOHN 16:29,30

The disciples respond with enthusiasm. They are swept up in the power and attractiveness of Jesus' words. Their emotions are stirred and their souls are animated. They do not realise that a foreboding Rubicon (a point of no return) must be crossed to really experience what Jesus is talking about. Jesus is fully cognisant that His disciples will be scattered and abandon Him. What lies ahead of Him, He must face alone. He advances towards the future, comforted only by the knowledge that His Father is with Him.

I HAVE OVERCOME THE WORLD

Jesus answered them, "Do you now believe? Behold, the hour is coming, indeed it has come, when you will be scattered, each to his own home, and will leave me alone. Yet I am not alone, for the Father is with me. I have said these things to you, that in me you may have peace. In the world you will have tribulation. But take heart; I have overcome the world." — John 16:31-33

Jesus knows too well that tribulation will inevitably come. While we are in the world we cannot escape it. Despite a lot of popular ideas about what it means to live in sonship, we must come to terms with the fact that it always involves facing tribulation. Being like Jesus means co-suffering with Him. This suffering and tribulation comes from being in the world but not of it. Persecution comes because, like Jesus, we originate from outside the world. The Orphan Spirit will always be intimidated by the sons of God and will try to stamp out sonship. Suffering also comes internally because we suffer with the Father about the orphaned state of His creation.

This tribulation is not intended to make us lose heart, however. Tribulation is not defeat; it is a sign of victory. The Son has overcome the world by living in the Father's love. Tribulation comes to try and dislodge us from our place in the Father's love; remaining in His love is to triumph over the world. Jesus has overcome the world by remaining always in the Father's love. Overcoming, then, is not by means of superior force or by the eradication of difficulty; it is by experiencing greater depths of love in the midst of trouble.

Is overcoming the world a goal for us to attain to in our sonship? Yes and no! It is not for us to attain outside of the fact that Jesus has already overcome the world. We do not need to overcome the world as much as to enter into Jesus' overcoming of the world. Every anxiety we feel, every pressure to fend for ourselves without looking to the Father, is evidence that we are not living in Jesus' victory over the world. What would it be like to be unaffected by 'the world?' What would it be like to resist the pressure of thinking, acting and living like orphans? Take heart, Jesus has already done it! He lives in the state of having overcome the orphan system, and we are invited to rest in Him.

CHAPTER SEVENTEEN

"YOU IN ME, AND I IN THEM"

∾

THE RECIPROCAL LOVE OF SONSHIP

I believe that John 17 may well be the most significant part of the biblical canon. It could be said to contain the purest revelation in the sacred text. The whole Bible is divinely inspired and profitable for teaching and instruction, yet there are different qualities of revelation contained in it. Here in John 17, we have one side of a dialogue within the Godhead itself. Jesus, the Son, talks to His Father. The relational flow within the Trinity is a family relationship. In this chapter, we stand listening to the inter-Trinitarian conversation. Here we stand in the heavenly room, hushed as divine light shifts and whirls in an interplay of revelation. Here we have the filial dialogue at the heart of the universe, the Son conversing with His Father. The Son, downstream from His Source, turns towards that Source and drinks. We overhear the Son, fully living in the Father's love, as He reciprocates that love back to His Father.

"He lifted up his eyes" (v.1) He averts His eyes from inward subjectivity and from the world to fix them on the heavenly reality of His connection with the Father.

"Father, the hour has come" (v.1) So much is contained in the word 'Father.' In breathing that word 'Father' as a first expulsion of His breath, He is receiving love, aligned with love, secure in love, and resting in love. This is the default stance of sonship.

"Glorify Your Son that the Son may glorify You" (v.2) Jesus knows how the life of sonship works. You *cannot* glorify the Father unless He *first* glorifies *you.* The deception of religion is that we think that we need to glorify God before He glorifies us. But here, Jesus shows that the source of glory is in the Father, and that the initiative in glorification comes from the Father. The Son (and sons and daughters) is glorified first by the Father, and reciprocates to glorify the Father.

To 'glorify' means to fully express, to fully display who a person is. A son cannot express fully who the Father is until the Father creates a capacity to do so. Only the Father's love can glorify a person, can bring out the full expression of who they really are. That full expression of a person loved by the Father will, in turn, show who the Father really is.

"…since You have given him authority over all flesh, to give eternal life to all whom you have given him." (v.2) The glorification of the Son (and, therefore, the Father) is to be in the arena of 'all flesh.' The Son sees with absolute clarity why He has come from the Father. He has come to bring eternal life from the heavenly dimension down to earth and to the whole creation. I believe that 'all flesh' includes

all material existence. The whole creation is waiting for sonship to be manifested, on earth and beyond the earth. I am suggesting that 'all flesh' is also a cosmic statement because the glory of the Father expressed in sons (both men and women) will ultimately fill all creation. And creation is still expanding. Sons cannot be glorified independently from the glory of the Father. The glory of the Father comes to all flesh through the Son.

"…to give eternal life…" (v.2) The Father has delegated to the Son the task of imparting, breathing, gifting, and generating the substance of the life that sustains the Trinity. This is the primordial life, the life from the beginning, the fountainhead of all existence.

"And this is the eternal life, that they know You, the only true God…" (v.3) The 'only true God' is *Father*. Every other description of God falls short of the true revelation. The Old Testament contains 'shadow revelation' but the task of the Son is to reveal 'the only true God' who is essentially Father. He has been Father from the beginning, before the foundation of all creation, and the Son has come to earth to declare what His nature really is—His nature is that He is Father. His substance is light and love. Not knowing God as 'Father' means that we do not know "the only true God." That does not make us atheists, pagans or heretics but it does mean that we are in the shadows still waiting for the light of revelation. We all await the increase of the knowledge of His parenthood but it *is* coming. The advance of the Father's love to all creation is inexorable. It cannot be halted in its tracks.

The absolute accurate and full revelation is given by the Son, by *"Jesus Christ, whom You have sent" (v.3)* It needs a Son to fully and unequivocally declare who 'the only true God' is. In His essential nature as Fountainhead of Love, He is Origin, He is Source, He is Progenitor. He is Father.

THE FIRST GLORY OF THE SON

"I glorified You on earth" (v.4) I, Your Son, your Beloved, have fully displayed and expressed Your entire personality on the earth. Glory is the shining forth of who a person is. The Son, throughout His life here on earth, has fully displayed the personality of the Father. Sonship's area of operation is to glorify *on the earth*. The Father is in heaven but is expressed through the Son (and through sonship) *on the earth*. He has declared Himself 'in son' (Hebrews 1:1)[32]. He has manifested 'son-wise'[33]. He has communicated using His 'mother-tongue' of 'Son.'

"And now, Father, glorify me, in Your own presence with the glory that I had with You before the world existed" (v.5) This glory is the first of three different 'glories' of the Son in this prayer. This is a glory before the world existed; it is a pre-incarnate glory. This is a glory before any downward movement into the human condition. This is the glory of the enclosed Father-Son-Spirit relationship. We do not yet know fully what it is. It is the Word, the Logos, the

---

32. The literal translation of Hebrews 1:2 does not include the words 'in the person of the" or "by the" Son, but rather says "...in these last days, He has spoken to us...in Son"

33. A. W. Pink has coined this term to explain God's mode of communication. He explains the use of Son here this way: "Were a friend to tell you that he had visited a certain church, and that the preacher 'spoke in Latin,' you would have no difficulty in understanding what he meant: 'Spoke *in* Latin' would intimate that that particular language marked his utterance. Such is the thought here. 'In Son' has reference to that which *characterised* God's revelation. The thought of the contrast is that God, who of old had spoken *prophetwise*, now speaks *sonwise*." from A. W. Pink, *An Exposition of Hebrews* [electronic ed.] Ephesians Four Group: Escondido, CA, p. 27.

inner core of loving and being loved. To be restored to *that* glory is to be restored to the first principle of all existence. For Jesus, it is the ultimate homecoming, an intimacy that exists between Him and the Father.

"I have manifested Your name to those whom You gave me out of the world. Yours they were and You gave them to me. (v.6) The Father is Source. He is the Original Parent. He gave those people to the Son, *because they previously belonged to Him.* They were originally the Father's possession but He gave them to the Son that the Son may reveal to them who they originally came from.

"Yours they were" (v.6) Jesus is referring specifically to the disciples here but *we too* have been given to Jesus out of the world. *We* previously belonged to God the Father. The Father has given us as a gift to the Son in order that the Son might bring us back to the Father, by breaking the orphan deception and showing us that we *always belonged* to the Father. Since the Fall (Satan's deception of humanity in the Garden), we have lost the reality that "Yours they were." When were they 'Yours?' They were 'Yours' before Creation, before the entrance of the Orphan Spirit, before the Son came into human flesh. You, beloved, were *His;* you came from Him, you belonged to Him, you were owned by Him, *before* He gave you to Jesus. The Father previously gave you to Jesus and Jesus leads you to back to the Father.

"...and they have kept Your word. Now they know that everything that You have given me is from You." (v.7) Jesus exposes the Source here. He takes us to the headwaters of eternal life and of divine existence. The Father gave everything to Jesus and the responsibility

of Jesus is to reveal the Giver of the gift. The work of Jesus on earth has been to reveal that *all is gift*, that everything is a grace-gift from the Giver. All this abundant giving is from the One who originally conceived us.

"For I have given them the words that You gave me…" (v.8) In chapter 12:49 of this same Gospel, Jesus asserted, *"For I did not speak of my own accord, but the Father who sent me commanded me what to say and how to say it."* (NIV) The Father's words are spoken 'in Son' through the mouthpiece of Jesus on earth. Jesus does not repeat these words mechanically; the Father's words are fully alive in the Son because His heart is aligned with the Father's heart.

"…and they have received them…" Many words had been given from heaven before, and many had heard the words from the Father that Jesus has spoken. However, it was those *who received them* to whom the doorway into sonship stood opened. The truth is, sonship is available to every person but the revelation of it must be received. The heart must open in humility to accept our personal need, our deep-seated orphanness and our need for parenting. John 1:11, 12 clearly lays out that the Father, in Jesus, came to His own but His own *"did not receive him. But to all who did receive him, who believed in his name, he gave the right to become children of God."* Receiving the Son and receiving the words of the Father that He speaks, brings the realisation that we are born of God (John 1:13)

"…and have come to know in truth that I came from You; and they have believed that you sent me." (v.8) The disciples came to understand the truth that the Son has not come of His own initiative, of His own accord, or of His own volition. They did not know

that 'everything is gift' from the Loving Giver, but *now they know*. Jesus has accomplished His mission by revealing that nothing is earned and that everything is given. To 'know in truth' is not the knowledge of information; it is the relational knowledge that comes by revelation and experience. Believing that Jesus is 'sent' is the opening of our understanding to knowing the Father. To know that Jesus is 'sent' is to know that He is the mediator, and that He has come *from the Father*.

PRAYING THE SOLUTION

"I am praying for them. I am not praying for the world, but for those whom You have given me, for they are Yours." (v.9) Jesus is focused in His request to the Father. He has drawn specific boundaries around what He is asking for. He is praying for something, and He is *not* praying for something. Faith is specific and it is measurable. Jesus has faith because He is asking the Father to protect what is already the possession of the Father's—"they are *Yours*." When you ask the Father to protect *His own* possession, and advance *His own* vested interests, the answer is guaranteed.

To intercede for the sons of the Father is to guarantee an answer for the problems in the world. Jesus is not praying for the world. He is praying, rather, for the revelation of sonship to be deeply embedded in the people given to Him by the Father. The problems that exist in humanity cannot be fixed within the orphan system that created them. The world's problem cannot be cured apart from sons of the Father incarnated in the created sphere. Jesus is effectively saying, "I am not praying for the world's problem, I am praying for those who are the answer to the problem."

The energy of prayer goes into the solution, not the problem. The energy and dynamism of prayer works in the positive, not the negative. Do not pray against the negative, pray *in* the positive. Do not seek to diminish what is wrong, but pray for the growth of the positive solution. Do not address the problem, make way for the energy and vitality of the solution. Do not pray against the darkness, pray rather for the dawning of the light. Sin and evil are not substantial reality, they are the *absence* of substantial reality. Love fills every void.

"All mine are Yours, and Yours are mine, and I am glorified in them." (v.10) This is absolute filial alignment, this is the union of sonship. Sonship has gained nothing for itself alone, yet it gladly receives everything. Nothing belongs to the Son that does not belong to the Father. Yet nothing belongs to the Father that is not given freely to the Son. Love holds nothing to itself but gives everything; yet paradoxically it also receives everything. Freely given, freely received. There is generosity between Father and Son, an eternal rotation of gift-giving from one to the other. The swirling whirlpool of the loving relationship between the Father and the Son is complete in itself, yet, at the same time, love always expands beyond itself.

"...and I am glorified in them" The Son is fully expressed when human beings display the glory of sonship. What is the glory of sonship? It is to receive, and then reciprocate, the love of the Father.

"And I am no longer in the world, but they are in the world, and I am coming to You, Holy Father. Keep them in Your name, which You have given me." (v.11) This is what Jesus is activating now, the promise given to His disciples in John 14:16, "And I will ask the

Father, and He will give you another Comforter, to be with you for ever." Jesus, the incarnated and tangible manifestation of the Father's love is about to leave. The suspense of the pause—the pause between one Comforter leaving and another arriving—needs a special grace from the Father. An intensity of trust and hope is called for when one Comforter leaves and before the other Comforter arrives. When the Comforter, the Holy Spirit, arrives, the Incarnation can continue again.

The indwelling Spirit of the Father is to bring an endless upsurge of comfort from within. Jesus has manifested the comfort of the Father to His own by external action, by words, by touch, by the glance and gaze of His eyes. But comfort is now to be manifested *internally*, by a substance growing in the heart, in the spirit. The substance of God in the inner being rises up and fills the human soul.

"They are in the world, but I am coming to You." (v.11) Jesus' desire here is for the Comforter to come. "Father, keep them safe until the Comforter comes." We will see the tension and anguish of the absence of the Comforter when Jesus is led away to the cross. The disciples will enter into a dark night of trauma, fear and anxiety. They will be shaken, they will flee and hide. Peter will vehemently deny any knowledge of Jesus. This is what Jesus is asking for now, praying that they will be kept through the darkest hour which descends just before dawn breaks. Everything make sense at Pentecost. The Comforter and the Teacher will be internalised. He will comfort and instruct from within. When the Spirit falls at Pentecost, the love of God will be poured out in the deepest interior of the human heart. But, Father, keep them safe until then!

"Holy Father, keep them in Your name, which You have given me." (v.11) The security of identity, of heritage and inheritance, is in the name of Father. Your name, Father, is given to Me, your Son. We are of the same DNA, we have the same heritage, the same genesis, and we have the same inheritance. This holds a universe of meaning, a galaxy of significance. Jesus matured in His sonship (as a man) here on earth. He inherited the Father's business. The name above the cosmic shop, fully displayed to Satan, and to the principalities and powers is "Yahweh and Son." Yahweh is actually a Father and He has a Son! The One who was Lord of Hosts, Lord of Angel-Armies, Ancient of Days, is my Father and I do business in His name, for He has full confidence in Me. Jesus is declaring that He can go to principalities and powers, to the depths of Satan's dominion, with the name of Lord of Hosts, who sits between the Cherubim. He can neutralise the demands of the Accuser to exact judgement on the disciples.

THE RESTORATION OF ONENESS

"That they may be one, even as we are one." (v.11) This is a mystery which will be unfolded eternally. How are the Father and the Son one? What is the oneness of the Father and the Son? They are primarily one in substance. The Nicene Creed stated that Jesus was "consubstantial with the Father" making use of the Greek word *homoousios*. Jesus and the Father are made of the same 'stuff.'

Jesus asks that they "may be one, even as we are one." He is asking that we too might become *light* and *love*. Paul the apostle was in "the anguish of childbirth" that Christ might be formed within the Galatian believers (Galatians 4:19). The metaphysical reality of Christ is the same substance as the Father—love. Of course He is fully human, but the point here is that when the love of the Father comes into our human heart, then Christ is formed within us. It can be no other way. The whole point of Christianity is the divine indwelling of the human person. It follows then, that the substance of Christ grows in us as a result of receiving the substance of the Father's love.

> *"While I was with them, I kept them in Your name, which You have given me. I have guarded them, and not one of them has been lost, except the son of desolation, that the Scripture might be fulfilled."* — JOHN 17:12

One of the most important functions of ministry is to 'guard' and protect the work of God. Often we meddle, probe and push, trying to grow people by management and duress. But the Holy Spirit is the agent of growth. When He fills our hearts growth is automatic, and happens much more easily than we think. The main reason why growth doesn't happen for some, is that it is hindered by something that is undermining it or actively destroying it. Exposed to water and light, in the right soil conditions, a plant will inevitably grow. The enemy of our souls seeks constantly to steal away the growth, by discouragement and heavy burdens. Any child, under love and nourishment, will grow, but the child has to be guarded and protected, to preserve their burgeoning yet vulnerable life.

"…except the son of desolation." Clearly, Judas's decision to betray Jesus did not originate in himself. He was 'the son of.' In that regard, a certain amount of self-determination was taken away from him. He may well have rejected the revelation that God the Father was his true father, and so he defaulted to his human identity. Something in

his background and culture would have *fathered* him in the ways of destruction. Maybe it was the toxic rage of religious zeal, desperate for a solution to the problem of the Roman occupation. Maybe it was a deep-seated prejudice stretching back many generations.

If we live out of our natural heritage it will yield good things but also bad things. My own natural background is bent towards destruction, but I have found a deeper DNA in my sonship to the Father of Lights and the God of Love. Fatherhood always reproduces itself. The question is, what fatherhood is a more virile reproducer? If you enter into the sonship of Christ, you will discover that the fatherhood of God is extremely potent to produce fruits of love, joy and peace and much more. Every son is a product of his father, and so it plays out down through the generations. You will never be any more than the product of who your father is. But when you get a revelation and enjoy the relationship that comes from being the 'produce' of God the Father, then you will be a product of *Him*—and there is nothing greater than that!

"But now I am coming to You." (v.13) This phrase is repeated by Jesus in this prayer. It seems to me that Jesus is accessing emotional comfort and stability here. He is steadying His human soul, which is beginning to be in distress in anticipation of the cross. Jesus is focusing beyond the cross to His reunion with the Father, to a literal homecoming back to the Father's arms. He has never departed from the bosom of the Father, but, in His human soul, He is longing to be caught up experientially in His Abba's arms, beyond pain and suffering. The earth-mission is complete; He has declared the Father's name. Now He engages in the cosmic endgame, to finally undo the orphan deception.

Of course, Jesus enjoyed intimacy with His Father as a Son here upon the earth. But it was an intimacy learnt in human experience. Jesus had to learn, as we do, to live within the human condition, to embrace weakness and the need for help. According to Luke 2:52, "… Jesus increased in wisdom and in stature and in favour with God and man." He had never been rebellious, but He had to learn to align His humanity (mentally, emotionally, and physically) with the Father. For that reason it was not automatic. I am not talking about a sin issue here but the coming to maturity of a human person. Jesus is sinless, but He has also been tempted with every temptation that we face. He had to grow in faith and in the ability to do and express with bespoke finesse exactly what the Father wanted to express. This is what has developed and grown in His life. He has needed to learn, with suffering, *to align His humanity* to fully express and carry out the Father's will.

Jesus' life on earth was a life of faith. He had to learn to do what He saw the Father doing, not because He was reluctant, but because His human body and soul needed to synchronise with the core reality of His spirit. Even though the fulness of the Godhead dwelt in bodily form within Him (Colossians 1:19), the declaration of the Father's name and the manifestation of the Father's glory was on an increasing continuum as His life on earth progressed. James Jordan has opened the truth to us by revelation, that it wasn't until the eve of crucifixion that the Son was able to express the words that the Father longed to express, in the way that the Father longed to express them, in John 14:18: "*I will not leave you as orphans; I will come to you!*" He had to mature in the use of His human faculties in the same way that we do.

The whole of Jesus' life here on earth was a growing incarnation, and now He has completed that phase and says to His Father, "…I am coming to You." What a reunion! The reunion of the Son, now eternally human as well as divine, with His divine Father.

> "…and these things I speak in the world, that they may have my joy fulfilled in themselves." (v.13)

Jesus is not speaking that we might understand or even share in His joy. He does so in order that the *selfsame joy*, the very substance of the joy that Jesus has because of His sonship to the Father, may be realised in His disciples and in all of us from then on. This is far greater than mere concept; it is to become a substantial reality. This joy is a fruit of being loved by the Father. The fulfilment of the joy is for the seed of promise to fully mature and become real. If there is a seed of promise within you, *it is* growing. The seed of the love of the Father within you is constantly growing in the soil, and it will produce fruit.

FREEDOM FROM THE ORPHAN SYSTEM

> "I have given them Your word, and the world has hated them because they are not of the world, just as I am not of the world." — JOHN 17:14

The 'world' that Jesus is talking about here is the system that has emerged out of orphanness. The world is the manifestation of the Orphan Spirit. It is a spiritual, systemic entity that is the manifestation of all that is orphan. It is bigger than the sum of every individual and holds the peoples of the earth in its grip. The orphan system of the world is based on self-preservation, self-aggrandisement, and fear. It conducts itself on the basis of greed and self-promotion. What we can easily miss, however, is that the religious system is every bit as much 'the world' as the secular system. To be engaged in a religious system that is motivated by orphanness is no different to being engaged in a secular system. They are both equally facets of the same orphan heart.

The world system (religious and secular) hates the weakness, incompetence and utter dependence of sonship. The world system strives for independence, betterment and excellence, and hates the absolute need of sonship for a Father. The world hates because it fears. Fear is a more basic emotion than hatred. From the perspective of 'the world,' sonship appears to be so foolish and so provoking because sonship is dependent on the Father. The world system hates sonship, but *creation* loves sonship. Creation is waiting for sonship to appear (Romans 8:19). The world system is destroying creation, but sonship, as it comes forth, will liberate and renew creation.

"I do not ask that you take them out of the world, but that you keep them from the evil one." (v.15) Jesus is careful here with what He is asking. He does not ask for them to be taken out of the world because He knows that the heart of the Father is for incarnation. He knows that the heart of the Father is to reveal sonship within the world to overcome the orphan system. The Godhead has utter confidence in its own love, its own peace, its own joy, its own life. Jesus asks that they are kept from "the evil one." The constant tactic of the evil one is to lure us back into orphanness and separate us from our connection to the Father. He does this primary through deceiving us with condemnation and unworthiness, thus luring us

345

into destructive and addictive behaviour. The antidote to this is to keep resting in our sonship, comforted as little children, depending on the Father to keep us safe from harm.

"They are not of the world, just as I am not of the world." (v.16) Those whom Jesus prays for have the same origin as He has. They originate from heaven, from the Father's realm. According to Hebrews 2:11, "…He who sanctifies and those who are sanctified all have one origin." That statement is astounding, but the more that you grow in sonship, it is confirmed to you that your origin is in the Father. The more that you grow in sonship, the reality that you have come from another world, the Father's house, establishes itself in your innermost being. As this reality grows you are ready to be sent and manifested to creation.

"Sanctify them in the truth; Your word is truth." (v.17) Let me consider this term 'sanctify.' The issue of sanctification is not a moral issue. It is not even a character issue as we have come to understand it. It is the 'setting apart,' the 'becoming other than,' of a son and a daughter. To be sanctified means to be 'other than' the norm. To be sanctified means to be 'other than' the predictable motivations and reactions of the orphan. Jesus asks the Father to "set them apart." The Father, by His Spirit, is the agent of sanctification. Part of a father's role is to establish identity and to propel a son and daughter forward into purpose. Purpose and function always flows from identity. That is why it is the Father who sanctifies. He establishes identity, and then purpose and creativity flow from that unique identity.

"Your word is truth." The definition of 'truth' is not primarily about conceptual or doctrinal accuracy. The biblical definition of

the word 'truth' is 'reality.' The foundational reality of all existence is the expression (the 'word') of the Father. Anything less than what Father expresses is not full reality. True reality is the Father's love. The Father's love is vast enough to fill the whole universe and beyond. As the Father's love is expressed, you will find that it sets you apart (sanctifies you) in that reality. This is the answer to issues of sin and temptation: to be brought by the Father into the environment of *His* reality.

The expression of the Father, in Son (sons) and through Son (sons) is truth (reality). The Word cannot contradict the Son. They (Word and Son) are one and the same (John 1:1). If our reading of the Bible appears to contradict the revelation of who Jesus is, and who He revealed the Father to be, then something is not aligned. In that case, we need more revelation about what the Scriptures mean. The Bible can only be rightly understood through the paradigm of the Son, the Beloved of the Father. The two disciples on the road to Emmaus were met by the risen Son. In Luke 24: 27 it tells us that, "Beginning with Moses and all the Prophets, he interpreted to them in all the Scriptures the things concerning himself." Jesus, as the Son in resurrection, opened up to them that the entire canon of the Old Testament (the entirety of the Scriptures at that time) was shot through with the revelation of sonship. That may not be obvious to us when we read the Old Testament. It takes the resurrected Son to interpret the Scriptures the way they are meant to be interpreted. In other words, the interpretative key to the Scriptures is the Son Himself. The Word (Logos) is the Son, and the Son is the Word. The Word, who is the Son, *is* the expression of the Father. That is the foundational reality. That is what you and I are sanctified in.

LOVE THAT SENDS

"As You have sent me into the world, so I have sent them into the world." (v.18) The sending of the Father is extended, no more and no less, through the commissioning of the Son. The sending of sons and daughters into the world is on the same basis as the sending of the Son into the world: they are to reveal the Father. When Jesus sends someone, He does not do it independently of the Father. Being sent by the Son is to be sent by the Father. The Father is to be manifested from heaven in the lives of sons and daughters here on earth. The sending is from Father's bosom, from heaven into the earth. The movement is a downward movement so that the kingdom (the dominion of the Father's love) will come on earth as it is in heaven.

"And for their sake I consecrate myself that they also may be sanctified in truth." (v.19) Here is the Son, having finished His mission on earth, about to go to the Cross to engage the principalities and powers and effect the work of redemption, then to return to heaven, and He *consecrates* Himself. At first glance, we may think that He is consecrating Himself through His death on the cross. I believe this consecration, however, is a consecration to be the Great High Priest. He is dedicating Himself, before the Father, for his role of interceding for humanity, for you and me.

The work of being Great High Priest is one of the main job descriptions of the Son in resurrection. He does not intercede for us before the Father because the Father is against us and reluctant to bless us. Rather, the Son in the Father's presence, intercedes *from* the Father, and He intercedes *into* the human condition.

The Son has experienced something personally that the Father never experiences. The Father has never (and will never) know directly in His own person what it is like to live within the restrictions of the human condition. The Son entered the 'swaddling clothes' of a human body and soul. He consecrates Himself before the Father for us that we may be set apart to the reality of the Father's love. He consecrates Himself to engage in a priestly work on behalf of the human race, to enable the human race to come into sonship to the Father. The main aim of the Orphan Spirit and of religion is to disqualify our human weakness. Most of us believe that our own humanity disqualifies us from being acceptable to God. The Son proved the opposite to be true. The Son proved that the temple of God, the temple of which all previous temples were but a sign and symbol, is the human person. The priestly work of Jesus is to give us confidence that our humanity is the abiding place of Almighty God. The book of Hebrews (much of which has yet to be opened to us in revelation) is all about this.

The Son consecrates Himself to intercede on behalf of the human race, so that the cosmic principalities and powers (under Satan) will not abort our place of acceptance before the Father. The prince of the power of the air, the author of religion, did not know that God had an ace up his sleeve in the spiritual battle for humanity. This winning hand is the Incarnation. I use the term 'Incarnation' in its widest sense here, meaning the entering of Godhead into the human condition. The Incarnation began with the birth of Jesus, and continued through His life, death, burial and resurrection. The Incarnation continues still, in heaven, because a Man is at the Father's right hand. The Incarnation continues on earth, as the Father is manifested in many sons and daughters. By becoming human, God has trumped Satan in a master stroke. The astonishing reality that God indwells the weakness of the human condition is something that the prince of the power of the air cannot deal with. Satan is defeated by the indwelling of God in human weakness. Jesus, consecrates Himself as Great High Priest, to maintain and grow the vibrant strategy of Incarnation.

"I do not ask for these only, but also for those who will believe in me through their word" (v.20) The vision of Jesus here extends as long and as far as humanity exists. Astoundingly, He trusts 'the word' of His disciples *as much as His own word.* If we take what He is saying at face value, it appears that, for Jesus, the word of His apostles is as high-fidelity and effectual as His *own* word. I find it staggering that Jesus trusted the Twelve, Paul and those beyond to have uttered the same word as Himself. There is to be no disparity between the word that Jesus preached and the word that His apostles are to preach. If Jesus doubted that, He would not have uttered this sentence, asking for those who will "believe in me through their word." Jesus extends the *same* request to the Father, for those who believe through *their* word as those who have believed through *His* word. He does not ask for extra protection from the evil one or more safety in the world for those who will believe in Him through the preaching of the apostles. The issues faced by those who have not encountered Christ in the flesh are not any different to the issues faced by those who did know Christ in the literal flesh. We do not face greater deception or attack than those who knew Jesus personally in the flesh. The cosmic issues remain the same: orphanness or sonship—all of the ramifications flow from that.

"...that they may all be one, just as you, Father, are in me,
and I in You, that they may be in us, so that the world may

believe that You have sent me." — JOHN 17:21

The core issue here is the Father-Son relationship in its primordial reality and in its stunning beauty. What the world needs to believe in is not so much the Son as an isolated figure, but in the One *behind* the Son, the One who *sent* the Son. The Son came to the world to open up a connection beyond what could be seen and handled. Those on earth "heard," they "saw with their eyes" and "touched with their hands," but a window was opened up beyond the physical and tangible to see "what was from the beginning...the eternal life which was with the Father." (1 John1:1,2)

The union of the Father and the Son, is that the Son lives in the bosom of the Father, and the Father lives His life in the person of the Son. Their lives intermingle but with a different purpose. The Son has His source in the Father; the Father has His expression in the Son. The Son abides in the bosom of the Father for comfort, for nurture, and resource. The Father abides in the Son, in order that the fulness of Godhead might find an outward expression to all creation. (Colossians 2:9)

"That they may be in us" The two poles of expression, the double loci of union, is to be shown in sons and daughters. Our being in the Father is for source-comfort, for security, identity, vitality, and growth. Our being in the Father is an inward abiding, an abiding into the Source. Our being in the Son, is an abiding that expresses, propels and sends, that compels us outward into fruitfulness and purpose.

Our abiding in the Father is a life that is "hidden with Christ in God." (Colossians 3:3) Our abiding in the Son is to manifest the love of the Father towards creation (Romans 8:19)

The Son abides in the Father *interiorly*, drawing from Source. The Father abides in the Son *exteriorly*, bursting outwards, urging expression.

THE SECOND GLORY OF THE SON

"The glory that You have given me I have given to them, that they may be one even as we are one, I in them and You in me, that they become perfectly one..." — JOHN 17:22

This is the *second* glory of Jesus' sonship (the first being "the glory that I had with You before the world existed"). This is "the glory that You have given me, which I have given to them." This is *incarnational* glory, the glory of sonship in the human condition. Jesus did not possess this glory before the world existed. This is the glory of the weakness of sonship. It *is possible* to fully express God in humanity. Jesus did it, and the corporate Body of Christ (consisting of sons and daughters) will do it when the Spirit completes His work to prepare the Bride for the wedding day. The Bride, prepared by the Spirit of the Father, will come to a maturity that will fully complement the Son.

"...I in them and You in me..." (v.23) The direction of the glory of the Incarnation is seen here. The Father is expressed in the Son, who is expressed in sons and daughters on the earth. If you look from the perspective of earth, you see Jesus in 'them.' If you look from heaven, you see that the Father is in Jesus. Heaven and earth is united within the human person. The human person is the meeting

point of heaven and earth. According to Paul (in Colossians 1:26, 27) the *"mystery hidden for ages and generations, but now revealed… the riches of the glory of this mystery,…is Christ in you, the hope of glory."* Christ *in* you. You only realise that Christ is "in you" when you come into sonship. This mystery, hidden for all ages, was that the Christ (in whom is hidden all the treasures of wisdom and knowledge) would exist within human persons.

"…so that the world may know that You have sent me and loved them even as You loved me." (v.23) The same love, the same substance of love, that the Son receives, is for us. The selfsame love that the Father loves the Son with, He *also loves us with.* When that love, as substance, resides within our hearts and radiates from us, we will know that He has sent us. To be loved is to be sent. This is not limited to a 'call to missions' or a 'call to service.' This is Love expressing itself; it is Love going beyond its own boundaries. Love always expands beyond itself to encompass its objects. Our limited vision and practice of 'service' can often restrict us but the universe is waiting!

The upshot of this is that *all* activity in the Father's love is a sending from the Father. Those who manifest the Father's love have been sent by the Father. This vaporises the 'sacred-secular' divide. When you see from this cosmic perspective, you laugh at sacred-secular dualism. When we realise our place in manifesting the Father to all creation, there is nothing secular left.

THE THIRD GLORY OF THE SON

"Father, I desire that they also, whom You have given me,

*may be with me where I am, to see my glory that You have
given me, because You loved me before the foundation of the
world."* — JOHN 17:24

This is the third glory of Jesus' sonship, the first being the
pre-incarnate glory of sonship, the second being the *incarnate* glory
of sonship. Now this is the *trans-incarnate* glory of sonship. This
is what James Jordan calls "the glorious freedom of the sons of
God." This is sonship, beyond death and resurrection, not confined
within the limits of this world. This is sonship appropriate to who
the Father is in *His* world. It is the display of His splendour to the
principalities and powers. Colossians 2:15 tells us that the Son, "…
disarmed the rulers and authorities, and put them to open shame,
by triumphing over them."

This glory is the glory of the sonship of Jesus as Cosmic Lord. This
is the glory of the name given to him at which every knee shall bow.
The submission of all things ('every knee') is not limited to earth, but
includes all principalities and powers, both 'angelic' and 'demonic.' This
will extend to the final undoing of Satan. What we have to understand
is this: the undoing of Satan is in the power of self-emptying love. It
is the Son, as expression of the Father, who undoes Satan.

We will be witnesses to the glory of the Son as it fills the universe.
The dominion of love is to expand beyond the earth, to bring
creative life to what is formless and void in the distant galaxies.
The love of the Father will, ultimately, renew the whole creation.
We cannot comprehend the extent of this, but Jesus here prays
that we will see His glory. This glory is a glory to display sonship.
This glory 'boasts' to the Orphan Spirit that the Father loved the

Son before the foundation of the world. This glory boldly asserts that independence from the Father is a road to nowhere! The glory that is given in resurrection is a glory that is anchored in the love that will carry Jesus through death. His anchor is the love that He is loved with since before the foundation of the world. When we experience the love of the Father, it is a love that goes back before the foundation of the world. This love precedes the fall of Lucifer, the fall of humanity, and the entire scope of history. The glory which Jesus desires us to see and share in, is the love that He knew before the foundation of the world.

"O righteous Father…" (v.25) O, Father, who excels in relationship! Righteousness is not to be understood as a code of moral behaviour but, rather, as a quality of relationship. Righteousness, in its biblical sense, is 'rightness of relationship.' Paul (in Galatians 3:6) gives an example of this. He says, "Abraham believed God and it was counted to him as righteousness." Before any commandment was ever introduced, to believe and trust the character of the One with whom Abraham related was *righteousness.* In His prayer here, Jesus addresses the Father as 'righteous.' The human relationship that the Son has with the Father is based on complete trust in the Father, because He knows the heart-motivations of the Father.

"…even though the world does not know You, I know You, and these know that You have sent me." (v.25) Sonship is epitomised in these words, "Father,…I - know - You!" This statement shows an exuberant confidence. There are two opposing realities: the world (including the religious world) which does not "know You," and sonship, which "knows You." We live in the world, and everything conveys the orphan message, either of a self-generated life or a life

resigned in despair. When we can say these words, '...I know You" they open up a door of hope and a new reality—the reality of sonship.

Sonship is completely assured of its identity. *I...*know...*You*. The subject and the object are fully present to each other. In sonship, the self is confident; it is neither the false ego nor is it trodden down or subdued. Sonship produces a secure and centred 'I' which comes from knowing 'You.' We see this in the apostle Paul, who confidently refers to himself with an astute self-knowledge. Paul's assessment of himself was clear-headed and level, not inflated yet not sublimated, but true, stating that he knew God and also knew himself. Paul had no illusions about himself so he was not disillusioned with himself. He had come to the realisation that, even though he was "less than the least of all saints" (Ephesians 3:8) and *even* the "chief of sinners" (1 Timothy 1:15), he "could do all things through him who strengthens me." (Philippians 4:13)

Jesus' affirmation here that, even though the world does not know the Father, yet He knows the Father, reassures us that there is no disparity between the Father and the Son. All that Jesus is, the Father is. The world will attempt to drive a wedge between the Son and His Father. We have all had confidence in Jesus but lacked confidence in the Father. That is how 'the world' (secular and religious) has influenced us. The Son, however, is revealing the true character of the Father to us.

"I have made known to them Your name, and I will continue to make it known." (v.26) The work of Jesus on this earth was nothing less and nothing more than to make known the true identity (the name) of the Father. He completed that task on earth but the

work continues unabated. His promise to the Father, out of filial relationship, is to fulfil His eternal vocation of making the Father known. Let me repeat that. The eternal vocation of Jesus, the Son, is to make the name of the Father known.

Intimacy with Jesus will inexorably lead to being introduced to His Father. Anyone who pursues intimacy with Jesus will find that He seeks to lead them to the Father. It is inevitable, because Jesus continues to "make it known."

"...that the love, with which You have loved me, may be in them, and I in them." (v.26) These final words sum up the essence of true Christianity. The New Covenant, in a nutshell, is this: that the love with which the Father loves the Son may be in us, and the Son Himself may be in us.

When we experience the substance of the Father's love, it *forms Christ in us*. Paul was in "the anguish of childbirth until Christ was formed" in the Galatian believers (Galatians 4:19). This is talking about the *metaphysical reality* of the substance of Jesus Christ being 'formed' in us. This is exactly what Jesus concludes His prayer of John 17 with. And what is more, He links the two things as cause and effect. When the "love with which You have loved me" is in us, then it automatically follows that 'I' (Jesus Christ, the Son of the Father) is substantially within us. If that wasn't true it would sound like heresy! The amazing thing, however, is that it *is* true!

Anything less than this, beloved readers, is *not* the New Covenant. Anything less than this is not what Jesus came to earth for, or went to the cross for.

James and Denise Jordan have often said, "If your Christianity is not working for you, there is only one conclusion. What you are living in is *not* Christianity." Christianity only began to actually work in my life when I came to experience the Father loving me.

"...that the love with which You have loved me, may be in them, and I in them." This is Christianity!

PART FOUR

A NEW CREATION

CONFRONTING RELIGION AND EMPIRE

∼

THE GARDEN OF GETHSEMANE

When Jesus had spoken these words, he went out with his disciples across the brook Kidron, where there was a garden, which he and his disciples entered. Now Judas, who betrayed him, also knew the place, for Jesus often met there with his disciples. So Judas, having procured a band of soldiers and some officers from the chief priests and the Pharisees, went there with lanterns and torches and weapons. Then Jesus, knowing all that would happen to him, came forward and said to them, "Whom do you seek?" They answered him, "Jesus of Nazareth." Jesus said to them, "I am he." Judas, who betrayed him, was standing with them. When Jesus said to them, "I am he," they drew back and fell to the ground. So he asked them again, "Whom do you seek?" And they said, "Jesus of Nazareth." Jesus answered, "I told you that I am he. So, if you seek me, let these men go." This was to fulfill the word that he had spoken: "Of those whom you gave me I have lost not one." Then Simon Peter, having a sword, drew it and struck the high priest's servant and cut off his right ear. (The servant's name was Malchus.) So Jesus said to Peter, "Put your sword into its sheath; shall I not drink the cup that the Father has given me?" — JOHN 18:1-11

T he closing scenes of Jesus' life on earth bring us, once again, to a garden. This place, Gethsemane, the court of the high priest, Pilate's headquarters, the Place of the Skull, and finally, another garden form the backdrop to the events that take place from now on.

"When Jesus had spoken these words, he went out…" (v.1) There is an intentionality about Jesus here. He has spoken to His Father. He has articulated the purpose of everything and, in doing so, has steadied His soul. His words now lead to the actions which bring Him inevitably to His arrest. Jesus may seem like a victim of men but God is the strategist behind this. It is not a cold and calculated strategy; it is a strategy in which Divine Love is passionately displayed. God the Father is continually manifesting Himself in His Son. Perhaps now more than ever, we need to see everything that Jesus goes through as a manifestation of who His Father is. The Father is 'in Christ' and is resolutely moving towards reconciling all things to Himself (2 Corinthians 5:19). In everything that happens, the Father is a full participant.

The garden of Gethsemane, across the Kidron Valley from the city of Jerusalem, is a familiar location for Jesus and His circle of friends. This garden is an evocative place, in which the air is tinged with the presence of the Father. The atmosphere still hums with what Jesus had previously told the disciples on their many visits there. The shrubs, bushes and gnarled olive trees in this garden are privy to deep and comforting revelation about who the Father is. This garden is a 'thin place.'[34]

Judas leads the soldiers of the high priest there because it is familiar. He hasn't been seen since he left the upper room (Mark 14:15) and now he reappears, accompanied by a posse of soldiers who are more than likely part of the Temple Guard rather than a Roman cohort. Judas, getting close to the nadir of orphanness, has done a deal with the full backing of the high priest and the Sanhedrin. He is supported by soldiers and officers, and equipped with weapons and flaming torches.

When He sees Judas, Jesus' heart must feel pierced. The prophetic significance of Psalm 55 is that it is a foretelling of how Jesus sees Judas:

> *"For it is not an enemy who taunts me—*
> *then I could bear it;*
> *it is not an adversary who deals insolently with me—*
> *then I could hide from him.*
> *But it is you, a man, my equal,*
> *my companion, my familiar friend.*
> *We used to take sweet counsel together;*
> *within God's house we walked in the throng."*
> — PSALM 55:12-14

---

34. In Celtic Christianity a 'thin place' is a place where the veil between this earth and heaven is thin.

Judas was once close to Jesus; he had been a 'familiar friend.' That friendship, however, broke down when Judas turned his heart against Jesus. He now comes, leading the soldiers of the High Priest, to identify Jesus with kisses.[35]

In contrast to the clattering band who have come to arrest Him, Jesus remains resolute and calm. He knows what must happen and He allows Himself to be carried along on the unstoppable tide of events, because it is the will of His Father. He faces Judas, the officials and the soldiers. When they confirm that they are seeking Jesus of Nazareth, He replies, "I am He." His reply causes a sudden reaction: they draw back and fall to the ground. Is it a reaction to supernatural power and presence? Is it a reaction of shock and bewilderment because He appears utterly different to what they are expecting? It must be a combination of both factors.

Jesus goes with Judas and the officers to be brought before the high priest who will cross-examine Him. He has fulfilled His promise to the Father (John 17:12) in ensuring that the disciples are not harmed. Peter, in a surge of reaction, draws his sword and promptly slices off the ear of the high priest's servant, Malchus. John does not record Luke's observation that Jesus healed the ear. Jesus, shining in His sonship, answers His persecutors by healing this man's ear. He is tuned into a greater reality, telling Peter sharply to sheath his sword and surrender to the inexorable course of the events which are taking place. These events are part of the 'cup' that the Father has given Him to drink.

---

35. John doesn't draw attention to the kiss of betrayal. Remarkably, the Greek rendering of Matthew's account is that Judas "covered Jesus with kisses." (Matthew 26:49.) This is exactly the same expression as Luke 15:15 when the father kisses the returning prodigal son.

CONFRONTING THE TWIN MANIFESTATIONS
OF ORPHANNESS

Jesus is moving towards His final showdown with Satan, the original Orphan Spirit. That will take place at the cross, but first He is brought into a head-to-head confrontation with the two major expressions of the Orphan Spirit on earth; Religion and Empire. Orphanness is supremely seen and experienced though these spiritual powers. They are both products of the Tree of the Knowledge of Good and Evil.

The entire edifice of the orphan system is propped up by the twin pillars of 'Religion' and 'Empire.' Wherever there is orphanness it will 'lord it over' others (Mark 10:42) and exert its will, either by domineering or by inducing guilt. It seeks to repress the freedom of those who are destined to be sons and daughters of God and desires to control the people by whatever means it can. The orphan system has been exerting its claim throughout history. When Israel cried out to be given a king like the nations, God warned them, through the prophet Samuel, of the consequences of seeking a human despot:

> *"These will be the ways of the king who will reign over you: he will take your sons and appoint them to his chariots and to be his horsemen and to run before his chariots. And he will appoint for himself commanders of thousands and commanders of fifties, and some to plough his ground and to reap his harvest, and to make his implements of war and the equipment of his chariots. He will take your daughters to be perfumers and cooks and bakers. He will take the best of your fields and vineyards and olive orchards and give them*

to his servants. He will take the tenth of your grain and of
your vineyards and give it to his officers and to his servants.
He will take your male servants and female servants and
the best of your young men and your donkeys, and put them
to his work. He will take the tenth of your flocks, and you
shall be his slaves." — 1 SAMUEL 8:11-17

The great forces of Religion and Empire have stolen extensively from God's creation. It is these systems of robbery that Jesus comes face to face with as He stands trial. Firstly, Jesus is brought before the court of religion: He is led to Annas, not officially the high priest now but a man who had held the position at an earlier time:

So the band of soldiers and their captain and the officers of
the Jews arrested Jesus and bound him. First they led him to
Annas, for he was the father-in-law of Caiaphas, who was
high priest that year. It was Caiaphas who had advised the
Jews that it would be expedient that one man should die for
the people. — JOHN 18:12-14

The narrative moves back and forward between the two scenes of Jesus' trial and Peter's experience. Imagine it as if you are watching a film: Jesus is led in to face Annas, then the camera switches immediately to focus on Simon Peter, standing in the courtyard.

SIMON PETER'S DILEMMA

Simon Peter followed Jesus, and so did another disciple.
Since that disciple was known to the high priest, he entered
with Jesus into the courtyard of the high priest, but Peter

stood outside at the door. So the other disciple, who was known to the high priest, went out and spoke to the servant girl who kept watch at the door, and brought Peter in. The servant girl at the door said to Peter, "You also are not one of this man's disciples, are you?" He said, "I am not." Now the servants and officers had made a charcoal fire, because it was cold, and they were standing and warming themselves. Peter also was with them, standing and warming himself.
— JOHN 18:15-18

Simon Peter stands shivering outside the door to the inner courtyard. He doesn't even consider trying to get through; deference to the Temple protocol has been ingrained in him as long as he can remember. The air is still and he draws breath quickly and exhales again. Try as he might, Simon Peter cannot quell the visceral tide of disappointment seeping into him. As he stands waiting, disillusionment engulfs him. Icy tendrils of fear clutch at his inner resolve. There is nothing he can do amidst the tremendous tension building in his soul.

The other disciple who goes into the court of the high priest where Jesus is being questioned is most likely John himself. Peter does not follow at this juncture but hovers outside the door. It appears that Peter and John stay longest with Jesus after the others flee (Matthew 26:26). Peter is still there, the 'other disciple' is still there and we know for sure that John ends up with the women at the cross.

Simon Peter's denial is rooted in fear of the religious authorities. Peter would have readily laid down his life in a struggle against the political occupier, the Roman Empire. He hesitates, however, when it comes to confronting the *religious* powers. Peter is unwilling to sacrifice his religious and Jewish identity at this point. Simon Peter identifies strongly and passionately with his Jewish culture. The vestiges of it cling to him for a long time. Paul confronts him about it years later in Galatia (Galatians 2:11-14).

Even though Peter has received a revelation of Jesus as the Son of God, he still harbours the hope that Jesus will call up the angels and rally a revolt against the Roman occupation. It is not to be. Peter must journey through the shattering of his illusions.

Simon Peter is one of the main protagonists in the Holy Spirit's story as told by John. We identify readily with Peter because he shows us aspects of ourselves. Peter wants success in this life. He desires justice, a radical political solution, and he does not want to ruffle the feathers of the religious status quo. As Peter holds out his hands to the heat of the brazier, the scene flicks back to Annas questioning Jesus.

RELIGIOUS INQUISITION

The high priest then questioned Jesus about his disciples and his teaching. Jesus answered him, "I have spoken openly to the world. I have always taught in synagogues and in the temple, where all Jews come together. I have said nothing in secret. Why do you ask me? Ask those who have heard me what I said to them; they know what I said." When he had said these things, one of the officers standing by struck Jesus with his hand, saying, "Is that how you answer the high priest?" Jesus answered him, "If what I said is wrong, bear witness about the wrong; but if what I said is right, why do you strike me?" Annas then sent him bound to Caiaphas the high priest. — JOHN 18:19-24

Annas, the 'emeritus' high priest, looks askance at Jesus. Here is the Nazarene at last; *now* He can be held answerable for what He has uttered. Why did He call God His Father, thus making Himself equal to God? How did the miracles happen? What about raising the dead? Is this man another Judah Maccabee who led an earlier revolt years ago? Annas' remit is to soften up the prisoner, to get more information out of Him. The real intention of the religious leaders is to see Jesus charged with blasphemy and put to death. The inquisition by Annas is motivated by fear; fear of the disruptive influence of Jesus. Annas focuses, not only on Jesus' teaching but upon His disciples. He knows full well that the revolution sparked by Jesus, once caught by others, cannot be controlled.

Jesus has not retreated from what the Father commissioned Him to do. He has declared openly in the synagogue and in the temple the true nature of God's kingdom. He has gone to the heart of the religious establishment and called it out for what it really is. Throughout all this, He has manifested the Father. He challenges Annas to question those who have heard Him, knowing that His preaching is irreversible. When the word is spoken out of the mouth of God, it cannot be neutralised, forgotten, or suppressed. It lives in the hearts of those who are open to receive it.

"They know what I said" (v. 21) This knowing is not intellectual, it is a perception by eyes that *see*. The words of Jesus do not inform; they enlighten and open up the paradigms of our understanding.

Jesus has always spoken His words to human hearts that, when receiving them, come into the true knowledge which only comes with spiritual insight. Religion cannot stop or control this. When Jesus tells Annas as much, one of the temple officers is enraged and lashes out at Him. A raw nerve is touched. Jesus cannot be accused of anything because He is blameless. This trial has now become an indictment of those who are seeking to accuse Jesus. They are being judged by the love and truth that is manifested before them.

REALITY DAWNS FOR PETER

Now Simon Peter was standing and warming himself. So they said to him, "You also are not one of his disciples, are you?" He denied it and said, "I am not." One of the servants of the high priest, a relative of the man whose ear Peter had cut off, asked, "Did I not see you in the garden with him?" Peter again denied it, and at once a rooster crowed.
— JOHN 18:25-27

Simon Peter stands by the brazier, holding out his hands to the heat. He is surrounded by the temple workers and the soldiers of the guard. These are working men, full of ribald jokes and engaged in banter with one another. Conversation that night was all about the arrest that had just happened and about the man who is in front of the high priest. They know that Peter is an outsider and focus on him, "Hey! Are you not one of His disciples? Were you not with Him earlier in the garden?"

Simon Peter is a man's man! He lets the old expletives well up and turns the air blue with curses. Maybe we are too sanitised today. Biblical parlance is much more earthy, colloquial and even banal than we realise. The Hebrew and Greek of the Bible has a sprinkling of language that we would consider borderline, to say the least. The words have only left his lips, when he hears the screeching cacophony of the rooster.

The crowing of the rooster announces a new dawn of realisation for Peter. His illusions about himself are shattered as he discovers with shock where his heart is really at. He now falls into a 'place of ashes,' descending into emotional blackness. He is now swallowed up in the full, horrible realisation that his zeal and enthusiasm for the kingdom of God has finally run out of steam.

This experience is a crisis of discovering that you are not the strong person you believed yourself to be. It is a very difficult place to arrive at, but it is probably the most liberating part of what it is to be a Christian. In my experience, I held out until I was forty-two years old, full of passionate zeal that I was willing to give everything for the kingdom of God. In late 2007, I was forced to look into the depths of my own heart in a way that I had never done before. In the light of reality, I saw that I was as capable as anyone else of denying Jesus.

The truth is; every person's heart is equally capable of Peter's denial because human enthusiasm can never be enough. The passion of the soul (the mind, will and emotions) is not sufficient to carry us to the cross and beyond. Even the allure of 'revival' experiences is not enough to bring forth Christlikeness. It is only the Father's love, coming to a human soul that sees its own inadequacy and humbles itself to become as a little child, that brings us to become like Jesus. After tasting the ashes of defeat, of disillusionment, even of despair, we will hear the crowing of the rooster as it announces a new dawn of divine love.

This new dawn is not yet the full sunrise of the resurrection morning. The resurrection dawn is unparalleled in its exuberance and the sheer joy of receiving Jesus again. *This* morning, however, which the rooster announces, does not liberate Peter from pain and grief. But it *does* liberate him from his illusions about himself. Depressing as it is for Peter, it releases him from a false sense of reality into *actual* reality.

We must plunge into the depths of disillusionment and arrive at the ground of our being, for it is only here that we receive a revelation of the cross. We finally realise that our human enthusiasm and endeavour cannot usher in God's presence. Jesus, the Son, has been rejected, not only by the secular and political system but also by the religious, 'God-pleasing' system.

THE EMPIRE STRIKES BACK

Then they led Jesus from the house of Caiaphas to the governor's headquarters. It was early morning. They themselves did not enter the governor's headquarters, so that they would not be defiled, but could eat the Passover. So Pilate went outside to them and said, "What accusation do you bring against this man?" They answered him, "If this man were not doing evil, we would not have delivered him over to you." Pilate said to them, "Take him yourselves and judge him by your own law." The Jews said to him, "It is not lawful for us to put anyone to death." This was to fulfil the word that Jesus had spoken to show by what kind of death he was going to die. — JOHN 18:28-32

Jesus is then led into the *praetorium* (the Governor's headquarters) to stand before Pontius Pilate. Pilate is the representative of the Roman Empire. Alongside Religion, the second great expression through which the Orphan Spirit is manifested on the earth is the spirit-system of 'Empire.'

Jesus is handed over to the Roman prefect because the religious system cannot bring itself to do the deed and kill Him. They have been trying to kill Him for some years now but, when He is in their hands, they shrink back claiming that it is not 'lawful' for them to do so. Judged by the system of Religion, the Son is now paraded before the political powers represented by Pontius Pilate. Pilate is the Roman prefect, governor of Judea, Samaria and Idumea appointed by the emperor Tiberius. Jesus is confronted with *the Empire*.

The imperial power of Rome that Jesus stands before is far from neutral and benign. It is an empire that stands in direct contradistinction to the benevolent rule of God. In Greek, the word 'empire' is exactly the same word as the word 'kingdom.' It is the word '*basileia*.' Jesus was proclaiming the *basileia* of God the Father; Caesar was proclaiming the *basileia* of Rome. The kingdom of God is the dominion of the Father's love. In Christ, we have been rescued from the "dominion of darkness and brought into the kingdom of the Son of His love. (Colossians 1:13)

When Jesus stands before Pilate, He stands as the Son of the

Father's love before the 'dominion of darkness.' Every system of rule and control that is founded upon orphanness can be identified as the spirit of 'Empire.' Jesus' confrontation of Religion and Empire is the final stage before He deals with the Orphan Spirit himself. Let me quote Wes Howard-Brook as he powerfully and cogently identifies what the spirit of Empire is:

> *"Broadly speaking, 'empire' refers to an organised system of power used against the many for the benefit of the few, which seeks legitimacy by claiming divine mandate."* [36]

This system is not only the norm in the political realm; it has also infiltrated the Church. Alienated from the love of the Father, our default has been to operate in the spirit of empire. Too often, it is the few who control the many, promising blessing to those who conform but keeping the power for themselves. Everyone called to leadership in the Body of Christ needs to be aware of this temptation for it cuts directly against the Kingdom of God. The Kingdom of God is a reality in which power is given *away*, in which life is laid down by the few so that blessing and privilege will flow to all. Jesus demonstrated this in calling attention to the marginalised, empowering the disempowered, healing the sick, and championing the poor and dispossessed.

In contrast to the manifestations of orphanness, Jesus stands in the peace and dignity of His sonship. Jesus is overcoming the world on the inside, even though He is outwardly being judged. Jesus does not meet the criteria of the system on the grounds of competence.

---

36. Wes Howard-Brook, The Church before Christianity, Orbis Books, Maryknoll, 2005.

He doesn't need to because He, in that precise moment, is the Son of the Father's love. He doesn't argue with the religious and political orphan system, because He is already energising a new humanity. When the new community is sufficiently gelled together, then the time for His arrest is ripe. The new community will be tested to the uttermost and scattered, but will flourish in a post-resurrection dawn. Jesus has manifested the Father to them: there is a sufficient spark in the tinder to light a fire when the Spirit comes at Pentecost.

THE NATURE OF THE HEAVENLY KINGDOM

So Pilate entered his headquarters again and called Jesus and said to him, "Are you the King of the Jews?" Jesus answered, "Do you say this of your own accord, or did others say it to you about me?" Pilate answered, "Am I a Jew? Your own nation and the chief priests have delivered you over to me. What have you done?" Jesus answered, "My kingdom is not of this world. If my kingdom were of this world, my servants would have been fighting, that I might not be delivered over to the Jews. But my kingdom is not from the world."
— JOHN 18:33-36

Pilate, the Roman governor, continues to press Jesus and bring a charge against Him. He wants to extract a confession from Jesus, admitting guilt to sedition, proclaiming Himself to be king of the Jews and plotting to overthrow the rule of Caesar. Pilate is confused and exasperated. He wonders what Jesus has done to make the chief priests and the Jewish people call for His crucifixion.

Jesus cannot be charged with trying to lead a revolt; the kingdom that belongs to Him is not identifiable by borders or a political constitution. The true nature of Jesus' kingdom is not of this world. If Jesus wanted to set up an earthly kingdom, He would do so by force; His servants would fight. Yet here, Jesus stands alone before Pilate bound, the ruler of a different kingdom, a kingdom that is not from the world. In the single event that one of His disciples attempted to fight by cutting off an ear with a sword, Jesus' response was to immediately heal the injured man.

The kingdom that Jesus rules over is a heavenly kingdom which exists in the spiritual realm. When the love of God pervades the atmosphere, His kingdom is extended to push back the powers of darkness. The truth is, God's kingdom is unassailable and cannot be defeated. The love of the Father is the most powerful and inexorable force in the universe. Love will ultimately overcome and prevail.

WHAT IS TRUTH?

Then Pilate said to him, "So you are a king?" Jesus answered, "You say that I am a king. For this purpose I was born and for this purpose I have come into the world—to bear witness to the truth. Everyone who is of the truth listens to my voice." Pilate said to him, "What is truth?" — JOHN 18:37-38

Jesus does not verbally answer Pilate's question, "What is truth?" He utters not a word. By His silence Jesus declares the demise of Empire. Standing before Pilate, seemingly helpless, allowing Himself to be under the control of His enemies, Jesus displays supreme confidence.

"What is truth?" is the futile query of the Tree of Knowledge. It is futile because truth cannot be found in knowing what is good or what is evil. Truth can only be found in becoming like God Himself. Too often, we have thought that we possess truth if we have correct doctrine or adhere to standards of good behaviour. Jesus' response to that misconception is to stand silently before us. If we have eyes to see and ears to hear, we will see Jesus, the Son, as the *embodiment* of truth. He is the embodiment of truth because *the love of God is truth.*

To be loved by God and to be transformed by His love is to enter into truth. The love of God is the fundamental reality of everything that is. Living in love is synonymous with living in truth because love cannot abide any deception. Love cannot deceive those whom it loves. Love cannot be deceived either, nor taken advantage of, because Love is willing to give everything unconditionally.

BARABBAS OR JESUS - THEFT OR GIFT?

> *After he had said this, he went back outside to the Jews and told them, "I find no guilt in him. But you have a custom that I should release one man for you at the Passover. So do you want me to release to you the King of the Jews?" They cried out again, "Not this man, but Barabbas!" Now Barabbas was a robber.* — JOHN 18:38-40

Pilate cannot find any guilt in Jesus. This does not mean that he is convinced of who Jesus really is. Rather, Pilate cannot find any legal basis to condemn Jesus to death. Under extreme pressure from the religious leaders, he finds a loophole whereby he can mollify them. According to custom he will let them choose a prisoner who can be set free for the Passover feast. Essentially Pilate lets himself off the hook. He will be able to wriggle free from his tight spot by putting the decision back onto the religious leaders. Their choice is between Jesus and the notorious bandit, Bar-abbas.

Bar-abbas means 'son of the father.' How remarkable is that! Here we have the Son of the Father, beyond reproach, being rejected in favour of Bar-abbas, a 'son of the father,' who is also a marauder and a bandit. John's terse description of Bar-abbas hangs in the air like the striking of a bell, "...***Now Bar-abbas was a robber.***"

Why does John write this sentence so starkly? Is he conveying something of great significance to us? John has highlighted this issue of stealing and robbery before in his Gospel:

- He has told us (John 12:6) that Judas was a thief who was habitually stealing money from the communal purse.

- He has recorded Jesus' speech (John 10:1,8,10) describing the religious leaders and false shepherds as thieves and robbers.

- He insinuates that robbery is taking place within the temple in Jerusalem (John 2:14-16; John 8:20). Mark is even more clear about this:

> *"Is it not written, 'My house shall be called a house of prayer for all the nations'? But you have made it a den of robbers."*
> — MARK 11:17

Throughout John's Gospel, John always contrasts the thief and the robber with the Son. Robbing and stealing are the ultimate orphan behaviours. Thieves take away because they have no capacity to receive gifts. In contrast, sonship will restore everything that has been stolen.

In choosing Bar-abbas, the orphan system chooses the 'father' of Bar-abbas; not his literal father, but his *spiritual* father, the Orphan Spirit. This is not about Bar-abbas the man. Bar-abbas is more significant for what he represents than for who he is personally. This is yet another sign to be read. The tragedy of humanity is that it chooses a 'son of disobedience' over the 'Son of obedience.' It chooses the Thief and rejects the Father's eternal Gift, His Son.

THE GREAT TRANSITION

~

We now arrive at the final hours of Jesus' life on earth. Everything has coalesced into this moment. This entire Gospel is proliferated with signs along the Way, to lead us to the Destination. We know that the door to relationship with the Father is the Son Himself. Throughout John's Gospel we have become acquainted with Jesus in His revealing of the Father, full of grace, truth, compassion and love. Now is the time for the *supreme* revelation of who the Father is.

My purpose for this chapter is twofold. Firstly, I will look at the events, focusing particularly on what John includes and the other Gospel writers leave out. Secondly, I wish to consider Jesus' death on the cross from a perspective that is consistent with the revelation of God as a loving Father rather than a God who wished to punish His Son for the sins that we have committed.

Then Pilate took Jesus and flogged him. And the soldiers

twisted together a crown of thorns and put it on his head and arrayed him in a purple robe. They came up to him, saying, "Hail, King of the Jews!" and struck him with their hands. Pilate went out again and said to them, "See, I am bringing him out to you that you may know that I find no guilt in him." So Jesus came out, wearing the crown of thorns and the purple robe. Pilate said to them, "Behold the man!" When the chief priests and the officers saw him, they cried out, "Crucify him, crucify him!" Pilate said to them, "Take him yourselves and crucify him, for I find no guilt in him." The Jews answered him, "We have a law, and according to that law he ought to die because he has made himself the Son of God." When Pilate heard this statement, he was even more afraid. He entered his headquarters again and said to Jesus, "Where are you from?" But Jesus gave him no answer. So Pilate said to him, "You will not speak to me? Do you not know that I have authority to release you and authority to crucify you?" Jesus answered him, "You would have no authority over me at all unless it had been given you from above. Therefore he who delivered me over to you has the greater sin."

From then on Pilate sought to release him, but the Jews cried out, "If you release this man, you are not Caesar's friend. Everyone who makes himself a king opposes Caesar."

So when Pilate heard these words, he brought Jesus out and sat down on the judgment seat at a place called The Stone Pavement, and in Aramaic Gabbatha. Now it was the day of Preparation of the Passover. It was about the sixth

hour. He said to the Jews, "Behold your King!" They cried
out, "Away with him, away with him, crucify him!" Pilate
said to them, "Shall I crucify your King?" The chief priests
answered, "We have no king but Caesar." So he delivered
him over to them to be crucified. — JOHN 19:1-16

Bending to the will of the religious leaders, Pilate has Jesus flogged with a Roman scourge known as the 'flagellum.' This instrument of torture was a whip of three thongs in which were embedded pieces of metal and bone as well as hooks. The victim was flayed, stripping flesh from bone. Having scourged Him, the Roman soldiers assault Jesus violently. Next, they mockingly put the symbols of imperial power on Him; a robe of imperial purple and a wreath, not of laurel, but of thorns. They make a parody of Him, accusing Him of claiming to be King of the Jews.

However hard he tries, Pilate cannot find any infringement of Roman law by Jesus at all, and so hands Him back to the mob. However, the chief priests are adamant, insisting that Pilate crucifies Him, because Jesus has blasphemed. This blasphemy is centred around 'sonship.' The Jewish leaders stir up the fear that Jesus is a political revolutionary. More fearful now, and wondering what exactly it entails to claim that one is the 'Son of God,' Pilate goes back to Jesus and attempts to assert his authority as the Roman prefect, the provincial governor of Judea.

The indictment of Jesus is twofold; it is both political and religious. On the political side, Jesus is indicted as the King of the Jews, having challenged the Empire of Rome. Pilate finds no guilt in Him; there is not enough evidence to support any fear that He is a political seditionist so He is handed over to the chief priests to be tried for blasphemy.

When Pilate interrogates Jesus again, asking "Where are you from?" he is met with silence. Jesus does not answer this question. Jesus sees through Pilate's claim to authority. Authority means nothing unless it is given from above. Where does the authority lie here? In the Roman governor or in the chained man standing before him? Spiritual authority always finds itself in direct contrast to titular authority. More often than not, spiritual authority stands in chains before authority based on title. Whether it is Jesus before Pilate or Paul before Agrippa, the spiritual authorities have little or no power in the arena of worldly influence. They appear as weak and helpless, handcuffed and in chains, yet they wield great authority in unseen realms.

> So they took Jesus, and he went out, bearing his own cross, to the place called The Place of a Skull, which in Aramaic is called Golgotha. There they crucified him, and with him two others, one on either side, and Jesus between them. Pilate also wrote an inscription and put it on the cross. It read, "Jesus of Nazareth, the King of the Jews." Many of the Jews read this inscription, for the place where Jesus was crucified was near the city, and it was written in Aramaic, in Latin, and in Greek. So the chief priests of the Jews said to Pilate, "Do not write, 'The King of the Jews,' but rather, 'This man said, I am King of the Jews.'" Pilate answered, "What I have written I have written." — JOHN 19:16-22

Jesus bears His own cross. He is ready to face death and He is not reluctant to embrace what lies immediately ahead of Him. He knows that the will of His Father must be done, and it is *His* will too. John doesn't mention that Jesus has any help carrying His cross. According to all three Synoptic Gospels, Simon the Cyrenian carried the cross at some point, but John is impressed with the resoluteness of Jesus. John portrays Him as taking full responsibility, exerting willpower (in spite of being flayed by the whip) and shouldering the weight of the wooden beam. He carries it to the place of crucifixion called Golgotha, the Place of a Skull.

A SEAMLESS ROBE

When the soldiers had crucified Jesus, they took his garments and divided them into four parts, one part for each soldier; also his tunic. But the tunic was seamless, woven in one piece from top to bottom, so they said to one another, "Let us not tear it, but cast lots for it to see whose it shall be." This was to fulfil the Scripture which says,

> *"They divided my garments among them,*
> *and for my clothing they cast lots."*

So the soldiers did these things, — JOHN 19:23,24

John is the only Gospel writer to mention the seamless robe. Again, he has the unique viewpoint of a witness. This is a very expensive tunic. Even the Roman soldiers can see that it is highly valuable because it is one piece of fabric, woven together from the top to the bottom. Unlike the veil of the temple which will be torn from the top to the bottom, the soldiers will not tear the robe of Jesus. The veil of the temple is ripped to remove the separation between God and us but this robe takes us a step beyond that into the all-inclusive unity of sonship.

Without a shadow of a doubt, this robe has spiritual significance. The fact that it is a fulfilment of prophecy means that we have permission to *interpret* it prophetically. For me, the seamless robe signifies that we are all one in Christ Jesus. When we identify ourselves with Jesus as sons to the Father, all dualism and division melts away. From the beginning, everything is in unison:

> *"There is no Jew nor Greek, there is neither slave nor free, there is neither male nor female, for you are all one in Christ Jesus."* — GALATIANS 3:28

> *"For he himself is our peace and has broken down in his flesh the dividing wall of hostility…that he might create in himself one new man…and reconcile us both to God in one body through the cross."* — EPHESIANS 2:14-16

> *"Here there is not Greek and Jew, circumcised and uncircumcised, barbarian, Scythian, slave, free, but Christ is all and in all."* — COLOSSIANS 3:11

The divisions (ingrained in us from the Fall) have been removed. There is *no* 'in-group' and *no* 'out-group.' There is *no* male-female rivalry. There is *no* clergy-laity divide. There is *no* sacred-secular divide. God has woven a seamless robe of sonship where all is grace, where everything interconnects.

BEHOLD YOUR SON! - BEHOLD YOUR MOTHER!

...but standing by the cross of Jesus were his mother and his mother's sister, Mary the wife of Clopas, and Mary Magdalene. When Jesus saw his mother and the disciple whom he loved standing nearby, he said to his mother, "Woman, behold, your son!" Then he said to the disciple, "Behold, your mother!" And from that hour the disciple took her to his own home. — JOHN 19:25-27

Once more, unique among the Gospel writers, John calls our attention to the women, in this case, those who stand by the cross of Jesus. Three Marys: His mother, His aunt, and Mary Magdalene. These women have followed Jesus to the very end. They did not flee like the disciples (who, as men, would have been under greater threat from the mob and the Roman authorities), but their feminine compassion for Jesus makes it impossible for them to abandon Him.

Throughout his Gospel, John has brought femininity into the spotlight. For him, women and the feminine have been redeemed by the Son. Jesus has acted on the Father's behalf to reverse one of the major results of the Fall: violence and marginalisation of all that is feminine in the image of God. In the Gospel of John, the Holy Spirit is very intentional about unmasking misogyny and reversing its effects. The place of women in the scheme of redemption is accentuated.

As Jesus looks around Him in the midst of His trauma, He sees His mother and John standing there with the others. From the cross, He addresses them and pronounces that they are, from now on, to be mother and son. In doing so, Jesus demonstrates His heart as a son to His mother. This is a very human emotion, for His mother and for His closest friend. In the midst of this supreme act of redemption, He gives His mother to John and gives John as a replacement son to His mother. This is completely consistent with His work of redemption and salvation. If the compassion of God is not demonstrated at this ordinary and intimate level, it is only a concept.

Immediately, a warm love and commitment is sparked within the heart of John and the heart of Mary. I see Mary's influence behind this Gospel. She and John must have spent many hours talking about the life of Jesus, reminiscing over what He said and did. Mary would have told John many things that she, as a mother, had observed in the life of Jesus. Mary knew, more than anyone, who the real Father of Jesus was. She didn't need a revelation, such as Peter did; she knew from the beginning that Jesus was fathered by God.

IT IS FINISHED!

After this, Jesus, knowing that all was now finished, said (to fulfil the Scripture), "I thirst." A jar full of sour wine stood there, so they put a sponge full of the sour wine on a hyssop branch and held it to his mouth. When Jesus had received the sour wine, he said, "It is finished," and he bowed his head and gave up his spirit. — JOHN 19:28-30

This is a remarkable perspective, as it were, from the inside. John, through the Holy Spirit and presumably through talking with Jesus post-resurrection, has inside knowledge of the workings of Jesus' heart and mind. "Jesus, *knowing* that all was now finished..." then says, "I thirst." The thirst of Jesus cannot be slaked by what He is given. He is given sour wine which, in reality, is vinegar. Are you thinking what I am thinking? The poor wine of John 2 has now turned totally sour. This is a sign that religion is finished and has turned sour.

"Jesus, knowing that all was now finished." Jesus says this *to fulfil the Scripture.* I am amazed at how intentional Jesus is as He hangs on the cross. He knows that the prophecies of Old Testament Scripture (Psalm 69:21) must be fulfilled, and so He sets about fulfilling His part. He knows that His work of manifesting the Father is finished. Hanging on the cross is the ultimate manifestation of the Father.

What else is finished? Orphanness is finished. Sonship is fully restored and reconnected because we can now enter into Christ's sonship to the Father. The Tree of the Knowledge of Good and Evil is finished. God is no longer remote and hard to access. Religion is finished. There is no need to pursue God, for He has come to us. Empire is finished. The weakness of sonship subverts and defeats all other authority.

Jesus bows His head and releases His spirit. He is in control of death, dictating when He will die. His spirit is not taken from Him; He gives it up, knowing that He has accomplished what He set out to do.

BLOOD AND WATER

Since it was the day of Preparation, and so that the bodies would not remain on the cross on the Sabbath (for that

Sabbath was a high day), the Jews asked Pilate that their legs might be broken and that they might be taken away. So the soldiers came and broke the legs of the first, and of the other who had been crucified with him. But when they came to Jesus and saw that he was already dead, they did not break his legs. But one of the soldiers pierced his side with a spear, and at once there came out blood and water. He who saw it has borne witness—his testimony is true, and he knows that he is telling the truth—that you also may believe. For these things took place that the Scripture might be fulfilled: "Not one of his bones will be broken." And again another Scripture says, "They will look on him whom they have pierced."— JOHN 19:31-37

John stands and watches as the Roman soldiers approach the three crosses to break the legs of those who hang on them. Death from crucifixion is agonisingly slow so the authorities take control by breaking the legs. The Roman authorities retain their control over death. They decide the moment when the crucified person dies.

By giving up His spirit before the Romans come to break His legs, the Son demonstrates that He, not the Romans, has control over His own death. When everything is finished, He will relinquish His life, but not until then. The usual process is arrested because Scripture (Psalm 34:20, Zechariah 12:10) *must be* fulfilled. God has stolen a march on the normal practice of the Roman authorities.

As he watches, a shaft of hope breaks through John's gloom. Things are not what they seem to be. Something else, determined by heaven and decided by the Father, is happening. John watches as the Roman legionnaires walk around the three crosses. They use a heavy iron club to shatter the bones. This act of breaking the bones is known as *crurifragium*. But there is to be no crurifragium for Jesus; His bones remain unbroken.

John, caught by surprise, watches as the soldier takes a javelin and thrusts it forcefully into the side of the dead Jesus. A torrent of blood and water bursts out, spraying onto the ground.

Throughout his account of the crucifixion, John is at pains to point out many details that fulfil Old Testament prophecy. This is a new day, of course, in which there is a departure from the old. It is also, crucially, a *continuation* of the Old Testament. In embracing the new, we are never fully cut off from what has gone before. What is new stretches back into history.

If we recall that John's Gospel is a 'new Genesis,' what springs immediately to mind, as we read that the solider pierced Jesus' side, is that God opened Adam's side and from it formed the woman, Eve, who would become "…the mother of all living." Out of Adam's deep sleep, the woman came forth. Blood and water are signs that accompany birth. Such is the vitality of spiritual life, that new birth inevitably comes out of death. The Church is that which is brought to life out of His death. The Church, the 'new Eve,' is born out of Christ's side.

Blood and water also represent 'life' and 'spirit.' When the blood of Jesus spills out, His life is poured out. But His life is poured out to then be poured into us. His spirit is poured out to infill us. As the blood and water seep into the earth, its effect impacts much more than humanity. It is also poured out to bring redemption to all of creation. In Genesis 4:10, the blood of Abel cried from the earth. Now, Jesus' blood speaks life back into the earth. All creation will be revivified by the life and spirit that comes from Jesus' death.

PERSPECTIVES ON THE CROSS

I now want to move away from my specific focus on John's Gospel in order to bring out some wider perspectives about the death of Jesus on the cross. So much has been spoken and written about this event in cosmic history that I am hesitant to regurgitate what is familiar and I do not wish to become too embroiled in theories about the Atonement. I wish to step away from that arena of debate and look from a different perspective.

As far as I see it, most of the atonement theories have not been based on a comprehensive revelation of who God really is as Father. This revelation, that we are now in, has shown that the real issue of God and the entire universe is an issue of orphanness and sonship. Therefore, we need to see the Atonement in relation to the Father and Sonship. I fully admit that I will not write a complete and balanced view. However, I want to point out some aspects, highlighting particular shapes and colours in the kaleidoscope of understanding about what the cross means. I believe this will give the Body of Christ a way forward for revelation within the paradigm of sonship and the Father's love.

When we come to look at the cross, I want to suggest a way to align ourselves to receive more revelation. Firstly, let me offer four 'foundation posts' that we need to build on:

i. **God is love. This is His substance and His essential nature.**
Everything must be viewed through the paradigm of God's
essential nature. Hans Urs von Balthasar has put it well,
"There will never be beings unloved by God, since God is
absolute love."

ii. **The Father and the Son are one in substance and purpose.**
There is no contradiction or dichotomy between the Father
and the Son when it comes to the cross. "God was in Christ
reconciling the world to Himself (2 Corinthians 5:19).

iii. **God is not willing that any should perish — 2 PETER 3:9.**
Therefore, Calvinism's 'limited atonement' theory is
heretical. If God is not a Universalist, He certainly
wants to be. That is not to say that some cannot *choose*
to remain outside the love of God. God has created free
beings. Love must always create beings that are free. This
leaves open the possibility that some may choose to remain
outside God's love. The fact remains that God *is* love.

A God of love did not want to punish humans for sins
committed. Jesus did not shield humanity from an angry
and vindictive Father God.

iv. **The fundamental understanding of the universe is through
the paradigm of orphanness and sonship.** Therefore fear
and love are the basic default paradigms that we view all
reality through. The Gospel is intended to restore humanity
back to sonship.

On the basis of these four 'foundation posts,' here is a suggested framework to work from. I suggest that we need to gain understanding in the following sequential order:

- **The reality of the Original:** Understanding God's true nature and His original intention for all creation.

- **The reality of the Problem:** Understanding what happened with Satan and 'the Fall' to disrupt the original intent of God.

- **The reality of the Purpose:** Understanding God's purpose for the future; a return to the original state of humanity in creation and progression beyond it to the full freedom of sonship.

- **The reality of the Solution:** Understanding the redemption of the original plan and the mechanism of salvation. I use the term 'mechanism' because this is where we need revelation.

We need to see soteriology (the theology of Salvation) through the paradigm of God restoring His children back into His family. The Father lost His children when they partook of the Tree of the Knowledge of Good and Evil. Jesus died on the cross to end accusation and condemnation from the Accuser and liberate us from the Tree of the Knowledge of Good and Evil. It is mostly condemnation and accusation that separate us from the love of God. Orphanness came in by what I call 'the upward movement' (I have written about this in detail in my book *Primal Hope: Finding Confidence beyond Religion*) and by partaking of the knowledge of good and evil.

THE CROSS AND THE TWO TREES

The paradigm of the two trees in the garden is an all-important one. It is only recently that this perspective has come into profile within the Church. Now we know that very little about life, about the Bible, about Christianity, makes sense outside of this perspective of the Two Trees. There are only two alternatives; we either eat of the Tree of Life or we eat of the Tree of the Knowledge of Good and Evil. How then is the death of Jesus on the cross viewed in the light of these two trees? This is the perspective that I am humbly offering.

When Jesus died on the cross, He died to deal with the insidious power of the Tree of the Knowledge of Good and Evil. Yes, He became sin for us, but the Church (lacking the perspective of the Two Trees) has not fully understood what sin actually is. Our definition of sin has been from the viewpoint of the knowledge of good and evil.

Historically, we have defaulted to view sin as 'moral evil' but this is incomplete. Sin must be viewed as 'moral good' too. We tend to equate holiness with 'good' rather than with *love*. Most atonement theories talk about the satisfaction of God's holiness as being 'total good' rather than total love. We have not seen God's holiness within the context of the Two Trees. Biblical terminology, such as "the spiritual forces of wickedness in the heavenly places," (Ephesians 6:12 NASB), is just a way of describing the knowledge of both good and evil. This is also what Paul talks about when he mentions "the law of sin and death." (Romans 8:2)

It is crucial to understand that self-righteousness is as sinful as all of the stuff on the wrong side of the moral standard. Being religious is as evil as being reprobate. If we only view sin as the 'bad stuff,' we will have a very lopsided view of the redemptive death of Jesus on the cross.

This is why we are also confused about Scriptures which talk about the 'wrath' or 'anger' of God. If we define sin, evil, or wickedness as the knowledge of good and evil, then God's wrath comes equally against the 'good' as well as the evil. God's wrath is against the knowledge of good *and* evil. The wrath of God is not a flaring up in anger or an outburst against our naughtiness. The wrath of God is a continual state of God's heart, totally consistent with His love. It is a passionate and burning indignation against the Tree of Knowledge of Good and Evil. God is not angry with humans, but with that which hinders us from being close to Him.

When Jesus became sin for us (2 Corinthians 5:21), He entered into the experience of what it was to be fully in the Tree of the Knowledge of Good and Evil. When He drank the cup, He drank the fulness of the knowledge of good and evil. This means that He became evil for us but, crucially, He also became *good* in the wrong tree for us. In other words, when He became sin, He did not only become morally repugnant; He *also* became morally self-righteous.

In the Tree of the Knowledge of Good and Evil, God is perceived to be eternally judgemental and eternally angry. Jesus fully experienced what it is to be in the wrong tree. In becoming fully filled with the knowledge of good and evil, He experienced what it was like to be abandoned by God because God cannot ever be reached in the knowledge of good and evil. This is why He cried out, "My God, my God, why have You forsaken me?" He did not say, "My *Father*, why have you forsaken me?" The Father had not abandoned Him but Jesus, having been made sin, *experienced what it was like* to be abandoned.

The writer of Hebrews tells us that Jesus "tasted death for us" (Hebrews 2:9). This was a consequence of Him participating in eat of the knowledge of good and evil. Death is inevitable for anyone who eats of that tree:

> "...but of the tree of the knowledge of good and evil you shall not eat, for in the day that you eat of it you shall surely die."
> — GENESIS 2:17

This is a crucial aspect of the death that Jesus tasted: He tasted the full consequences of eating from the Tree of the Knowledge of Good and Evil.

However, God was in Christ reconciling the world to Himself. (2 Corinthians 5:19) Jesus went from the Tree of Life over to the Tree of the Knowledge of Good and Evil in order to end the knowledge of good and evil and open the way to the Tree of Life again. His substitution was that He took our place in the knowledge of good and evil. When Jesus became sin, He experienced what it was to be "falling short of the mark." (Romans 3:23). He could not get to God, and felt abandoned by the God who was unreachable. But the Father raised Him from death to life (Romans 6:4, Colossians 2:12). After tasting death for us (Hebrews 2:9), the Father restored Him into life because it was not possible for Him to remain in the grip of death (Acts 2:24-28).

THE MECHANISM OF REDEEMING
OUR RELATIONSHIP WITH THE FATHER

If this revelation of the Father's love and sonship is the Gospel (which I believe it is), then forgiving from the heart to regain the heart of sonship is a crucial aspect of it. James Jordan has made a crucial breakthrough for the Body of Christ in communicating this. Heart forgiveness and the heart of sonship are the central lynchpins of restoring our connection experientially to the Father. In forgiving from the heart and opening our hearts to sonship again, we are applying the work of the cross in our lives. This is our repentance, our *metanoia*, in which we turn away from our orphanness and turn back to sonship. We change the direction of our heart-attitude towards our parents, and towards the Father.

A full Trinitarian gospel includes receiving Jesus as Saviour, the infilling of the Holy Spirit, *and* the reconnecting of the parental relationship to God the Father. These are all meant happen through repentance and baptism. A full gospel, to bring a person back into a sonship relationship with the Father, presents 'heart-forgiveness' and the 'heart of sonship' as part of repentance. Baptism is a baptism out of orphanness and into the sonship of Christ. Those who are baptised in water realise that they are entering into death, dying from orphan ways and emerging again into sonship. Anything short of this is an incomplete representation of the Good News.

Jesus must go to the cross to expose Satan and the orphan system. Jesus hanging on the cross will display what God is really like. He is still "the radiance of the glory of God and the exact imprint of His nature" (Hebrews 1:3) when He hangs on the cross. When Jesus is lifted up, God will be in Him, reconciling all creation to Himself (2 Corinthians 5:19). Creation is not reconciled through power and domination, but through self-giving love. God will pour out His life on the cross and invite humanity to receive that life. To stand and look at the One who is lifted up is to be invited to drink the life that He is pouring out. The lifting up of the Son on the cross is an invitation to participate in receiving the substance of God's love.

On the cross, Jesus experienced the full gamut of what it felt like to become orphaned and disconnected from His Father. He experienced what it is to count the cost of everything that was stolen, to enter into heart forgiveness, and find the heart of sonship again. The Father had not abandoned Him, but He *experienced* a rupture in His sonship to the Father.

Jesus plumbed the depths of orphanness on the cross. He faced the full cost of what had been stolen from humanity when Adam and Eve were pushed out of the garden. His cry expressed how they felt, "My God, my God, why have you forsaken me?" He was able to forgive from the heart those who crucified Him, praying, "Father, forgive them for they do not know what they are doing." His heart of sonship became operative again when He exhaled with His last breath, "Father, into Your hands I commit my spirit."

The cross is an eternal disposition in the heart of the Trinity. It is a display of the love that self-gives to the nth degree, that lays down its life to bring others into freedom. The love of the Godhead (Colossians 2:9) is at its fullest expression as Jesus hangs on the cross. James Jordan says, "The love of God is not an expression of the cross. The cross is an expression of the love of God." The love of God required His Son to die on the cross so that we can be reconciled with the Father.

THE BURIAL OF JESUS

After these things Joseph of Arimathea, who was a disciple of Jesus, but secretly for fear of the Jews, asked Pilate that he might take away the body of Jesus, and Pilate gave him permission. So he came and took away his body. Nicodemus also, who earlier had come to Jesus by night, came bringing a mixture of myrrh and aloes, about seventy-five pounds in weight. So they took the body of Jesus and bound it in linen cloths with the spices, as is the burial custom of the Jews. Now in the place where he was crucified there was a garden, and in the garden a new tomb in which no one had yet been laid. So because of the Jewish day of Preparation, since the tomb was close at hand, they laid Jesus there. — JOHN 19:38-42

This chapter finishes with the words, "They laid Jesus there." There is a strange rest that comes with utter powerlessness. When all human energy is exhausted, there is no other option but to wait for divine intervention. Jesus is buried and disappears permanently from the world. The Resurrection and Life submits Himself to being buried. He is *really* dead. The secret disciples, Joseph of Arimathea and Nicodemus, come out of hiding to care for the body of Jesus. It is anointed with expensive perfumes, fulfilling Mary of Bethany's prophetic action in John 12. This is an immense quantity of spices of staggering monetary value, fulfilling the prophecy of Isaiah:

"…He was with the rich in his death." — ISAIAH 53:9

Jesus always had the heart of a son towards His Father and, out of that intimate love relationship, He pleased the Father during His time on earth. The Father never turned His back on the Son, even during the hours of darkness. It was the Son, passing through the dark tunnel of being made sin, who took on the abandonment of orphanness that the human race experiences.

Since the great disruption of the Fall, humanity has been orphaned. We feel lost and alone in the world. Without the love of the Father at the deep essential core of our being, we are abandoned and utterly alone, disconnected and confused, without direction in this life. There is an existential homelessness at the core of our humanity. Jesus identified with the feelings of that abandonment.

In my preface, I wrote that John's Gospel is all about transition from the old to the new. The death, burial and resurrection of Jesus is the ultimate transition. As Jesus is buried, we plunge to the depths of transition. In every transition there is a low point when all hope seems lost, when the past is forever gone and we cannot see the future. Everything that Peter, John, His mother, Mary Magdalene and the others had believed in is shut into the tomb with the body of Jesus. They have followed Jesus too far to ever return but they are left not knowing what will happen now.

This is a necessary part of the process of transition. The burial of Jesus means that there can be no investment in anything that is not of the Spirit. This was the lesson that the disciples had to learn. They would realise that, "Even though we have known Christ according to the flesh, yet now we know Him thus no longer," (2 Corinthians 5:16). Everything that Jesus had promised them would happen on the basis of resurrection, *in* the Spirit. The promises of God are realised beyond the perception of orphan eyes.

Even though it may seem impenetrably dark at times, the reality is that the Father has never stopped loving us and watching over us. In the same way, the Father kept watching for Jesus to re-emerge, having defeated the powers of darkness. The Father is intensely watching as His Son is put into the tomb. The Father is moved in His emotions but confident knowing that the Son will re-emerge with the treasure of many sons and daughters.

BACK TO THE GARDEN

~

John's Gospel—the new Genesis, the 'book of beginnings' for the New Creation—brings us back to a garden. Human life on earth began with a relationship with God in a garden. Human life in the new creation begins in a garden too. Here, in John, we are taken to a garden to announce the resurrection.

> *"Now in the place where he was crucified there was a garden, and in the garden a new tomb in which no one had yet been laid. So...they laid Jesus there."* — JOHN 19:41,42

The garden of resurrection is located in the place of crucifixion and burial. The body of Jesus is laid in this tomb because it is close by and readily available. But if we are to take seriously John's theme of signs and their significance, there is a deeper meaning here. From God's perspective, the stage setting is orchestrated to bring particular 'sign-ificance' to the events.

Death, burial and resurrection all happen in the same place! The location of death and burial is also the location where resurrection happens. The truth is, resurrection can only happen where there is already death and burial; only what is already dead and buried can be the subject of resurrection. New life springs from the same place where the old life has died, but the new life has an entirely different quality than the old life.

DEATH AND RESURRECTION
IS INTEGRAL TO SONSHIP

Christianity only functions on the basis of resurrection. True Christianity is something that occurs beyond death. In my meditation on John 20, I want to extend meaning beyond the death and resurrection of Jesus. I want to look at the importance of the experience of resurrection life, asking the question: What does resurrection life actually look like?

The life of sonship is a life that is lived in the power of resurrection. A lot of emphasis has been put on the soteriological (pertaining to salvation) quality of Christ's death, burial and resurrection. This is absolutely right and necessary. In this chapter, however, I do not wish to focus strongly on that aspect.

The point I wish to emphasise is that sonship is only embarked upon through death and resurrection. Through this, different levels in the experience of sonship are entered into. In opening our hearts to the revelation of God's divine parenthood, there must be a willingness to die to our human default which is the paradigm of orphanness. To open the heart to receive the love of God involves a letting go of the deeply seated orphan mindset. To forgive our natural parents radically enough from the heart, to release them from all responsibility in the area of parenting, and to open our hearts to receiving parenting from God, involves a dying to the rights of the self for justice and vindication. To have the heart of sonship reactivated by having compassion on our natural parents (who could never give us the parenting that we needed) is to enter upon a death to our normal and natural way of doing things. It is not a normal human response to have a heart of sonship towards those who have failed to love us as we deserved to be loved. But that is what is required and enabled by supernatural grace.

To be loved experientially and continuously by the Father is to experience resurrection life. Connection to the Source of love and growing in the life of sonship cannot happen within the confines of natural, human life. It happens spiritually in resurrection power.

It is clear from Scripture that Jesus Himself also transitioned through different levels of sonship through death and resurrection. He was eternally the Son in the Father's bosom before creation. To become a Son in humanity, however, He had to pass through the birth channel from heaven into the womb of Mary, dying to functioning in His divine essence, to experience what it was like to be a Son in human weakness. The fifth chapter of Hebrews confirms this. To enter another level of sonship after defeating Satan, overcoming the principalities and powers, and sin and death, involved His death and resurrection. It is only post-resurrection that Jesus ascended to sit at the right hand of the Father, and was made cosmic Lord (Ephesians 1: 20-23). Death and resurrection is integral to sonship, for Jesus and us.

From this perspective, let me consider what happened on the morning of the resurrection.

EXPERIENCING SPIRITUAL CRISIS

The resurrection scene opens with the main protagonist, Mary Magdalene, coming to the tomb in the garden. She comes, before dawn, wrapped tightly against the night cold. As she approaches the tomb, something doesn't look quite right. To her shock, she discovers that the tomb has been broken open and the body of Jesus is missing. Her immediate assumption is that the body has been stolen.

The grievous finality of Jesus' death is now deepened with the disappearance of His body. For Mary, and for Peter and John, this discovery plunges them further into crisis. Mary's consternation is clear in her outburst to the other two, "They have taken the Lord out of the tomb, and we do not know where they have laid Him."

Mary uses the same terminology again, in verse 13, when speaking to the angels. It is very emotive language, a cry of anguish and confusion, even more personal:

"They have taken away my Lord, and I do not know where they have laid Him." As her distress deepens she expresses her heart. The most precious thing to her is the person that she calls "my Lord."

We all, without exception, can identify with Mary. A spiritual crisis of any sort, whether it is major or minor, is an experience of the absence of the Lord in the place where you look for Him. You go through the circumstances of life and previously the Lord has been there for you. He has helped you and given you the grace to get through; you have experienced Him to be very close to you; you have witnessed the excitement of Him moving supernaturally. Then, one day something happens, and in the place where you expect Jesus to be, He is no longer to be found.

When we enter a time of spiritual crisis, we expect to see something of what the Lord has done for us. But the tomb contains only the linen cloths that had been wrapped round the body of Jesus. These are the vestiges of what had once contained the person of the Lord.

Similarly, in times of spiritual crisis, we can look into our circumstances and into our hearts, and we can see only the residue of a past spirituality. We can see only the residue of what had been a vibrant relationship with the Lord. The linen cloths in the tomb do not contain anything, not even the dead body. It seems to us to be a hopeless situation. However there is a hint of resurrection when we read the following verse:

> *"Simon Peter…saw the linen cloths lying there, and the face cloth, which had been on Jesus head, not lying with the linen cloths but folded up in a place by itself."* — JOHN 20:6,7

This little observation about the face cloth neatly deals with any theories that the body of Jesus had been stolen. The face cloth has been set aside deliberately from the winding sheet and intentionally folded. This was either done by the angels or by Jesus to give a sign that resurrection had happened. If a body, lying in a tomb guarded by Roman soldiers, had been stolen, would the thieves have taken the time to fold up the face cloth? Of course not! Why would they even think about doing such a thing? This little observation, recorded by John years later, neatly dismisses all alternative theories of what might have happened to the body of Jesus. The deliberate folding of the face cloth is a clear confirmation that there has been a resurrection. However Peter, John or Mary do not notice it or find it significant at the time.

John, calling himself "the other disciple," enters the tomb and he sees and believes. (v.8) It is important to note that what John believes is *not* that Jesus has risen from the dead. What John believes here is the report of Mary that the body has apparently been stolen. Verses 9 and 10 clearly state that it is *not* the resurrection that he believes in. Peter and John return to their homes in fear, grief and disillusionment, leaving Mary Magdalene alone in the garden.

OUR ARDENT LOVE FOR GOD
CAN ONLY TAKE US SO FAR

"But Mary stood weeping outside the tomb..." (v. 11) Mary is still the main protagonist in this unfolding scene. Mary, like other women in the Gospel of John, becomes a catalyst for a major revelation of the Father and what sonship is.

Mary of Magdala personifies what it is to be an ardent lover of Jesus. Encountering Jesus had saved her from a life that was, ostensibly, in the gutter of society. Some theologians have suggested that she had been a 'loose woman' and a prostitute. Scripture does not actually specify this but it does say in Luke 8:2 that seven demons had been cast out of Mary. It is enough to say that she came from a lifestyle where she had been seriously demonised.

Mary's affection for Jesus is extremely passionate. Her love is so ardent, in fact, that she is willing to lift up and carry the body of Jesus all by herself (v.15). The strength of her emotion is enough to drive her beyond her physical capabilities.

This sort of ardent love is admirable, but it is actually misplaced. There is no need for her to re-bury the body of Jesus. Often, we can be so zealous in our love for God that we volunteer to bear burdens far beyond what is actually required of us. Many mystics and devoted believers have utterly spent themselves trying to carry the spiritual burdens of the whole world—burdens which they are not intended to carry. I fell into this trap myself. I was so on fire in my love for the Lord and in my zeal for His kingdom that I was willing to take on burdens that I was never graced to carry. In my intensity, I made promises to the Lord and others which were impossible to fulfil. Mary, weeping at the tomb, is consumed with an ardent fire but it is a zeal, nonetheless, that comes from ignorance. She is unaware of the fact that she doesn't actually need to locate and bury the body of the dead Jesus.

What Mary doesn't know, at this point, is that her Lord has *already* overcome death itself and has *already* been resurrected by the glory of the Father. Unknown to her, her resurrected Lord is standing right behind her!

Our love of God, out of our own zeal, will not last. If our love for God, no matter how devoted and passionate it is, is energised by our own selves, it will come to an end. Mary is desperately in love with the Lord but this has to come to a point of crisis so that she can *receive* the love of the Father. The whole point of the new creation and the new covenant is to *receive* Source-love, the love that originates in the Father and is energised by His Spirit. Our love for God can only be true love if it is a *response* to our experiencing of Him loving us. This is what Mary is about to enter into.

WHAT DOES RESURRECTION LIFE LOOK LIKE?

> *"Having said this, she turned around and saw Jesus standing, but she did not know that it was Jesus. Jesus said to her, 'Woman, why are you weeping? Whom are you seeking?'"*
> — JOHN 20:14,15

This now brings me to my original question: What does resurrection life look like?

Before I offer an answer, let us imagine Mary weeping at the empty tomb. She has lost everything. The passion in her heart that burned fiercely enough to lift up and carry the dead body of her Lord, has come to an end. Her Lord, who she loved more than anything else, is absent from her. Her hope has died.

The stranger who appears behind her, whom she supposes to be the gardener, puts a question to her, *"Woman, why are you weeping? Whom are you seeking?"*

That question pierces to the heart of Mary's problem. She is seeking closure and she is determined to give herself the closure that she needs. When she found the body she would take it, bring it to a particular place of closure, and create a memory around it. But that is not to be.

So, what does resurrection life look like?

Here is the answer:

The first appearance of resurrection life *doesn't look like anything out of the ordinary.*

Firstly, she *does not know* that it is Jesus.

Secondly, she *supposes* Him to be the *gardener.*

This is crucial. When the resurrected Christ appears to you in a way that you have not experienced Him before, at first you will not recognise Him. Resurrection life does not initially appear with an explosion of supernatural power and glory. The resurrected Christ does not bedazzle Mary. He is not surrounded by a heavenly company of angels; He is not in a glorified state as He was on the Mount of Transfiguration.

No: He just looks like the man who tends the garden. He appears as an ordinary working man.

As we go through the death of the old, when our past experience of the Lord has run its course and we find ourselves weeping and looking for the Lord who is not there, we will find that He is *actually* standing behind us. Then, turning around, we suppose Him to be the gardener.

One of the problems of the culture of the Pentecostal and Charismatic movements, that many of us have been part of, is that it has given us an expectation to look for God only in the spectacular and the extraordinary. If Mary had been looking for a supernaturally spectacular epiphany, she would have missed the resurrected Jesus. *The Son of God in resurrection life looked like the gardener.*

Let me suggest to you. If you identify with Mary in her grief and her loss of the experiential presence of the Lord, I exhort you to look at your life full in the face, and cry from your heart, "Tell me where you have laid Him!" In spiritual crisis, the circumstances of our daily lives can appear to be as mundane as the man who does the gardening. But, out of that mundaneness and disappointment, resurrection life will call your name.

> *"Jesus said to her, 'Mary.' She turned and said to him in Aramaic, 'Rabboni!' (which means Teacher)".* — JOHN 20:16

When the Spirit of resurrection life, the resurrected Christ—whom we mistake to be the gardener—calls us by name out of the humdrum of our ordinary lives, we will be able to recognise Him as our Teacher. You will be able to see your life as containing 'Rabboni,' as containing the ability to teach you how to enter into sonship on the other side of spiritual death. You will recognise that resurrection life, appearing within something which you assume to be ordinary, is able to lead you into new spiritual realities.

THE ROLE OF SONSHIP IN THE GARDEN
OF THE NEW CREATION

There is more, however, to the risen Son appearing as a gardener. In the first chapters of Genesis, man and woman were placed in a garden. They were commissioned to tend the garden and to extend the dominion of love throughout that garden and into all of creation. Then, by the loving action of the Father to save them from eternal death, they were expelled from that garden. Here, in resurrection life, they are restored to the garden and there is a revelation that the Son is a gardener. The task of the risen Jesus, among others, is to restore all that was lost in the original garden of Eden. What was begun in Eden, then interrupted by the Fall, can now be taken up again. The purpose of the Father to parent *all creation* can now be resumed in resurrection life.

The work of redemption is meant to extend beyond the human race into the whole of creation. And the work of redemption is to be carried out on 'resurrection ground,' by the sons and daughters of God, in whom the spirit of the Father resides. The manifestation of the Father to all creation will involve 'gardening.' Gardening is a vocation requiring love for the earth, the knowledge of what is good for the earth, and following the rhythm of the seasons. Gardening involves the acceptance of death in the sure hope of resurrection, the connection between seed-sowing and fruit-bearing. Gardening necessitates love, hope, vigilance and joy. The ministry of manifesting the Father's love is very much like tending a garden. This vocation of 'gardening' applies to all callings in life. To be a 'gardener' is to have dominion, not domination.

One of the principal vocations of sons and daughters in relation to the groaning creation, is to carry out the Father's work in loving that creation. The manifestation of the sons and daughters of God to the groaning creation will free it from futility and decay. Romans 8:19-21 makes this clear. This freedom from futility and decay will come about through the spiritual charism of 'gardening'; of having once again the dominion that was given to man and woman in Eden (Genesis 1:28). Denise Jordan has crucially pointed out that this dominion is the rule of love rather than power, and it can only be given to the image of God, to the complementarity of the true masculine and the true feminine.[37]

RESURRECTION RESTORES
THE TRUE FEMININE

The fact that Mary is the first witness to the resurrection of the Son brings out another significant reality in the new creation: the redemption of the feminine from the grip of misogyny.

Mary is the primary witness to the restoration of the Tree of Life in the Garden. The death of Jesus delivered the final blow to the Tree of the Knowledge of Good and Evil. The resurrection of Jesus has made the Tree of Life available again. The love of the Father is the life source of everything. Humanity is able, once again, to feed freely from the Tree of Life, and to administer the leaves of the Tree for the healing of creation.

The approach of the Risen Son to Mary Magdalene is a direct answer to the approach of the serpent to Eve. Satan, the Orphan Spirit, approached Eve to invite her to eat of the Tree of the Knowledge of Good and Evil. He has attacked the feminine characteristics in the image of God ever since.

---

37. Denise Jordan, *The Forgotten Feminine*, published by Fatherheart Ministries, Taupo, 2013, p 31.

Jesus, the Son, approaches Mary to offer her to eat of the Tree of Life. The femininity of God's image is restored to its true place. Mary, like the other women in John's Gospel, is a catalyst and a witness to divine in-breaking and revelation.

"Jesus said to her, 'Do not cling to me, for I have not yet ascended to the Father...'" — JOHN 20:17

In urging her not to hold onto Him, Jesus propels Mary further into resurrection life. She has recognised Him to be the Jesus that she knew very well, her beloved Lord whom she loved with ardent passion. She is now clinging to that reality. But there is more to come. She is not to remain in this place of personal affection for Jesus. Resurrection life is to open up something to her (and the disciples) that can only come from Jesus ascending to the Father. It is only when He ascends to the Father that the Holy Spirit of sonship, who will make resurrection life real inside them, can be poured out.

Mary accepts the miracle that Jesus has risen from the dead. To her delight, she has no choice. She is touching Him, recognising Him, hearing His voice. It would not have be strange for her to hear Him tell her that He is going to return to the Father.

The other half of the sentence, however, brings an explosive new reality to Mary:

"...but go to my brothers and say to them, 'I am ascending to my Father and your Father, to my God and your God."

In this instant, Jesus speaks her into union with Him! By His words, Mary is caught up into sonship. She is included with Jesus in *His* relationship to the Father. She is also given the substance of this to pass on to the disciples. This is the first time that Jesus has referred to His disciples as His brothers. In resurrection, they are brought into the Father's family.

The words of Jesus are never merely words. They are never just sounds that communicate concepts. Every word that God speaks carries with it the creative force to make the words real in our experience. In saying, "My Father and your Father, my God and your God," the revelation of sonship has entered into the heart of Mary Magdalene. The God and Father of Jesus is, in stunning reality, her God and Father too!

REDEMPTION GIVES BIRTH TO SONSHIP

The Son came from heaven to earth through the birth channel, the womb of His mother, also called Mary. He came to this life, to creation, through the womb of a virgin.

The revelation of sonship ("*My Father and your Father…my God and your God*") then comes to Mary of Magdala.

This Mary is, most likely, the epitome of the 'fallen feminine.'[38] She had been delivered of seven demonic strongholds. She may have been a prostitute in her previous life; she was certainly a woman with a bad reputation. Nevertheless, she is a *spiritual virgin*. She has

---

38. You need to be familiar with the teaching of Denise Jordan to really see what I am bringing out here. The chapter entitled 'The Restoration of the Image of God' in Denise's book, *The Forgotten Feminine*, brings this out.

a heart that is pure and untouched by any other spiritual influence, therefore, she is able to be impregnated with the revelation of sonship.

The resurrected Son, by including her with Him, uniting her in sonship with the words, "I am ascending to my Father and your Father," includes Mary in the sonship that He enjoys with the Father. In hearing of her inclusion in the sonship of the risen Jesus, she now experiences in her heart the reality of the final words of Jesus in John 17:26:

> "...that the love with which you have loved me may be in them, and I in them."

Mary Magdalene, who has personified the fallen feminine, is the first one to experience the substance of the Father's love for her in the reality of sonship. In announcing the resurrection to the other disciples, Mary is a witness to resurrection life. More than that, however, she is a carrier of the substance of resurrection life itself. She manifests the Father's love, which has been imparted to her by the risen Son, to the other disciples. She had been injected with the revelation of her union with Christ in His relationship to the Father.

I believe that this section of John, narrating Mary of Magdala's experience in the garden on the morning of the resurrection, contains much to instruct us. It shows us that sonship comes in the place of resurrection. That gives us great hope, because crisis is part of our human experience. We all go through circumstances when our experience of God is lost to us. In the Father's love, however, there is eternal hope. The love of the Father carries with it the hope and the reality of resurrection life. But remember, resurrection life does not look as we may expect it to. Resurrection life appears in the guise of the ordinary. It needs to do so because the sons and daughters of God are called into the whole creation.

In His death, Jesus gathered all the orphanness of humanity (as well as the orphanness of creation) into himself. In rising again, He reconnects humanity (and creation) with the Father. The words, "I ascend to my Father and your Father" articulate the resolution of the whole orphan issue. In Christ, full redemption of the parent-child relationship to God the Father is accomplished. After expressing the ultimate orphan cry on the cross, "My God, my God, why have you forsaken me?" redemption is expressed in the words, "I am ascending to my Father and your Father, to my God and your God." These words, *my Father and your Father, my God and your God*, envelop us in union with Christ, in His relationship to the Father.

THERE IS A NEW CREATION!

~

THE FIRST SIGNS OF A NEW ERA

R isen and alive, Jesus goes to His disciples. With breathless excitement, Mary Magdalene has already announced to the disciples what she has experienced in the garden. Now Jesus visits them to announce the beginning of the new epoch:

> *On the evening of that day, the first day of the week, the doors being locked where the disciples were for fear of the Jews, Jesus came and stood among them and said to them, "Peace be with you." When he had said this, he showed them his hands and his side. Then the disciples were glad when they saw the Lord."* — JOHN 20:19,20

It is the evening of the day of resurrection. In Jewish understanding,

---

39. Chapters : John 20:19-31 and John 21

this evening begins the first day of the week. The disciples are locked indoors, fearing the reprisals of the religious leaders and the mob. After the crucifixion, they must be fearful of being rounded up and killed as well. Immediately Jesus speaks peace to them. In actual fact, He is giving them the usual greeting that friends exchange on meeting each other. In Hebrew it is "Shalom Aleichem," though it is likely that Jesus would have spoken it in Aramaic. It is a casual, familiar greeting but when Jesus speaks, an infusion of serenity and wellbeing fills the room.

Let me assure you of this: locked doors cannot stop the entrance of God. Jesus disregards the locked doors and enters the room to speak 'Shalom' to those who are full of fear. Oftentimes, in ministry, we put the onus on people to open their hearts, saying it is their responsibility. However, this incident tells us that Jesus overrode the disciples' fear and entered the room anyway. Many times the doors of a person's heart can be shut through fear and they cannot open those doors. The reality is, anointing and the powerful love of God can walk through a wall even if the doors of the heart are locked. We, as preachers, need to ask the Lord for enough spiritual power to emulate Jesus and enter the 'room' of the human heart, even if the doors are locked.

The doors are locked because of fear of the Jews. And rightly so, because the old always resists the embryo of the new. But now, the first signs of the new epoch, the first shoots of spring are appearing. The green shoot of sonship in resurrection comes through the wall irrespective of locked doors. Resurrection life cannot be thwarted. Peace comes in the first light of a new era.

Jesus shows them His hands and His side. It is still the same Jesus. He has carried His wounds through death, and, most importantly, through resurrection. Even in resurrection life, the scars of crucifixion remain. I love this! The God (Father, Son and Holy Spirit) that I know is not afraid to carry through the marks of crucifixion into resurrection glory. God is not trying to clean us up so that the scars and wounds disappear. No! The wounds *leak* resurrection life. There is continuity through the rupture. He is the same person that they always knew. His humanity remains.

Whenever we pass through suffering, wounding, and the death of the old, we can be assured that resurrection will, inevitably, come. However, we should not expect to come out on the other side without the evidence of our past brokenness. In my opinion, many people are expecting to be healed enough so that scars and wounds completely disappear. This is not the case. We are intended to carry the vestiges of past wounds (the pain of which have been healed, of course) so that others may be reassured and gladdened through seeing them.

THE BREATH OF LIFE

Jesus said to them again, "Peace be with you. As the Father has sent me, even so I am sending you." And when he had said this, he breathed on them and said to them, "Receive the Holy Spirit. If you forgive the sins of anyone, they are forgiven; if you withhold forgiveness from anyone, it is withheld." — JOHN 20:21-23

As Jesus reiterates peace, wholeness and wellbeing (Shalom) to His disciples, He speaks the words of sonship to them: "As the Father has sent me, even so I am sending you." He is not sending them as a commander; He is sending them in the way that the Father sent Him. The Father sends the Son, and the Son sends other sons. There is an uninterrupted thread. The sending of Jesus by the Father was not by directive command; it was by the infilling of love. When the Father's love fills us, its water level rises so much that it overflows, and that overflow becomes a sending. Nothing more is needed; love sloshing over and spilling out *is* the commission.

Jesus breathes upon them. He exhales His breath over them and says, "Receive Holy Spirit!" I believe that they receive the Spirit here. This is the *indwelling* Spirit who fills them on the inside. It is not yet the *empowering* Spirit who will fall upon them in the Upper Room on the day of Pentecost. In my experience, it is one thing to have the Spirit of God welling up from inside, but it is another thing to be clothed with power. The Spirit breathed on the inside will, undoubtedly, witness with our spirits that we are God's children (Romans 8:16). That is a wonderful and ongoing reality, but it does not equate with being empowered and anointed to effectively work miracles.

This breathing of the Spirit of life into them is indicative of the new creation. John's Gospel is a 'new Genesis' and here we have new creation taking place. Jesus breathes into them the Spirit of Life. As God breathed His love and life into Adam in the garden, His love and life are breathed into the disciples and new creation begins in their innermost spirits. They are now seeded with resurrection life on the inside. The first thing they are empowered to do is to wield the power of forgiveness.

EMPOWERED TO FORGIVE OR
WITHHOLD FORGIVENESS

*"If you forgive the sins of anyone, they are forgiven; if
you withhold forgiveness from anyone, it is withheld."*
— JOHN 20:23

Immediately upon receiving the Spirit being breathed into
them, the disciples are given power to forgive sins and to withhold
forgiveness. Why does the promise of the Holy Spirit primarily
involve forgiveness?

The forgiveness of sins is a very powerful weapon in the ministry
of sonship. In ministering to others, I have recently discovered
the dynamic power of the sacrament of reconciliation. Like the
confessional familiar to Catholics, I have been given the grace
to listen to some of the most shameful secrets of people's lives,
and then to pronounce absolute forgiveness of their sins. When a
person confesses the most shameful secrets of their past and they
receive not a smidgeon of condemnation in return, that is more
powerful than prayer ministry or the casting out of demons. In fact,
people are instantly set free from demonic oppression because the
demonic no longer has any landing ground within them. Shame and
condemnation are the habitat of demonic, emotional and mental
oppression. The sacrament of confession and absolution of their sin
and shame, removes the rug from under the feet of the Accuser in
their lives.

Why withhold forgiveness? This is not to be seen as some sort
of mean-spirited callousness. Rather, it is the prerogative of those

who know what forgiveness really entails to ensure that people come to a place of true forgiveness. James Jordan has given to the Body of Christ a breakthrough in this area of forgiveness, when he distinguishes forgiving from the heart from forgiving from the will. The only genuine forgiveness is forgiveness that is from the heart. To withhold forgiveness is to ensure that a person is able to come to a place of being able to forgive from a heart that loves mercy. Wielding the power of forgiveness is granted to those who are living in sonship. Forgiveness is a rudimentary anointing in the life of sonship. The initial evidence of receiving the indwelling Spirit of the Father's love is the supernatural grace to experience and live in forgiveness. Greater works need the *empowerment* of the Spirit falling *upon* us. Mature Christianity is the synthesis of the Spirit within us rising up in love, *and* the Spirit falling upon us in power.

BEYOND SIGHT AND SENSE

Now Thomas, one of the Twelve, called the Twin, was not with them when Jesus came. So the other disciples told him, "We have seen the Lord." but he said to them, "Unless I see in his hands the mark of the nails, and place my finger into the mark of the nails, and place my hand into his side, I will never believe."

Eight days later, his disciples were inside again, and Thomas was with them. Although the doors were locked, Jesus came and stood among them and said, "Peace be with you." Then he said to Thomas, "Put your finger here, and see my hands; and put out your hand, and place it in my side. Do not disbelieve, but believe. Thomas answered him, "My Lord

and my God!" Jesus said to him, "Have you believed because
you have seen me? Blessed are those who have not seen and
yet have believed." — JOHN 20:24-29

Our friend, Thomas, makes an appearance again. As I have observed earlier, disciples such as Thomas the Twin and Simon Peter are there to help us connect with our humanity and our struggle to go beyond our sense world into the realm of faith. The Biblical writers do not disparage the reactions of Thomas and Peter (Thomas is never called 'Doubting Thomas' by the biblical writers). The reaction of Thomas is there to give us hope. Thomas is rationalising, needing evidence in order to believe. But there is even hope for rationalists in resurrection.

Yet again, the doors are locked. The Spirit breathed within them is birthing them into new life, but they are still afraid. The blast from heaven at Pentecost will shatter the door locks and they will burst boldly out into the street. For now, they are closeted indoors. However, Jesus does not condemn them. He knows that they are newly born of the Spirt, so He takes the initiative to come again to them. Again, He speaks peace and wellbeing to them. He is feeding them, nurturing them with the comfort of the mothering love of God. These disciples, who before the crucifixion were 'mature' Jesus followers have now been 'born again' and are infants who cannot feed themselves. Their old enthusiasm and bluster has died; now they are weak and vulnerable infants, who need constant nurturing. They are in an enclosed space; this room is a nursery.

In our religiosity and ignorance we tend to snigger at Thomas, despising him for being full of unbelief and doubt. Doubt is not the issue. Thomas was not there when Jesus breathed the Spirit into the disciples earlier. Thomas, therefore, is not born of the Spirit yet. Jesus invites Thomas to witness that it is truly Him, Jesus. I do not believe He speaks words of condemnation to Thomas. I believe that Jesus breathes the Spirit into Thomas in the same way that He had exhaled on the others. Believing cannot come by seeing the evidence. Yes, Thomas is reassured, but true belief only comes by the Spirit imparting faith on the inside.

"Blessed are those who have not seen and yet have believed" (v.29) The new epoch is *beyond* the physical senses. If we are looking to our natural senses or to our intellect for spiritual answers, we will always struggle with belief. In light of that, it is absolutely understandable for a rational person to be an agnostic or an atheist. Connection to God can only be established by faith, and faith is something produced in the heart.

Jesus tells Thomas that it is not enough even to be able to place his hands into the wounds. That will not carry him into the era of the Spirit. When Jesus leaves, which He will shortly do, faith must be activated. Thomas Aquinas, in his Latin hymn, *Tantum Ergo* says:

> *"Let faith provide a supplement*
> *For the failure of the senses."*

This expresses it well. Our senses are limited and faith leaps beyond them. The senses tell us what is true or what is not true according to our *natural* deduction, but faith is not limited by that. What is true is not necessarily *truth*. When we are filled with supernatural love, faith is created within us and we begin to believe in a different reality. A word spoken from God is creative. True faith does not look for evidence; it *creates* the evidence.

> *Now Jesus did many other signs in the presence of the disciples,*
> *which are not written in this book; but these are written*
> *so that you may believe that Jesus is the Christ, the Son of*
> *God, and that by believing you may have life in his name.*
> — JOHN 20:30,31

The words written by John have become Scripture. These words, like the entire written corpus, are not an end in themselves. They are intended to *help* us *believe* that Jesus has come from the Father. When we read what Jesus said and did it opens our hearts. Belief is not something that we drum up by willpower or positive affirmation; belief is automatically consequent on having an open heart. John's Gospel is unique in opening our hearts to Jesus Christ's sonship to the Father.

"Life in His name" is the life of sonship. Jesus is the Anointed One sent by the Father to restore all creation into harmonious relationship with His Father. We can now see clearly that the title of 'Christ' (the Sent and Anointed One) is a title of sonship. Eternal life is not found within Jesus as an isolated individual; that is the limited revelation of Evangelicalism. Eternal life is to be found within the *sonship* of Jesus to the Father.

John's Gospel only contains a sample of the signs that Jesus did. As amazing as it is to read about them, they are only a mere sprinkling. John tells us now that the whole of Jesus' life and ministry on earth has been intended as a sign to point us to the Father. There is no doubt in John's mind, as he brings his writing to a conclusion, that the Father *must* be known.

THE SACRAMENT OF THE SECULAR

Now we come to John's final scene, Chapter 21. Seven of the disciples are together and what happens now is indicative of what the new epoch of Spirit-filled sonship will look like:

> *After this, Jesus revealed himself again to the disciples by the Sea of Tiberias, and he revealed himself in this way. Simon Peter, Thomas (called the Twin), Nathanael of Cana in Galilee, the sons of Zebedee, and two others of his disciples were together. Simon Peter said to them, "I am going fishing." They said to him, "We will go with you." They went out and got into the boat, but that night they caught nothing.*
>
> *Just as day was breaking, Jesus stood on the shore; yet the disciples did not know that it was Jesus. Jesus said to them, "Children, do you have any fish?" They answered him, "No." He said to them, "Cast the net on the right side of the boat, and you will find some." So they cast it and now they were not able to haul it in, because of the quantity of fish. That disciple whom Jesus loved therefore said to Peter, "It is the Lord!" When Simon Peter heard that it was the Lord, he put on his outer garment, for he was stripped for work, and threw himself into the sea. The other disciples came in the boat, dragging the net full of fish, for they were not far from the land, but about a hundred yards off.*

When they got to the land, they saw a charcoal fire in place, with fish laid on it, and bread. Jesus said to them, "Bring some of the fish that you have just caught." So Simon Peter went aboard and hauled the net ashore, full of large fish, 153 of them. And although there were so many, the net was not torn. Jesus said to them, "Come and have breakfast." Now none of the disciples dared ask him, "Who are you?" They knew it was the Lord. Jesus came and took the bread and gave it to them, and so with the fish. This was now the third time that Jesus was revealed to the disciples after he was raised from the dead. — JOHN 21:1-14

Simon Peter's fishing expedition highlights something that is innate to sonship. Many commentators say that Peter acts out of unbelief, in hopelessness and resignation that the dream of building the kingdom with Jesus is now forever finished. I do not see it like that anymore and I want to offer an alternative view.

It is true that the disciples' first attempts at fishing were fruitless. They have fished throughout the night but have caught nothing until the resurrected Jesus appears to them. Jesus appears to them "in this way" *within the ordinary.* Like Mary in the garden, at first they do not recognise Him. Mary Magdalene mistook Him for the gardener; here, He appears as a fisherman. Resurrection life is transforming the ordinary. The mundane is shot through with eternal life.

If we, as Christians, begin to realise that resurrection life is resident within us, it will transform everything. Resurrection life cannot always be felt, however, emotionally or physically. Mostly, it takes faith to believe that we have the life of God within us. One of the huge dichotomies that exists in Christianity today (and has done so for millennia) is the sacred-secular split. In resurrection life, there is no such thing. The question I wish to pose is this: Does Simon Peter remain a fisherman while also functioning as an apostle? Does he set up 'a ministry,' or does he *become* the ministry?

Somehow, I don't think that Peter will rent out office space in Jerusalem with the nameplate "Simon Peter - Apostle" on it. I am being a little facetious but I am making a point. How about, when Simon Peter announces that he is going fishing, he is going to what his true calling is? Could it even be that Peter returns to fishing in order to become a fisher of men? Maybe Peter's apostleship is woven throughout his fishing. Is that possible? Many scholars now take the view that Paul established a full-time business making tents in Corinth, and worked in his shop for 12-14 hours a day, and that many of his converts were customers and business associates. This now makes perfect sense to me.

Resurrection life is not a departure from normal life. Rather, it transforms it! It is the glorious freedom of...........going fishing! What we thought of as 'secular' is actually a sacrament; it is a natural activity which imparts spiritual graces. Life, in all its joy and sorrow, its excitement and mundaneness, is shot through with heavenly, spiritual substance. The death and resurrection of Jesus announces the collapse of another historic dualism. This dualism still plagues the Church, but let it be stated unequivocally: *There is no sacred-secular divide.*

One of the problems of contemporary Christianity is that it is largely attempting to bring a business paradigm into spirituality.

Ministries are run like businesses, spiritual leaders have the title 'CEO' or other titles used in the business realm. Don't misunderstand me: business is good and God-given. My desire, and I believe I can say this prophetically, is that we will see that God is moving in the opposite direction. Rather than putting a business model into the Body of Christ, God is filling every son and daughter with His spirit of approval so that they bring a *spiritual* paradigm into business, or indeed, whatever area they are called to. What will this look like in practice?

First of all, a revelation of sonship makes each person secure in their identity. Instead of striving to be in 'ministry,' they will see that they are *already* in ministry. People will see that they do not have to become a 'pastor' or be involved in a missionary organisation to be in ministry. Ministry is the overflow of the life of God in *your* calling, and according to your particular bent, whatever that is. As we bring the life of Spirit into our work, we will find that the 'haul of fishes' will exceed anything we ever dreamed of.

I believe that the Church needs to cast the net on the other side of the boat. Instead of people leaving what they enjoy and are gifted at, to join organisations and programmes of ministry (which are labouring in the 'night' of lack of revelation and catching nothing), they need to cast the net out in unprecedented areas. If you are in a profession, in business, or a manual labourer, cast the net out for supernatural intervention in *that* arena. Accountants can receive revelation too! All vocations and occupations can be permeated with the miraculous grace that brings in the haul of fish. The Lord blesses Peter in his work and uses it to show that he can be a fisher of men.

THERE IS A NEW CREATION

What is abundantly evident in resurrection life is that a new beginning has emerged out of death. John reiterates this new genesis, the new creation coming from the Father. New life is breathed upon us and as we open our eyes we see the eyes of our Father gazing longingly into us. In this new creation, eyes that were closed are opened again. The time after the crucifixion, when the body of Jesus was laid in the tomb, was a time when the eyes of natural perception were blinded. Those eyes of soulish judgement, on an intellectual and moral level, were never meant to see. But see they did, and they need to become blinded again so that the eyes of the heart can be reopened.

Saul of Tarsus experienced this after his blinding encounter with the Light on the road to Damascus:

> *"Saul rose from the ground, and although his eyes were opened, he saw nothing…and for three days he was without sight."* — ACTS 9:8,9

Saul went through the essential process of becoming blind. He needed to 'un-see' what he had seen so that he could see the unseen.

After three days, Ananias visited him, laying hands upon him:

> *"And immediately something like scales fell from his eyes, and he regained his sight."* — ACTS 9:18

Paul lost and regained his physical sight but he lost his 'Tree of Knowledge' sight permanently. His eyes were opened to see an entirely new reality. He saw through the eyes of love. This is what new creation does: it brings the perspective of love to the restored eyes of the heart. Paul explains what is happening to the disciples here, after the resurrection of Jesus:

> *"For the love of Christ controls us, because we have concluded this: that one has died for all, therefore all have died, and he died for all, that those who live might no longer live for themselves but for him who for their sakes died and was raised. From now on, therefore, we regard no one according to the flesh. Even though we once regarded Christ according to the flesh, we regard him thus no longer."*
> — 2 CORINTHIANS 5:14-16

What Paul is saying here is exactly what has happened to the disciples. They have known and followed Christ "according to the flesh." That was legitimate and essential. When Jesus went to the cross and died, the disciples' 'knowing' was shattered. By all accounts, He had let them down and failed their expectations. However, their expectations were misplaced. They didn't realise that they need to relate to Him within the environment of 'new creation.'

Paul then follows with a crucial statement:

> *"Therefore, if anyone is in Christ he is a new creation."*
> — 2 CORINTHIANS 5:17

That is what most translations say. But that is *not* what the original language says. The original Greek actually says:

"If anyone is in Christ—**new creation!**"

In other words, if anyone is in Christ, *there is* a new creation. This goes beyond individual renewal. This statement shows unequivocally that being 'in Christ' opens up our eyes to see the entirety of new creation. It also means that we see everything with 'new creation eyes.' What was 'fallen' no longer looks fallen, what is cleansed was never vile; what is redeemed, in actuality, was never lost. Father has always been Father; Jesus has always been victorious, the Spirit of Life has eternally gushed out from the Godhead. The death of Jesus and His resurrection has reestablished that absolute, original and final reality in our vision. Our eyes have truly been opened. When we are on resurrection ground, *everything* is new.

THE NATURE OF LEADERSHIP
IN THE NEW ERA

When they had finished breakfast, Jesus said to Simon Peter, "Simon, son of John, do you love me more than these?" He said to him, "Yes, Lord; you know that I love you." He said to him, "Feed my lambs."

He said to him a second time, "Simon, son of John, do you love me?" He said to him, "Yes, Lord; you know that I love you." He said to him, "Tend my sheep."

He said to him the third time, "Simon, son of John, do you love me?" Peter was grieved because he said to him the third time, "Simon, son of John, do you love me?" and he said to him, "Lord, you know everything, you know that I love you." Jesus said to him, "Feed my sheep. — JOHN 21:15-17

They sit around the charcoal fire, which Jesus has prepared, eating the fish for breakfast. Resurrection life is fully engaged with the ordinary. The resurrected Son demonstrates His ability and willingness to tend to their human needs. Then Jesus turns His attention to Peter. Peter has been through a rough time. His expectations and ideals were high and noble, then he went through extreme disillusionment. He is humbled and deflated. Jesus is searching in Peter's heart to see if there are still any vestiges of kingdom-passion in it.

When Jesus puts the question to Peter, "Do you love me more than these?", I think He is saying, "Do you love me more than these other disciples love me? Is that *still* what you are claiming, Peter?" Peter has demonstrated his devotion before; he has always surpassed the others in his passion for following Jesus. Now, Jesus is probing Peter for any residue of spiritual grandiosity and elitism. Personally speaking, I can identify with Peter in this regard. I always viewed myself as being more radical and more willing to give everything for the kingdom than anyone else. I really believed that I loved God "more than these." Like Peter, I have been disillusioned and humbled.

Peter *does* love Jesus in his heart. There is no question of that. But his devotion has been tested to the point of him denying three times that he ever knew Jesus. Now Jesus asks him three times, "Peter, do you love me?" Peter is upset that he is being tested again but Jesus is teaching Peter that the fruit of love will be different to what it was before. In the old era, Peter showed his devotion by claiming he would follow Jesus to the end and lay down his life for Him (John 13:37); he demonstrated his passion for Jesus by slicing off the ear of the high priest's servant (John 18:10). Now, Jesus says to him that the true evidence of love will be the tender nurture of the Father's flock.

Peter's earlier devotion was religious zeal. As the love of the Father fills him, it will overflow into others under his care. This is how his love for God will be demonstrated. Jesus lays out to Peter the criteria for leadership in the *basilaea* (dominion) of love. Leadership in love is not like the false shepherds who steal and rob. True leadership does not lord it over, it does not drive, nor does it use flattery or induce guilt to manipulate the results that it wants. True leadership does not drum up passion, or call for ever greater levels of commitment to 'the big vision.'

True leadership cares for the sheep and the lambs. It feeds, nurtures and protects. God is more than capable to accomplish His work in and through people. When the life of God is released within people, they do not really need to be led, in the sense of achieving the fulfilment of a vision. David, the Shepherd of Israel understood this:

> *"Your people will volunteer freely in the day of Your power…"*
> — Psalm 110:3 (NASB)

Leadership is to be an expression of what God the Father is like. More than that, it is God the Father manifesting Himself in tender care:

"He will tend his flock like a shepherd;
he will gather the lambs in his arms;
he will carry them in his bosom,
and gently lead those that are with young." — ISAIAH 40:11

The evidence of loving God is to care for His sheep and the lambs. It shows that our love is not based on religious zeal, but that we are receiving love from the Source and it is pouring through us to the sheep and the lambs. Peter is now learning this: to truly love God is to also love others. He is learning what John astutely observes in his letter:

If anyone says, "I love God," and hates his brother, he is a liar; for he who does not love his brother whom he has seen cannot love God whom he has not seen. — 1 JOHN 4:20

We only have spiritual authority to the extent that we are filled with the Father's love. If you are not able to feed and tend the sheep and lambs, it is only a matter of waiting until you have received enough love to let it overflow. This is why we should never try to grasp at ministry before we are established in our experience of the love of the Father.

"Truly, truly, I say to you, when you were young, you used to dress yourself and walk wherever you wanted, but when you are old, you will stretch out your hands, and another will dress you and carry you where you do not want to go." (This he said to show by what death he was to glorify God.) And after saying this he said to him, "Follow me." — JOHN 21:18,19

Jesus now prophesies to Peter how he, Peter, will die, and He calls Peter to follow Him. The path of following will lead Simon Peter through Pentecost into mighty deeds of power. It will lead to the rooftop where he will eat what God has cleansed, accepting what is not kosher to prepare the way for the Holy Spirit to fall upon the Gentiles. This following will bring Peter to experience increasingly what it is to "partake of the divine nature." (2 Peter 1:4)

Simon Peter is called to follow Jesus into participation in His nature. In other words, he will realise that divine nature is fully expressed in the laying down of a life in love for the sake of others. Ultimately, this will lead Peter to the same type of death as Jesus, that of crucifixion. My point is this: Peter's leadership is not diminished or abandoned when he is old. His powerlessness in the face of his own martyrdom is *supreme* leadership. It is the laying down of his life for his friends. In this he becomes like his Lord.

ONLY LOVE REMAINS

Peter turned and saw the disciple whom Jesus loved following them, the one who had been reclining at table close to him and had said, "Lord, who is it that is going to betray you?" When Peter saw him, he said to Jesus, "Lord, what about this man?" Jesus said to him, "If it is my will that he remain until I come, what is that to you? You follow me!" So the saying spread abroad among the brothers that this disciple was not to die, yet Jesus did not say to him that he was not to die, but, "If it is my will that he remain until I come, what is that to you?" — JOHN 21:20-23

Peter turns around and notices John following them. Peter is processing Jesus' prophetic hint about his future martyrdom, and now he wonders about his friend, John. They are close. It was to these two men that Mary Magdalene first turned when she discovered the empty tomb. They raced each other to the tomb that morning. John outran Peter and reached the tomb first, though he hesitated about going into the tomb. Peter, maybe older and heavier, arrived after John but there was no hesitation for him; he plunged directly into the tomb. These two have the highest profile among the disciples. They loved the most fervently and were the most dedicated. Perhaps there was a rivalry between them about who was the most devoted.

Somehow I don't think John really wants to be noticed. Maybe he kicks a stone or scuffs his feet on the gravel and Peter turns around and sees him. John wants to garner as much information as he can. I reckon he is already thinking about writing his Gospel which will take many years to complete.

> *"When Peter saw him, he said to Jesus, "Lord, what about this man?" Jesus said to him, "If it is my will that he remain until I come, what is that to you? You follow me!"*
> — JOHN 21:21,22

Jesus, quite sharply, tells Peter not to compare himself with John. He is abrupt with Peter because He knows that comparison is one of the things we do when we are steeped in the knowledge of good and evil. When we want to ascend higher and become better, we compare ourselves with others. In the Father's love, everyone is equally favoured.

Jesus tells Peter not to even think about what will happen to John. The disciples latch onto this and think John will not have to face death. That, however, is not the point. The point that Jesus emphasises is that Peter must resist falling into the age-old temptation of comparing himself with John. Comparing ourselves with others is what orphans do. Orphanness creates rivalry; receiving the love of the Father creates contentment.

> *This is the disciple who is bearing witness about these things, and who has written these things, and we know that his testimony is true.*

> *Now there are also many other things that Jesus did. Were every one of them to be written, I suppose that the world itself could not contain the books that would be written.*
> — JOHN 21:24,25

Only love remains. John now knows that. He signs himself off, fully realising that the whole point of Jesus coming into the human condition, is to declare the reality of where He has come from. Jesus, the Son, has been sent from the centre of all that is, the bosom of the Father and He has brought us to where He lives, in that very place. John has witnessed an abundance of signs which point to this reality. He only records a sampling of the signs, and that is all that is required. There is so much in all that Jesus has said and done that countless books have been written about the few incidents that the Gospels actually tell us about. The book you are reading now is yet another one. John (and I) urge you: Don't depend on books to take you to the heart of what is written. John's writing, and my own offering, are there to help you open your heart to have your own relationship with the Father, the Son and the Spirit.

If you look into your heart, you will find a spring of living water there already.

"Launched Full Sail Upon the Waves of Confidence and Love"[40]

~

We have come to the end of our odyssey in John's Gospel. Now we are launched out into the ocean of the Father's love as we live our daily lives. With the words of John's Gospel ringing in our ears; we can joyfully embark upon the life of sonship. Confident that we are going into the ancient future, and completing the eternal circle of our redemption into the Trinitarian family. In the light of God's purpose, the orphan condition has been shown to be a mere blip. The coming of the Son, His declaring of the Father, His death and resurrection, and the presence of the Spirit of truth has eradicated that blip. From eternity and into eternity, we *belong*: We are His.

---

40. This is adapted from a quote by St. Therese of Lisieux, *The Story of a Soul*, translated. by G. M. Day, Burns and Oates, London 1951.

In his writing, John has shown the Way and the Destination. Interwoven through everything, the golden thread leads back to the Source. The primordial reality has been revealed. The Word who was with God in the beginning, declared His revelation from a specific place, the bosom of the Father. In the Gospel of John the way to the Tree of Life is opened up once again. We can eat of its leaves, imbibe its nectar, and come forth as sons to heal creation.

We have had our water turned into a wine that will never run out, the wine of sonship. Now we see that the temple has become incarnated in sonship. As we look within our flawed humanity we see, with joyful surprise, a fountain of living water at the core of our being. From our innermost spirit, the Father's love bubbles up in an everlasting well from which we can continually slake our thirst. Learning to eat the substance of who Jesus is, the Father's approval becomes eternal food and we are set free from the condemnation of the accusers.

As we read this Gospel, the eyes of our hearts begin to see clearly. Spiritual dimness is removed, and we realise that we were once blind but a man called Jesus touched our eyes, and now we see. We see Jesus as perfect representation of the Father, the true Shepherd who lays down His life for the sheep. Not only does Jesus lay down His life to serve; His serving reveals a fully accurate picture of who the Father is: the original and ultimate Servant. All true service flows from the Father's love. Knowing this sets us free to love and serve others, not lording it over them but lifting them from beneath.

We know that death is not the end. It is simply a portal whereby we enter into resurrection life. In the garden, as the Son (sun) rises, we look around and see Jesus standing as a gardener. Then

He appears on the shore helping us catch a mighty haul of fish. Resurrection life is evident in the ordinariness of life. There is no need to fear, the itch to escape life's difficulties is settled because we can experience the resurrected Son wherever we go and whatever our circumstances are. By the Spirit, the Father and the Son make their home and relax within our humanity.

In John's Gospel, the systemic problem of misogyny, with its roots in the very beginning of creation, has been reversed. The true feminine is restored once again as the pathway into revelation and divine encounter. For revelation and divine encounter come by way of the heart. The Holy Spirit through John has intentionally highlighted women, and the feminine, as catalysts for spiritual breakthrough, and as pioneers into new frontiers of revelation. And not just any women, but women who have suffered at the hands of the aggressor against the feminine. Redemption has reached to the outsider. The woman who was a teenage mother, pregnant outside of marriage, has become the prototype human container for Incarnation. I like to think (and increasingly believe) that Mary of Galilee, the mother of Jesus, is a hovering presence behind this book written by John. She has become John's mother and he has become her son in a very real way.

The 'illegitimate' mother, the promiscuous Samaritan woman, the woman caught in the act of adultery, the demonised and possible prostitute Mary Magdalene, the forgotten women who have sacrificed their own happiness for love, Mary and Martha of Bethany, all find redemption in sonship. All are witnesses to signs, and all are signs in themselves. All of them are shown what the signs point to. To these women, the mystery hidden for ages and generations is revealed.

God *really* is the original Parent, and our home is within His bosom.

John has brought us into that place where he has learned to rest. Now we are in Christ, in the bosom of the Father. This can be known fully, in life beyond religion and beyond death. In His resurrection life, we are included and embraced within the Trinity. In Christ, we see from *inside* the loving circle of the Trinity through the perspective of Jesus Christ the Son. Within us, the Holy Spirit continually reveals that speech of the heart which words cannot express. We bask in the loving gaze of the Father and gaze back into His face. And, in this reality, we are launched into life, full sail upon the waves of confidence and love.

RESOURCES

More resources can be found at:

WWW.ANCIENTFUTURE.CO.NZ